A TEXAS WOMAN'S CHILDHOOD NIGHTMARE—
AND HER ESCAPE FROM HELL AS A SEX SLAVE.

survivor.

I am
ABIGAIL

JAMIE COLLINS

TRIGGER WARNING

This book depicts real events that deal with trauma and the difficult emotions experienced by a survivor of childhood abuse and sexual assault. Parts may be triggering for some trauma survivors.

TO CHEVO & LAURA:

Upon the altar of truth.
Black words across ivory pages.
Ugly truths over pretty lies.
Exposed for all to see.
ALL of me. ALL of you.
The power you wielded over me,
now GONE,
like all the things you took from me.
Standing defiantly in the light of day,
claimed page by page.
Today, I stand in the sun. Head held high.
No longer afraid to speak your names.
The keeper of memories.
The bearer of scars.
Set free.

To the voiceless, the faceless, the silent,
and the burdened. This is for YOU.

*Most little girls dream of fairies, castles, and
the slaying of dragons in far-away lands.*

*My nightmares were born from the faintest beam of light
spilling through the sliver of a crack in the doorway.*

— **JAMIE COLLINS**
(For Abigail)

Behind big brown eyes,
she hides.

Tucked between shadows.
Standing in the light of day.
Flinching. Flailing. Falling.
Through the darkest of nights.

Silent.
Suffering.
Hopeless.
A girl.

Tortured. Broken. Empty.
A woman.

Waiting.
Suffering.
Silent.
A survivor.

Innocent.
Faultless.
Now found.
Standing before you.
Soul stripped bare.
Empowered.

Behind big brown eyes,
she RISES.

—JAMIE COLLINS
(For Abigail)

A NOTE FROM THE AUTHOR

Jamie Collins

y name is Jamie Collins. I work as a litigation paralegal by day and an author by night. I often tell people that I was born a writer, but I just failed to realize it somewhere along the way. Thankfully, I did eventually discover—or perhaps, rediscover—my love for putting words on the page, that obsessive tug within me to tell a great story in a unique way. All this is to say, it's important that I tell you how this story came to be.

I published my first book, *I Am Jessica: A Survivor's Powerful Story of Healing and Hope,* in April of 2019 to tell my cousin Jessica's tragic story. As a family story, it was one to which I had close personal ties mixed with an undercurrent of residual trauma, and one that, 30 years later, still wielded power over me.

Jessica returned home from a sleepover at age nine to find her house surrounded by crime scene tape and her driveway filled with squad cars and police officers. She learned that her entire family had been murdered while she was away. Tragedy upends people and trauma changes them. Telling my cousin's story proved to be therapeutic, healing, and pivotal—for both of us.

On the heels of publishing my first book, I promised my best friend, Krishna, that I would not start anything new for at least a year. Still, I believe the perfect story finds those who are willing to tell it. I don't consider myself to be a religious person but more of a spiritual one. On the night of my 44th birthday, as my head hit the pillow, I took a moment to quietly ponder, pray, and meditate before drifting off to sleep. I ended my prayer with, "Please bring any people across my path that I'm supposed to help or show me anything that I'm meant to find." I was ready for whatever came next. I just didn't have any idea what it would be.

The night I uttered that prayer, I had officially reached the year-and-a-half mark of my solemn oath to my best friend. Promise kept. More wishes thrown into the universal ether.

The next day, I awoke to find an email in my inbox from a man named Jeff Ferris, a fellow writer from Ohio whom I had never met. He saw me and my cousin on an episode of *48 Hours* one evening. He bought my first book. In his words, he was so captivated that he began reading parts of it aloud to his wife and considered it an exceptional read. That eventually led him to reach out to me about another story.

Jeff knew a survivor named Abby with a riveting story to tell. While he initially entertained the idea of writing her story himself, after more than a year it hadn't gone anywhere. Abby wasn't ready to share her story. Jeff felt that a female writer would be better suited to tell her story since it delved into sexual abuse.

As a person, I was curious to learn more about Abby. As a writer, I was intrigued. I found myself on the phone with Rudy Alvarado the next day and we formed an instant connection. Our conversation was capped by a brief introductory call with Abby. She had a kind persona and a calm, shy demeanor. Similar to when I worked with my cousin on her story, I could feel Abby encumbered by her trauma, holding her thoughts and guarding her words, almost clinging to them. The past's grip on Abby was palpable.

I wanted to help Abby free herself from the horror that had consumed her life as best as I could. That would require me to not only sit down with Abby—the sad, guilt-ridden, shame-filled little girl—to walk through the dark corridors of her past, but to also take a long, unadulterated look at Abby, the woman, the one who shouldn't feel an iota of guilt or shame because of the terrible things that happened to her.

Silence often becomes shame's playground. I would have to sit with her as she recounted the moments of abuse and not flinch or look away. It was an undertaking that would require the highest degree of trust and reverence between us. As an author who writes for trauma survivors, I know this type of creative collaboration to be one of the truest forms of emotional intimacy that exists. It is my role to listen fully, without judgment, and to intuitively hear everything that is said as well as everything that sits lingering beneath the words so that, as a human conduit, I can translate it onto the page.

A remarkable story? One thousand percent, yes. And after hearing the main pieces of it, I knew it was a story that I could not turn down, walk away from, or *not* tell. This was a story that *needed* to be told. It had darkness, but it also had a lot of light, and I knew it wielded the power to help so many people. It pulled me in. I knew that Abby's story was a perfect match for me and the way that I would tell it.

Some would call how this story came to be a coincidence. Others would refer to it as luck. But for Abby, Rudy, and I, it was fate.

Before we dive in, it's important for you to know that reports written by Child Protective Services (CPS) are shared in this book. The first report shook Abby to the core. These CPS reports were an unexpected piece of Abby's life's puzzle. They are gut-wrenching and emotionally jarring, and hearing of them proved to be a trigger for her.

One evening, I called Abby to tell her about the CPS reports that I had received in the mail. I began reading parts of them aloud over the phone. Upon hearing the first few sentences—and specifically, a particular man's name—panic surged within Abby. She immediately threw the phone down and ran to the bathroom in a state of horror. Someone else who was in the room with Abby at that time had to pick up the phone to explain to me what had just occurred.

Post-traumatic stress doesn't always arrive in vivid flashes or expected moments, but it does tend to linger on the inside, like poison, even when its boundaries become blurred over time or the trauma itself is forgotten—intentionally or as a means of self-protection. For Abby, hearing a certain man's name sent her spiraling into panic. These are memories she would rather not recall. But it is important to know that the first CPS report is not the abuse that forms the basis of her life's story. It is merely a pre-cursor and unfortunate background for all that would transpire.

Abby never realized that her sister or brother had also suffered abuse. That knowledge hit her hard. She had spent all her life—34 years at the time we wrote this—feeling alone and thinking that she was the only one of the three that had endured mistreatment. But they were children. She likely blocked out certain pieces of her past in order to survive it.

Abby didn't realize the perilous nature of her early years spent with her biological mother. Granted, she had no way to compare her experience to normal life. They just lived how they lived, ate what they ate, and existed the way they did—somewhat feral. Abby never wondered if growling stomachs were normal. She never questioned the empty cupboards or the constant hunger. She didn't know it wasn't normal to not have toys or clothes. She didn't know that smoke billowing in a living room full of strangers, beer cans, and white lines of powder on tables was not the norm. It was just her life.

The events contained in first CPS report became the catalyst that would set Abby's horrific fate into motion. Parents make choices and children are left to live with the consequences. While Abby can't give her biological mom a free pass for the choices she made all those years ago, there is no way that her mother could have known what would come next. No one could.

No matter what happened, Abby was slated for the hard path. Her life was never going to be easy. She has often wondered about the divergent fork in the road and whether being raised by her real mom would have been as harrowing.

These are things Abby will never know.

The abuse would mark her mind and heart indefinitely.

This is her story.

PROLOGUE

ABIGAIL

AGE 25
July 21, 2014

"*My* name is Abigail Castillo."

Those are the first words I say after swinging the door open and walking into the brown brick building of the San Antonio Police Department.

The police officer led me away from the glass encased front desk at the entryway and the sterile waiting area filled with a throng of uncomfortable black plastic chairs, back to a rather non-descript office to hear what I came here to report. Sitting across the table from him, I take a deep breath, hoping to steady my nerves, and continue, "I've been abused—badly abused—for the past 16 years . . . my entire life. I was beaten, stalked, and sexually assaulted. I was held prisoner by a man who raped me almost every single day of my life—and it wasn't just him. I finally got away. I know what he did is wrong. I'm scared for my life. I'm here to document the abuse—everything that happened to me—to make a police report . . ."

There are defining moments in one's life that serve as a poignant, unforgettable marker of the person you used to be, punctuated by the one you have become. That person, blurred at the edges, with her boundaries now clearly defined, stands in the room an entirely different woman than the one she otherwise might have been. One who feels weaker in some regards, but stronger in others. A survivor of evil acts. A teller of brutal truths. An echo in the darkness not to be forgotten. One woman forged by another's sins and standing strong to hold the space of survival. That's who I am today: a survivor. And this was the moment where I would stand up, step forward, and take my power back.

I didn't have to name myself publicly. It was a choice, both then and now. As a survivor of sexual assault, the authorities agreed to shroud my identity within the black ink keystrokes of anonymity to keep my name out of the public record. But in the sweltering Texas heat of that day in July, nine years ago, I was prepared to publicly claim my identity. It was finally time that I own the shame-filled-ugliness that had consumed my life up to that point. It was something I wanted—*needed*—to do after enduring 16 years of hell at the hands of two demented people masquerading as normal that I somehow survived. Some in positions of power would call it one of the worst cases of child abuse they had ever heard. I would call it my life story.

No shame. No fear. No filter. Unshackled by the truth, as I lived it. Now inscribed onto these pages to serve as a permanent record.

Admittedly, there is nothing more terrifying than telling a haunting story, like mine. There is also nothing more liberating. So, I am finally going to tell it.

We should probably start at the beginning . . .

ABIGAIL

AGE 8

Life With Mom

*M*y name is Abigail (no-middle-name) Rodriguez, but most people call me "Abby." My mom—a single, Hispanic woman—gave birth to me at a hospital in San Antonio, Texas in September of 1988. On my birth certificate, where my father's name should appear, no name is listed. I have a sister who is two years older than me and a brother who is one year younger. We each have different dads. I grew up not knowing anything about mine.

My mom was born in San Antonio and grew up in a large family alongside five half-brothers. I live with my mom and siblings in a little brown house in San Antonio. We used to live in a sky-blue house, but this is our new place now. We don't have much. My mom is a hard worker who struggles to pay our bills, buy our clothes, and keep enough food in the fridge, but somehow, she does.

Our house is always filled with people. There is always Tejano music—that's Mexican music—blaring through the speakers of our home. It is never quiet here. People are everywhere. A few we know, but most are strangers. They laugh, and they drink, and they dance. A haze of smoke billows in the air. Sometimes, we even see the grown-ups kissing on the couch. They don't ever seem to go to sleep—these people in our house. They just party, party, party all night. It doesn't matter what day of the week it is, or whether we have school the next day. It is rarely ever quiet here. And it is almost *never just us*. During one party, when I was only five or six, Tejano music was blaring and my mom turned to me and said, "Mija, get up on this table and dance for us! Let everyone see how you dance!" (Mija is a term of endearment in Spanish for "my daughter.")

It seemed a bit weird to stand up on the coffee table in our living room, but even more so to dance for a room full of strangers, especially unfamiliar men in the room. It made my stomach turn. Because my mom asked me to, I climbed up onto the table and I danced, even though I didn't want to.

My mom sleeps a lot during the day, probably because she's tired from staying up all night partying with her friends. I wish she would spend more time with us—me and my brother, and sister. I don't feel like she pays much attention to us. It's like we're just around. Like we just live here. Like we don't really matter. At least not in the way I wish we did, like we are important to her.

But one fun thing about my mom is that she throws the world's best birthday parties. My brother and I always celebrate our birthdays on the same day, since our birthdays are just days apart. On that day, Mom likes to spoil us.

In the living room, Mom always hangs up a big sign that says "Happy Birthday" with our names written on it. She blows up balloons, covers the table with a colored tablecloth, and we open birthday presents wrapped in bright wrapping paper. Then we have a pretty cake with icing and sprinkles. Birthdays are my favorite days. On our birthdays, the nightly parties we usually have with strangers become one big, fun, special *family* party, instead. Everyone we know comes over. We get to see all our aunts, uncles, and cousins.

We have a really big family. Kids of all ages play together while waiting for yummy food. Soon, my mom fills our plates with slices of cheese pizza, hot dogs, and chips. When we're done eating, she gives us all a big piece of birthday cake that we gobble up. The grown-ups talk and tell stories to each other. The kids run around outside and play games, chasing one another, playing freeze tag, and giggling.

My sister, brother, and I don't always get along. We all get on each other's nerves because we are always together. My brother sometimes picks on me, and they both like to call me a "crybaby." When we aren't playing in our front yard or running around in the backyard, we usually pick at one another. We argue about stupid things.

One year, my brother got a new skateboard for his birthday. I begged him to ride it, until my mom finally got tired of hearing me whine. "Mijo, just let Abby ride it for a minute," she said. (Mijo means "my son" in Spanish.)

We went to the driveway, and I stood over the skateboard. Before I could hop on, it rolled out from under me and into the road, straight into the path of an oncoming car. The skateboard was destroyed. My brother was so mad at me. "See Mom, that's why I didn't want to let her ride it! She ruins everything." (Perhaps he was right just that one time.)

As the middle child, I don't remember having many friends as a kid. I had my siblings around, so they kind of took the place of them as built-in friends at home. We were always together. Laughing. Playing. Picking at one other. Bickering and squabbling. Fighting. One of us pinching or poking the other when Mom wasn't looking. We always made up afterward, some of the time because Mom made us. But let an outsider try to pick on one of us, and they were gonna get the whole bunch. It was typical sibling rivalry blended with a thin undertone of we-are-related-by-blood-and-we-protect-one-another mentality.

But there are some things that even family cannot protect you from . . .

ABIGAIL

AGE 9

A Knock on the Door

One day in May of 1998, a knock on the door of our home would forever change our lives. Child Protective Services had received a report expressing concern for the well-being of my brother, my sister, and me. My guess is that somebody probably told them about mom's parties. One of my aunts once described me, as a toddler, as "todo tirado," which is Spanish for "looking a mess." She didn't mean it as a put down, just an accurate descriptor of my appearance. My hair was usually unwashed and messy, hanging in my face, while my soiled diaper sagged around my legs.

My mom seems to remember it differently. "Remember how I always used to dress you in those pretty pink dresses with your hair up in pigtails, Mija? You always looked so pretty!" That didn't seem to be the image that anyone else had of me as a kid. And not much changed as we got older. We pretty much took care of ourselves. When we were hungry, my older sister would make us sandwiches, or we would rifle through the cupboards looking for something to eat, which often consisted of a packet of noodles, can of soup, or a box of generic macaroni and cheese. We pretty much lived on that stuff. The smoking, drinking, and partying seemed to come before we did, as did the house full of strangers, the cans full of beer, and whatever else it is that the grown-ups "did." Someone had finally noticed it and reported it.

And that brings us to the day someone knocked on our front door.

There are two people on the front stoop talking to my mom right now—a man and a woman. I heard them say they are "from Child Protective Services." I don't know what that means or why they are here. Mom just keeps saying, "Please don't take my kids. Don't take my kids. I'm just going through a hard time right now." I'm confused and I feel scared. I'm not sure what is going on.

These people are strangers. Where are they going to take us? This doesn't make any sense. Why would they just take somebody's kids? I don't know what is going on right now. I don't even know who these people are. I want to stay with my mom.

One of them utters, "Ma'am, I'm sorry, but we have to take your kids with us today. That's why we are here."

I didn't hear the rest of what was said. I didn't need to.

I begin to cry, "I don't want to go. I don't want to go. I don't want to go. Please don't *make me* go! I don't *want to* go. I just want to stay here with my mom. [gasp] With my mom. Please don't take me. I don't want to go. . ." I am attempting to cling to my mom's side holding onto her, to stop this from happening.

Mom turns to me and my brother, "Kids, just go with this lady and man, like they are asking. I will get this all worked out. I will get it all straightened out. I will see you all soon. I love you."

The lady and the man walk us out to an SUV parked outside. They open the backdoor and we climb in. We put our seatbelts on because they tell us to. They drive away from my house, away from my mom. I can't stop crying. I don't know where they are taking us, or why. Here we are, riding in a SUV with two strangers, who are acting like they get to be in charge of us. I don't know where they are taking us. "I don't want to go with you. We don't even know you!" I cry out in a bitter tone to the two stranger-adults. I am gasping with each breath I take from crying so much.

"I [gasp] juuuust [gasp] want [gasp] my [gasp] mom."

INVESTIGATION REPORT
(Pertinent portions included below)

**All major typographical errors contained in the original report, abbreviations spelled out, with some names intentionally withheld. **

Case: 25014731

Intake Narrative

Intake Received: 5/14/1998
Reporter Name: Crossland, Holly
Stage ID: 24335088
Rel/int: School Personnel
Stage Type: SXAB2
Person ID: 24867438

Person Notes: Oldest victim's teacher at Storm Elem. Rep wouldn't give the name of the neighbor who saw the children being beaten because the neighbor wants to be anonymous. Rep agreed to ask the school nurse to examine other victim's brother too & to call back if the victims have injuries.

GENERAL INFORMATION/DESCRIPTION

Oldest victim [Abigail] is 9 years old. About 2 weeks ago, oldest victim was out of school all day. Oldest victim went back to school with a note that she had been at San Antonio Police Department all day long because her mother's boyfriend had sexually abused her. Oldest victim said her mother's boyfriend, name unknown, made oldest victim "put his thing in her mouth and in her privates." Oldest victim said the mother's boyfriend told oldest victim if she told her mother about the sexual abuse, he would keep doing it to oldest victim. Oldest victim said her mother's boyfriend was in jail.

Today oldest victim was an hour late to school. Oldest victim said she was late because her mother's boyfriend had hurt the mother real bad, and the police had to come get the boyfriend. Oldest victim said the family overslept. Unknown if this is the same boyfriend who sexually abused oldest victim. The mother lives with two men. Reporter doesn't know the names of either of the men.

A neighbor of the family said that last night the mother was very drunk. The mother was hitting and kicking oldest victim and her first grade brother. The boyfriend was trying to stop the mother from hitting the children. The mother then turned around and hit the boyfriend. The boyfriend then hurt the mother.

Reporter didn't know if oldest victim or her brother have any injuries. The school nurse at other victim's school is going to look at oldest victim.

Diane Hill, Intake Spec. IV

CONCLUSIONS:
P. 1—SXAB [sexual abuse], PHAB [physical abuse]—mother's boyfriend allegedly SXAB oldest victim; the incident was disclosed to police about 2 weeks ago. The boyfriend was allegedly in jail at that time, but oldest victim is saying the mother's boyfriend assaulted the mother last night. Unknown if this is the same boyfriend who sexually abused oldest victim or not. The mother also was allegedly hitting and kicking on oldest victim and her brother last night, unknown if the children have injuries.

LOCATING INFORMATION: Directions. When the family is home. Where the victim can be seen. Both oldest victim and her brother attend Storm Elem. Oldest victim is in second grade, and her brother is in first grade.

INVESTIGATION REPORT
Abigail
Neglectful supv. [mother's name omitted]
Reason to believe Serious NA

Abigail
Physical Abuse [mother's name omitted]
Reason to believe Moderate NA

[brother's name]
Physical Abuse [mother's name omitted]
Reason to believe Moderate NA

Abigail
Physical Neglect [mother's name omitted]
Reason to believe Moderate NA

Abigail
Sexual Abuse
Ruled out NA

IMPACT History for All Principals
Abigail
Case: 25014731
Stage: 16462798
Intake Date: 5/28/1996
Allegation: Neglectful Supv [CPS]
Role: Victim
Disp: Ruled Out

Sev: [left blank]
Allegation: Sexual Abuse
Role: Victim
Disp: Ruled Out
Sev: [left blank]

Investigation Contacts

**All typographical and grammatical errors are contained in the original transcript. Some names intentionally withheld. **

Date of Contact:	5/18/1998
Date Entered:	5/18/1998
Person[s] Contacted:	Abigail
	[brother]
	[mother]
	[mother's boyfriend]
Purpose:	Assessment

NARRATIVE:

Telephone call from Shelly [last name omitted]. [Mother] and [mother's boyfriend] had a fight. [Boyfriend] was taken to jail by San Antonio Police Department. Evidently, both were drunk and [boyfriend] assaulted [mother]. Abigail and [brother] witnessed the fight. [Mother] has left [boyfriend's] home. It is not known where she is living. Shelly will find out and call me.

Date of Contact:	6/10/1998
Date Entered:	6/10/1998
Person[s] Contacted:	Abigail
	[brother]
	[mother]
Purpose:	Gather/Obtain Info

NARRATIVE:

Shelly [last name omitted] called concerned about Abigail and [brother] since she had not heard from [the children's mother]; also, to let me know that [the children's mother] has not called to ask about [sister] in the past 10 days. [Sister] does not want to go home to live with her mother and [mother's boyfriend].

NARRATIVE:

I met with [mother], Abigail, and [brother] today. I asked that the children be placed with others. This is the result of mother's long history of neglectful supervision of the children due to drug and alcohol use. I called Shelly [last name omitted] who is keeping [sister]. She was willing to take Abigail and [brother]. An alternative placement was to the maternal grandmother's [name and phone number omitted].

[Mother] says that she is living with Patsy [last name omitted], a reported long time drug user, at [exact address omitted] Lombrano, a high-crime, drug infested, high poverty neighborhood on the west side. When I made the home visit Patsy's phone had just been disconnected for non-payment. Patsy had "just had open-heart surgery and needed my help," [the children's mother] said.

When I mentioned that the children needed to leave, [the children's mother's] response was without empathy or concern for her children. She focused on herself and how depressed she was. She cried briefly, but for herself and the sadness she feels toward her life circumstances. The children looked thin and malnourished. There was little food in the house and benefit checks had just been sent. [Brother] has a malformed mouth. He needs a dental evaluation of his condition and follow up services.

All of the children require ACAC assessment to further pin-down their outcries of . . . abuse, and when the . . . abuse occurred.

———

ALLEGATIONS/DISPOSITION:
There were multiple allegations for this referral.

There was an allegation that Abigail had been sexually abused, however, this allegation was reported and investigated previously by Yadira Salinas, Investigations [March and April, 1998]. Disposition was RTB [reason to believe].

The second part of the allegation was for physical abuse of Abigail and [brother]. [Mother] hit and kicked Abigail and [brother]. [Mother] was drunk. There was a domestic disturbance and [children's mom's boyfriend], her paramour was arrested and taken to jail by the San Antonio Police Department. [Children's mom's boyfriend] was trying to stop [mother/wife] from hitting the children when she turned on [him] and hit him. It was then that [he] evidently did something to hurt [mother/wife] but it is not clear what. [He] was taken to jail after the SAPD responded to the domestic disturbance call made by neighbors. He did ten days in jail time. Disposition was RTB [reason to believe].

The third facet of the investigation was found at the time of my investigation. I validated for physical neglect and for neglectful supervision due to [mother's] increased drunkenness and the deteriorating hygiene and physical condition of Abigail and [brother] over the past two weeks. [Mother] made one suicide attempt of May 7, 1998. She was hospitalized for less than 24 hours. The children were cared for by [mom's boyfriend]; however, there was a previous allegation that one of [mom's boyfriend's] friends, [name omitted] had fondled [one of the children]. [Name omitted] is a Mexican national whose whereabouts are unknown.

INTERVIEW AND EXAMINATION:

Comments for each victim and or other children at risk and their response to all allegations / other pertinent information:

Abigail and [brother] have chronic lice infestations. They have few clothes and they are always dirty. The children look like they have not bathed in days on virtually every occasion I have seen them. They complain that there isn't a lot of food in the house. Both children look thin and poorly cared for. Due to the domestic fighting between [mother] and [her boyfriend], who both drink to excess, [mother] was "kicked out"; therefore, the children have no home. [Mother] has just moved into the home of a known long-standing cocaine, crack user, Patsy [last name omitted].

It appears that there have been multiple occurrences of . . . abuse of all of the children over the past six years due to mother's drug and drinking problems. Both Abigail and [brother] have made outcries. Also, they complain of their mother not having food; of being drunk a lot; and of the children not liking the mother's friends. Abigail age 9, has been asked to table dance for money and attention from [mother's] guests who are drinking in the home. Abigail is a precociously sensual child in a sexual sense. She moves her physical body in such a way as to encourage the attention of men.

The children have one or two articles of clothing and one pair of shoes. They have no other physical possessions, like beds for example.

OBSERVATIONS OF HOME ENVIRONMENT:

Conditions that involve risk to the child: The children and [mother] had moved in with Patsy [name omitted], an old friend of [mother's] with a long history of cocaine use. The home was dirty and there was little food. The telephone had just been disconnected [6/10/98] for non-payment of the outstanding bill.

INTERVIEW WITH EACH PARENT AND/OR PERPETRATOR:

[Mother] denied that she knows anything about the allegations. She complains of being "too depressed." She admits to bouts of drinking. She responded without emotion or empathy when I asked her if it would be possible to place Abigail and [brother] with a relative as a safety plan until the sexual abuse referrals and other matters where more thoroughly investigated. She agreed to place [brother] with Shelly [last name omitted]. Abigail initially wanted to go to her maternal grandmother's home, but later decided to go with Shelly after she remarked that her grandmother never has any food.

[Mother] never asked questions that one would expect a mother to ask like, for example, why it was being done and for how long. [Mother] has no physical possessions.

INFORMATION ABOUT ABSENT PARENT:

[Mother] has refused to provide information on Abigail's absent father. No one in the family knows who is Abigail's father.

[Sister's] father is a Mexican national of unknown name allegedly living in California. He has expressed no interest in [sister] since birth. She has never seen him.

[Brother's] father is [name omitted]. He is physically disabled and he receives SSI payments. Whereabouts are unknown.

COLLATERAL INFORMATION:

Shelly [last name omitted] has corroborated much of the information obtained from the children and from school sources over the past two years. [She] has been involved with the family off and on over the past six years.

DOCUMENTATION SUPPORTING RISK ASSESSMENT: PAST ABUSE/NEGLECT:

CHILD FACTORS:
There are no child factors contributing to significant risk. Twelve-year-old [sister] refuses to go home and deal with her mother; drunkenness and her anger. She is living with Shelly currently. [Sister] has been with Shelly since March or April, 1998.

PARENT FACTORS:
[Mother's] alcohol and drug addiction and her inability to supervise her children properly when she is drunk. Her continued association with paramours, friends, and acquaintances who . . . abuse her children. Her low motivation to parent; coupled with depression and one known recent suicide attempt. Loss of housing, possessions for herself and her children.

OTHER PERTINENT INFORMATION:
[Mother's] family has multiple incidents within the family . . . For example, [mother's] brother allegedly raped his wife in front of their children. Status of this case is not known at this time. Also, [Mother] claims that she was sexually abused [had sexual intercourse] by her father and by other family members as she was growing up.

—

COURT AND PLACEMENT ACTIVITIES:
All children voluntarily were placed out of the home, as a Safety Plan, as the investigation into the old sexual abuse allegations continues; and, to assure the reasonable provision of the basic needs of existence [adequate food, shelter, and clothing] of the children while other aspects of the cases are investigated.

ABIGAIL

AGE 9

Shelter Life

They drive us to a shelter in San Antonio called "BCFS." I quickly learn that a *shelter* is a place for kids who don't have a home. That must be who we are now: kids who don't have a home. They say we don't get to live with our mom anymore because "the judge is worried about us." They say they "think things will be better for us here." That makes no sense to me. After all, we have a mom, and—up until today—we had a house, until they came and took us away. Now, we are going to have to live here, in this shelter, with a bunch of strangers. This shelter looks like one big building, but is made up of several. I realize this once the staff begins showing us around. The lady who welcomed us calls it "a tour."

There is a main building and a school building. There is also a boys' building and a girls' building, a gym, and playground. The boys' building and girls' building each have five or six bedrooms and four bathrooms. I get to share a room with my sister. I am happy about that. But we don't get to see my brother much because he has to stay in the boys' building. We only see him at school and at recess. I feel sorry for him having to be alone in the boys' building.

My sister and I share a room. Everything looks the same here. Bare walls. No decorations. The bed, the tile floors, it's nothing special. Every room is the same. It feels more like living in a hospital or a school building rather than a real house.

At night, I tell my sister, "I miss Mom. I want to go back. Why did the judge say Mom can't call us, or even come see us? It's not fair."

She tries to comfort me saying, "Abby, maybe, they got it all wrong. Maybe they will bend the rules a little bit and let us talk to her soon."

I cry myself to sleep in this place. I miss my mom.

The people at the shelter are nice to us, for the most part. Like anything else, some of our caretakers are friendlier than others, but I am sick of being here already. I don't understand why we are in this place, or why they took us away from Mom. I just want to see her, to talk to her, to hug her. I cry a lot. But we do always have meals prepared for us here. All the kids sit down and eat them together. We go outside after. I really like the playground. My favorite part of this place is the weekly field trips that we take to a local ice rink to go skating. I'm not very good at it and my ankles get wobbly when I try to glide across the rink on ice skates, but it's still fun.

Here, there is no blaring Tejano music, no dancing strangers, no smoke billowing in the air, no empty bottles of alcohol laying on the floor. They make sure that we take a shower, put on clean clothes, and walk over to the school building each day. In some ways, this place is better. We are taken care of, we get to play with other kids, and we always have enough to eat now. But I still miss my mom. I really want to see her. It doesn't seem fair that some people could just come and take us away from her.

Married couples sometimes come to visit the shelter during the day to interview the kids here. That part is weird and kind of freaks me out. I am shy. I don't feel comfortable talking to strangers. They usually walk into the shelter holding hands, smiling and happy, and they tell the people in charge what *type* of kid they have in mind. "We are looking for an 8 or 9-year-old girl, who is smart, and who knows how to clean her room." If you fit the bill, they then call you into the office to do a meet-and-greet with the couple. The shelter worker will say, "Mr. and Mrs. Smith—This is Abby. She is nine years old. She's a smart, sweet girl who is kind of shy and loves to play outside." The couple will then ask you a bunch of random questions to determine whether you would be an ideal kid for them or not. I don't want to be anyone's kid, neither do my siblings. We have a mom. And we used to have a home. We don't understand why we are here, in this shelter for homeless kids. And we certainly don't want new parents. These people are *strangers* to us. They are *nothing* to us. We aren't interested in anything they have to offer. They can take the others and leave us.

Whenever a couple seems to take interest in us, my sister—with a storm brewing behind her brown eyes—always quips, "They either take *all three of us*, or *none* of us!" She fears us being split up. The problem is none of these foster couples ever want to take in three kids. They usually come in looking for one. For that reason, we are fairly safe from the fake-new-parents-picking-out-their-fake-new-kids process, but we worry that they could one day try to split us up.

We have been at this shelter for quite a while now. The days have stretched into weeks, and those weeks have turned into months. One day, my sister turns to me and says, "You know what? We should ask them to call Uncle Eusebio—Mom's half-brother—to see if he is willing to take us in. All of us!" I'm not sure how she came up with this idea. We don't know him well. I have only seen him maybe a time or two. His real name is Eusebio, but everybody calls him "Chevo." If he does take us, at least we will get to stay together. That is important to us.

My sister tells the social worker her half-baked idea. It takes the shelter worker some time to pull things together, but she does eventually call our Uncle Chevo. Surprisingly, he and his wife, Laura, agree to take all three of us.

At the time, I remember thinking this was a blessing for us, since we found ourselves living in a shelter without family around us. But this—this choice, the agreed acceptance of us, this plan set into motion—would become the pivotal moment in my life that would upend and forever seal my fate in the worst ways imaginable. It was the precursor to what would become the erosion of my innocence. The undoing of a little girl.

I never saw the evil making its way to me.

No one did.

ABIGAIL

AGE 9

Goodbye, Mom

Today, my mom gets to come visit us at the shelter! I am so excited! She is coming to tell us goodbye before we go live with our Uncle Chevo and Aunt Laura in Hawaii. I am so happy that I finally get to see her!

When Mom walks into the shelter, we run up to her and give her a big hug. I don't want to let her go. I have missed her so much. More than I even realized. I am so happy to see her, to touch her, to hear her voice, to hug her tight, to be with her. She is smiling and looks happy to see us. It makes me feel important, like she really missed us. Like she really missed *me*.

We get to sit in a room with her today for a few hours to play games, watch a movie, and talk—just the four of us. We play the board game Chutes and Ladders. I try to beat my brother and sister up the ladder. I whine when I spin and the arrow lands on a bad color, so I have to slide back down the board. "Stop being such a crybaby about it, Abby. It's not a big deal. Just move to where you're supposed to be," my brother says. He doesn't say it in a mean way, he just says it like I get on his nerves.

We sit down together and watch *The Lion King*. I'm not really watching the movie though. I can't stop looking over at my mom. It's almost like I'm trying to soak her in and memorize every single thing about her. I'm so happy to finally see her. To know that she is right here, with me, with all of us. I've missed her wavy black hair pulled halfway up that sits at her shoulders. Her dark brown eyes. Her red lipstick. Her laugh. This is the best day I've had since they took us away. I feel like I belong somewhere, with someone—with her. Like we get to be a real family again, even if it is just for today. I can tell my mom is sad, but she is trying not to show it. She tries to force a smile, but it doesn't feel real. I'm excited to be moving to Hawaii, but I'm sad to be leaving my mom because I'm not sure when I'm going to get to see her again. Hawaii is far away from Texas—far away from everything and everyone.

When it's time for my mom to go, I start to cry. We all cry. For once, it's not just me. My brother, sister, mom, and me—we sob and hold one another. My mom wraps her arms around us. "I love you. I will see you soon. I will call you as soon as I can. I love you." It's the hardest thing to watch my mom walk out the door. We are all gasping and calling out to her. I can't see anything through the tears streaming down my face.

"I'm [gasp] going [gasp] to miss [gasp] mom."

Me and my brother and sister hold each other until my brother has to go back to the boys' building. We cry harder because he doesn't get to stay with us. My sister and I walk back to our room. My sister tries to cheer me up. "Don't cry, Abby. Hawaii is going to be so beautiful. We are going to love it." She always tries to make me feel better whenever I'm sad. I fall asleep crying. But when I wake up, things seem better the next day.

When I think about Hawaii, I am happy that we get to move there. Everyone says the ocean is beautiful. One of the social workers said, "I'll bet y'all are excited to see Hawaii, to go live with your aunt and uncle. Y'all are gonna be moving to paradise!"

To which I replied, "What is Hawaii?" I don't know anything about "Hawaii." The shelter worker seems to sense my confusion. She pulls out a map and slides her finger across it to point to a chain of tiny little pieces of land across the blue water.

"Hawaii is an island. See, there are other islands right next to it. Hawaii is the big one, right here," thumping her bright red fingernail down onto the map, she taps it twice over the biggest yellow blob. You have to cross the ocean to get to Hawaii. This ocean right here."

I can tell that Hawaii is *really* far away. That means we have to fly on an airplane to get there. We've never done that before. I'm nervous about that, but kind of excited. We get to go live on a cool island! We are so lucky. I bet the other kids wish they could go to Hawaii.

I wonder if I'll still share a room with my sister? I wonder if I'll like my new school? I wonder if we'll like it there? Is there a big yard to play in? Will we live on a military base, since Uncle Chevo is in the Army? Is their house nice? I can't wait to find out.

ABIGAIL

AGE 9

The Uncle Flashback

*T*onight is my last night sleeping at the shelter. After putting on my pajamas and brushing my teeth, I climb up the ladder of my bunk bed and flop onto my mattress, feeling excited about the move. Our room is dark and quiet. I think my sister is already asleep. I'm too excited to sleep. I keep tossing and turning in my bed. I can't get comfortable. The only real memory I have of Uncle Chevo begins to play in my mind.

I'm five or six. I'm with my mom, Aunt Laura, and Uncle Chevo. My brother and sister are there, too. We are swimming at a pool at the Holiday Inn in El Paso. We are having fun together as a family. Uncle Chevo and Laura seem nice. My mom just left to walk my brother and sister back to their hotel room. We are still in the water together, just Uncle Chevo and me. He looks over at me and says, "One day, I am going to marry you."

I'm not sure what he means, or why he says that to me. He's my uncle. I'm just a little girl. I'm not sure if I ever want to get married. Maybe one day, when I'm a grown up. But he's my uncle. I don't think I would ever marry my own uncle. I don't even think that is allowed. Plus, why would he even want to marry me? He already is married—to Laura. He's a grown up. I'm just a kid. I don't understand . . .

My eyelids get heavier and heavier. Lying on my belly with my head turned sideways across my pillow, my breathing begins to slow, until finally—on the heels of my only memory with Uncle Chevo—I fall asleep.

ABIGAIL

AGE 9

Hello, Hawaii

A lady who is a social worker comes to the shelter to pick us up and drive us to the airport. We never met her before. She is Hispanic, like us, and she is really pretty. She wears a gray pantsuit and her hair is black. I like her right away. She looks like someone important, someone people would pay attention to. And she's really friendly to us.

We are on our way to the airport right now. We had to make sure we had all our stuff packed into bags before we went to bed last night, so it would be ready to bring with us today. The Lady walks us out to the parking lot, where there is a shiny black SUV. We swing the doors open and hop in. She is going to drive us to the airport. She will make sure we get to Hawaii okay, then she is gonna fly back to Texas. I'm glad she's flying with us, even though she's a stranger. It makes me feel better, safer, like nothing bad will happen to us.

Uncle Chevo and Aunt Laura are going to meet us at the airport. I feel excited to see them again. I hope they are glad that we are gonna be living with them. I know they already have a son. They are gonna have four kids now.

She parks the big, black SUV in a parking lot that is filled with cars. We hop out, slam our doors shut, and start to walk toward the airport. It's a HUGE building. There are a bunch of lights all around it. Every few minutes, we hear the roar of an airplane flying overhead.

They are so big when you're right under them, like we are. It's pretty cool. "This way, kids. We're gonna head in through those doors right over there."

We walk through the entryway, then the Lady checks us in, and a man working behind a long counter takes our bags. We then walk to this place where there is a big sign that says, SECURITY. I guess they want to make sure there aren't any bad people trying to get on an airplane to fly somewhere.

We walk through a big body-scanner-thing one by one. It beeps at some people, but it does not beep at us. There are walls of windows everywhere around us. You can look out and see everything—all the planes, some moving around on the runway, others parking next to the building. When it's finally time for us to get on the plane, the Lady hands all our tickets to the woman at the desk, who says, "Have a nice flight, y'all!" We walk down the long aisle of the plane. There's not very much room to walk between seats. We keep having to stop so someone can heave their bag up into the bin thing. I thought it looked a lot bigger from the outside than it really is once you're actually on the airplane. The Lady makes sure we find the right seats to sit in and says, "Right here, kids. It's these four seats. I'll take this one and you sit in those right there. Put on your seatbelt, like this," she clicks hers together, then continues— "then you pull it tight across your lap."

I'm so happy to be sitting on an airplane! When it starts to move forward, then takes off, I feel scared, but it's also exciting! Once we are in the sky, my ears hurt. I can't hear right. I hear a rushing noise and I feel kind of sick. After a few minutes, I get used to it. Flying isn't so bad. I like looking out the window to see the land so far beneath us. All the streets, cars, houses, and farms look like part of a miniature playset. It's hard to believe how high up we must be to make it all look so tiny.

When our plane finally lands, I feel relieved and happy that we didn't crash, and we made it. I'm glad to be back down on the ground. We exit the plane and walk up the little hallway to make our way into the airport. We see Aunt Laura and Uncle Chevo waiting on us.

They are both smiling and look happy to see us. They hug us and say, "You made it! Welcome to Hawaii!"

After the Lady talks to our aunt and uncle for a few minutes, we turn to say "goodbye" to her, then we leave the airport with our aunt and uncle. When we step outside the spinning airport doors. I can't believe how beautiful everything is. It looks like a picture from a book. The sky is bright blue and there are palm trees everywhere. I look around to see green grass, bushes with the biggest, prettiest flowers, and palm trees swaying in the warm breeze. I feel the warmest sunlight on my face. I stand there and take it all in. It does look exactly like everyone describes it, like a paradise. Laura and Chevo walk us up to a white SUV and we all hop in.

They talk to us a lot on the drive to their house—our new home—and make us feel welcomed, like they really want us to be with them. I think this is going to be great. We are going to have a real family again.

Uncle Chevo drives us to the military base where they live. He pulls in, stops the SUV, and shows his ID to a guy wearing a military uniform who is standing by a little booth at the entryway of the base. The man lifts his hand to his forehead to salute Uncle Chevo, and Uncle Chevo does the same thing back. I've never been around a person in the army before. I guess that's just something they do. The further we drive on the base I notice that it looks like a big apartment complex. There is a group of army guys running and singing out chants on the roadway, as we drive past them. They look sweaty and tired, like they've been running for a long time. I guess that's another thing that army people do. There are a bunch of tall, white-brick buildings with green trim all over. They all look the same. There are so many of them.

We pull up to the white-brick apartment building where they live. Our apartment has two floors and three bedrooms. It is nice. I am going to share a room with my sister, like I always do. My brother is going to share a room with Uncle Chevo and Aunt Laura's son, our new stepbrother. He is one year older than me. He is half Hispanic and half Black. He is short and slightly pudgy with dark brown eyes and curly hair. He is really Laura's son, but Uncle Chevo acts like he is his dad, even though he isn't. He seems nice. Since he doesn't have any brothers or sisters, I wasn't sure what he would think about his mom and dad taking in the three of us. I know if I was an only child, I don't think I would like it, but he seems to be okay with it and is excited to have us as siblings.

We are standing in the big living room downstairs. There is a kitchen by the living room that has a bar counter that divides the rooms and a sliding door off to the side of the kitchen. All the floors are wooden downstairs.

Laura tells us, "Come upstairs and I'll show you your rooms." We walk up an L-shaped stairway to the top floor. The carpet is gray. Our bedroom has cream walls and bunk beds and a small desk. There are colorful 3-D flower decorations hanging on the wall in shades of pink, blue, and yellow. The comforters on our beds are covered in pretty flowers and butterflies. It is beautiful. *I love this room! I've never had a bedroom like this before. It's so pretty! I can't believe that I get to live here. I am happy to share this room with my sister.* The top bunk is mine, like always. My sister is going to sleep on the lower bunk.

My brother is going to share a room with our new stepbrother. They each have their own separate beds, not bunk beds, like ours.

Later that night, my sister and I lie in our bunk beds and talk about our day. I tell her, "I really like it here. I love our new room so much!" She replies, "I know. See? I told you everything would work out for us, Abby. I really like Hawaii, too. It's cool here." With my head on my pillow, I fall asleep thinking about my mom and missing her, but I feel happy to be here. I am lucky. We all are. This is going to be the best thing to ever happen to us. I just know it.

ABIGAIL

AGE 9

Getting Settled

A unt Laura and Uncle Chevo seem pretty cool, like they're going to be good parents. We get to play outside a lot here. We like to run around in the big backyard behind our apartment building. We play tag. It is nice to have so much room to run and explore. Today, Aunt Laura took us shopping for costumes because it is almost Halloween. I am going to be a "good" witch. My costume is black with purple with a tall, pointy hat with sparkly, silver glitter all over it.

I am nervous to start at my new school, which is located here on the base. I am really shy. I don't talk to many people and don't make friends very easily. I don't know why. I'm nice. Maybe because I'm quiet, but I can't help it. I never know what to say. It's hard to meet new people. It's the way I've always been. I don't like talking to strangers—kids or grown-ups— especially in groups. I also don't like to try new things. That's part of what always gets on my brother's and sister's nerves and why they pick on me. "Just try it, Abby," they always say. "Stop being such a baby, Abby." "Why do you always make such a big deal over the smallest things, Abby?" But, sometimes, I really don't want to. They can taunt me all they want, but they can't make me try things or like people I don't know.

I worry that there won't be other Hispanic kids, like us, at our new school. In Texas there were all kinds of Hispanic people where we lived and a lot of Hispanic kids went to our school in San Antonio. We fit in there. But in Hawaii, we live on a military base, where people come from all over the world to live. I have no idea what to expect. *I just hope we aren't the only Hispanic kids there.*

We walk to school. It's on the base about ten minutes away. Since we are surrounded by military people, it seems really safe here, like nothing bad can happen to us. There is always an Army guy sitting in a tiny shack at the front of the base who checks people's IDs to make sure they belong here. Once he allows them inside, the sliding iron gate pulls back, and lets in military families and their close friends. I like that there is always someone on guard outside to protect me. I never had anyone to protect me back in Texas.

On my second day of school at Halekula Elementary, a girl named Jessica walked up to me on the playground and said, "Hi. I know you're new here. Do you wanna be friends with me?" She seemed nice and I really needed a friend. I felt relieved to have somebody I know and could hang out with every day. Now, she is my best friend and the one person I always look forward to seeing at school.

The school here isn't so bad. There is a mixture of kids from all over the world, all kinds of people. There are a lot of Samoans—people from Hawaii—at our school. Some of our teachers are from Hawaii, but some are from other states. I am glad there are Hispanic teachers here too, just like I'd hoped.

I have math in the morning and language arts in the afternoon. I especially hate—like, really hate—having to read aloud. I'm shy and I'm not very good at it. I get nervous and fumble over my words. I worry the whole time about messing up as my heart beats three hundred miles-per-minute. I get so nervous, to the point that I am shaking and breathing weird because I'm scared about looking and sounding stupid. I hate being called on by the teacher. I'd rather just hide. But other than reading and math, I enjoy other subjects. I really like art, especially drawing, but I'm not very good at it. My teacher says I'll get better with more practice. I hope she's right.

I know a girl who lives in the apartment building across from ours. Her name is Brittany. She's really nice. We play outside together a lot. I like that she lives across the street because it makes it easy for us to spend time with one another. We are pretty much together all the time when we aren't at school or spending time with our families.

Things at our new home seem good. We are getting used to living with Aunt Laura and Uncle Chevo. We have to do chores now. We have to clean our rooms, wash dishes, do some laundry, sweep and mop the floor, and scrub the bathroom. We don't have to do all these things at once. We each take turns on what chores we have to do each week. Aunt Laura writes on a calendar that tells us our job for each week. We just have to do our chores Monday through Friday, not on the weekends. If we do all of our daily cleaning, we get $1 a day—that's $5 every week! I never had an allowance before. We like to spend our allowance money at a little store located on our base. They have soda and snacks there. We get to buy whatever we want, since we earned the money by working for it.

Doing chores is okay, until I get assigned the bathroom duty. That includes the toilets. My brother and stepbrother are disgusting. They pee all over the place, on the floor, all over the back of the toilet, on the seat. When it's my week to clean the bathroom, I think they do it on purpose. I cry because it's gross in there, which is pretty much every single time that it's my turn to clean it. They act like I'm a brat. Really, I just think it's the nastiest thing someone could ask me to do and I don't want to do it. Usually, the boys and my sister tell me "Stop being such a crybaby, Abby. Just go do your chores." When it comes to the bathroom, Aunt Laura sometimes gets tired of me whining and crying about it and lets me out of cleaning the dirty toilets. It's so disgusting that I'd rather do any other chore, or even a bunch of other chores than to clean the stupid toilet. I may not get my dollar for it, but I also don't end up having to clean up a bunch of smelly pee, either. I think of it as a win. My siblings think of it as annoying.

Aunt Laura is a good cook. She always has tasty meals for us here. We eat at the table together most nights. We eat a lot of Mexican food: rice and beans, enchiladas, and foods from the mainland. I had never tried salmon before moving to Hawaii. It is delicious. The thing I don't like about meals here is that we aren't allowed to get up unless we eat everything on our plate. I mean, everything—even the gross stuff. I'm not a picky eater, but if there is something that I don't want to eat, I sometimes sit at the table for a really long time picking at it with my fork, hoping that it disappears. My siblings and I don't like vegetables—at all. Aunt Laura always says, "They're good for your body. Carrots make you see better. Eat them, or you'll be sitting there all night." Depending how gross something is, I will stubbornly sit at the table until bedtime. Other times, I just suck it up and shovel the gross vegetables into my mouth while trying to plug my nose or pretend I can't taste the nastiness on my tongue as I try to just gag it down faster. Broccoli and carrots are the worst. If those are on my plate, I know that it's gonna be a looooong night. Who in the heck wants to eat broccoli? The stuff is green and looks like miniature trees. So nasty. I have no idea why Aunt Laura wants to serve us mini trees and then makes us spend the whole night at the table.

Our Aunt Laura works as a childcare worker. She works during the day and is home with us after school. She is very organized, like a teacher. Everything is always planned, labeled, in the right spot, and kept neatly. Her son seems to like having us around, especially my little brother. They play football and basketball together outside all the time. I guess my brother is like the brother he never had. I'm glad they get along. It would be terrible if they didn't.

Uncle Chevo is nice. He works a lot, but when he is around, he talks to us and tries to teach us things, including some things a lot of men might not try to show a girl, like how to fix something, how to change a tire, or how to change the oil in a car. He says, "Abby, I'm going to teach you how to do *everything*. You aren't ever going to have to rely on a man to do things for you. You will always be able to take care of things for yourself." I like that he wants to teach me things. It's pretty cool.

Another thing I like about living here is that we get to have "family night." Once a week we all gather as a family in the living room to play fun games, like Candyland and Monopoly. Most of the time, it is all of us and Aunt Laura and Uncle Chevo play, too. Other times, it is just us kids. Either way, I really like family night and always look forward to it and try to beat my brother and sister at board-games.

This feels like a normal life for us. There are no late-night parties, drinking, smoking, and blaring Tejano music. We are just a normal family, doing normal family things. I feel like I belong here, with them. I feel like they are going to always take care of me.

Me and my brother seem to miss our mom the most. I'm not saying my sister doesn't, but she is older and probably better at hiding it. She tries to help me to feel less sad anytime I talk to her about how much I miss mom and wish that we could see her again. She tells me, "The judge says we aren't allowed to, we live here now." I'm not sure when we'll get to see our mom again, or if we ever will. I try to focus on the good things: Hawaii, sunshine, palm trees and hibiscus flowers, Aunt Laura and Uncle Chevo, being a family, my best friend Jessica, my newest friend Brittany, my "new normal" life. I get to have a fresh start here, with them.

ABIGAIL

AGE 9

Seeing the Sights

*I*n our new life, we do a lot of things together as a family. On the weekends, we all go out to eat together. Laura takes us to the ocean often. Sometimes, we wear our swimsuits to school under our clothes because she takes us to the beach right after.

I absolutely love going to the beach! Hawaii is *so* beautiful. I can't stop staring at the clear blue sky, the waves as they crash on the sandy beach, the colorful hibiscus flowers on green plants everywhere. There are times we spend a day at the beach, and other times when we get to rent a cottage and spend the whole weekend with my friend Brittany's family. I like the beach trips best. It's fun to have a friend come along. We lie in the sand on our towels to soak up the sun. We run into the crashing waves. We look for seashells. Sometimes, we get lucky and there is a sea critter lying on the sand or in the shallow water where we can see it. I always look forward to seeing the ocean. Aunt Laura takes us to see all the beaches here.

The coolest thing I've seen so far in Hawaii is Diamond Head. It is a volcano. It's not black and rocklike from past eruptions. It is so big, like a giant dome that is covered in greenery. We get to climb it. There are small steps that lead you all the way up. I have to stop to take breaks at times because my legs start to cramp after a while. Once I get up to the top, I can see everything from here. I see all of

Hawaii, crystal blue water lapping at the sandy shore, houses dotting the horizon, boats sailing across the water, colorful cottages, and huts.

Aunt Laura and Uncle Chevo once took us to a thing called a luau. That was really cool. All of the ladies were wearing traditional Hawaiian dresses and hula skirts. The men do a Mosquito Dance, where they tell a story through their motions while a translator tells what they are singing about. At the end all the men would race all the way up to the top of palm trees. It was the coolest thing to see. At the luau, they bury a whole pig in the ground and cook it. They always put an apple in the pig's mouth. I think that part is kind of funny looking and weird, but the meat is delicious. It's like a big celebration with dancing, singing, and eating. Everyone is happy. I love learning about the culture here. It's like we are in another world. This place is *way* different than Texas, but in a good way. Not everybody even gets to visit Hawaii, but I get to live here. Hawaii truly is paradise. And now, it is *my* paradise.

I wonder if we'll get to stay here forever.

ABIGAIL

AGE 9

The Adoption

One day, about three months after we moved to Hawaii, Aunt Laura and Uncle Chevo call us all down to the living room. Laura says, "Sit down, kids. We have something important that we need to talk to y'all about." I have no idea what it could be. *Are we in trouble? Are we moving? I have no idea.* Laura continues, "We just wanted to tell you that we are going to officially adopt you all—legally—so you will be *our* kids. All we have to do is fill out the papers, write down your 'new' names and turn in the paperwork! Isn't that exciting news?"

From now on, my new name is going to be "Abigail Olga Castillo." I have a new middle name—it is the same as Laura's mom's middle name. I don't really like the name "Olga" at all. I think it sounds dumb, but Laura seems really happy about it. She said it is a "family name" and acts proud of it, so I pretend to be okay with it. At least people will still call me by my first and last name. It's not like you ever really have to tell anyone your middle name anyway. We all share the same last name now, like a family. We are the "Castillos." Instead of calling them "Aunt Laura" and "Uncle Chevo," me and my brother and sister now call them "Mom" and "Dad." (If I talk about my real mom, I'll refer to her as "Real Mom," so you don't get confused.)

My mom and dad seem happy to adopt us. In a way, I think it's strange that our last name is no longer "Rodriguez." That's the name we've always had. It's the name my mom gave us. But I guess this is just the way things have to be now. We are here, with them. They do take care of us, like real parents. We get to live here, in Hawaii. We have a beautiful home. We get whatever we want. They are our new mom and dad now.

To celebrate our adoption, Mom invites a few of her friends over to celebrate by eating dinner with us. She keeps calling it, "an adoption celebration." It feels good to be adopted. It isn't a big party, like we used to have with Real Mom, but it's still fun to have a dinner with company. Everybody seems happy about it. They are talking, and laughing, and we are all having a nice time sitting around the table together. My mom's friends say nice things to us, like, "Congratulations!" "You guys are going to be a real family now!" "It's so awesome that they adopted you!"

And they are right—our new life is good.

ABIGAIL

AGE 9

Home Alone

This afternoon, I am home alone with my "dad." No one else is here. It's just the two of us. I kind of like how quiet it is when my real brother, stepbrother, and sister are gone. I don't get to have time alone very often or be by myself with just one of my parents. We are in the living room downstairs watching TV. I am lying on the dark brown couch with my legs stretched across a few of the cushions. My dad sits on the cushion at the end of it. We are just relaxing, watching a show together, and one of us occasionally says something or makes a comment about what just happened on TV.

My dad grabs one of my socked feet which is lying next to him and begins to give me a foot massage. *It feels so good. It's pretty cool that I have a new dad that likes to give me foot massages.* He is rubbing the bottom of my foot and making small circles and pressing into my heels with his thumbs. There are times when him pushing his thumb into my foot almost hurts, but not all the way, and it makes my whole body feel relaxed. When he is done rubbing my foot, he sets it back down on the couch cushion and picks up the other foot. He begins to massage that one, too. *It feels really good to get your feet rubbed.* He turns to look at me and says, "I know you had a long day. I just want to help you relax." I did have a long day. I am happy he wants to try to make me feel relaxed.

My dad then starts to massage my ankles. *He is going to give me a leg massage, too!* He is rubbing back and forth across the backs of my leg. Back and forth. Back and forth. His hands go from my ankles up toward my knee, still rubbing across my skin. He keeps rubbing back and forth, back and forth, then slides his hand up to rub my thigh. I am wearing shorts, so he can touch my whole leg. He is using his fingers to rub up and down my leg in long lines and then making small circles in certain spots. It feels good to get my legs rubbed, but not as good as it felt when he was massaging my feet. Each time he moves his hand back down to my ankle, on the next pass up the back up my leg, he seems to go a bit higher. *That's kind of weird, but it's my dad. I'm sure it's fine. He said he just wants to help me relax.*

His hand slides down the back of my knee to my ankle. Then, one of his hands goes way higher up my leg than he'd gone before, skimming across the very bottom of my panties. *Okay, this is weird. Something about this isn't right. I know this is wrong. It feels wrong. Why is he doing this?*

Everything is fine, until the moment when it's not. His fingers run up my leg and across the front of my panties. I ask, "What are you doing?" I'm confused about what is happening right now—what he is doing. He says, "Oh, I'm just rubbing you to help you relax." *But this feels wrong.* I look at my dad and his face looks totally normal, like nothing strange is going on. His hand runs across the tops of my legs and across the top of my panties in the front of them, rubbing me there, over and over. *This is weird. I think this is wrong. This is a bad touch. I know a grown up isn't supposed to touch someone like this. Why is he doing this?*

My dad's hand eventually stills. He pulls it away and stops touching me. He looks me in the eyes and says, "Don't tell your mom." *Why doesn't he want me to tell my mom? Because she would be mad? Because he knows he shouldn't be doing this? Would she be mad at me, or mad at him? Was this wrong?*

The rest of the family eventually comes home. The rest of the night my dad acts like everything that happened between us was normal, or maybe more like nothing happened at all. But it did happen—something did—and I'm not sure how to feel about it. I think it was something bad that happened to me. *Should I tell my mom? He did tell me not to tell her. Did I do something bad?*

I guess more than anything, I just feel confused about it. It's like I now have a secret to keep because of that—what he did—whatever that was. But I don't even know exactly what the secret means, or why it has to be a secret at all. And why would he touch his hand on my panties? That's a "bad touch." They taught us about that at school. That you should never let anyone touch you there. But it's my dad. He didn't go under my panties. He said he was just giving me a massage. That he was trying to help me relax because he knows I had a long day today. I guess I just won't say anything.

I guess I'll just pretend that it never happened. The secret thing. The thing-that-feels-kind-of-bad-and-wrong-between-us that we aren't going to tell anyone about.

ABIGAIL

AGE 9

The Mind Trip

$\mathcal{A}$fter the-thing-we-aren't-going-to-talk-about happened with my dad, he acted totally normal, like nothing weird or bad ever took place. I'm not sure what really even did happen, what it means, what he meant by it, or if there is anything actually wrong with it. But it feels wrong. I feel like I am bad, like I did something wrong. Like it's something he shouldn't be doing. I don't know why he wanted to do that, and I hope it never happens again.

I know I'm not supposed to tell anyone. I don't know what my mom would think about it. I wonder if she would be mad about the thing that happened between me and my dad. Maybe it was just a one-time thing, and I don't have to worry. I hope so. I don't want to be around him now. I am afraid that he'll do it again. I don't want to be alone with him anymore. I know he won't do bad things to me if other people are around, but there are times when no one else is home. Times when it's just me and him alone when I start to worry that he will look at me with his cold brown eyes. And touch my body when he shouldn't be touching it at all. I think he is sick. There has to be something wrong with him to want to do this to me. He has a wife. He needs to just leave me alone.

But then there is a crack in the door to our bedroom. I hear his footsteps. He is walking toward me. He is walking closer to me. Closer. Even closer. I'm holding my breath trying to pretend to be asleep. *I just want him to leave. Please just leave. I am asleep. Please don't come in here.* He stops beside our bunk bed. He climbs up the slats on the ladder and lies down beside me. *Does my sister hear? Maybe she will wake up and say something. Anything.* He brushes my hair off the side of my face. He gently runs his hand down my neck. I can smell his breath. He lies beside me. I feel the warmth of his body near mine. The idea of him being in here, in my bed, beside me, makes me want to throw up. I don't know what is wrong with him, but there is definitely something wrong with him to want to do this. I wait for it—for this—night after night. I fear it, day by day. I worry. And I wait.

The crack in the door.

The footsteps.

The ladder.

His breath.

Him lying beside me.

His fingers roaming.

I now fear the dark. I fear that crack in the door even more. The light spilling in.

And I hate him. I really hate him.

I just want him to leave me alone. To go away. Forever.

He is a monster.

And I am just a girl in the dark. Stuck in her bed, with terrible thoughts running through her head, waiting for it all to be over.

ABIGAIL

AGE 9

Telling Mom

I am at home with my mom today. I decide that I need to tell her about what has been happening to me, about what my dad has been doing. The big, bad, ugly thing that I'm not supposed to talk about. The secret he warned me not to tell anyone. I don't want to keep it anymore. I need my mom to help me. I need her to make him stop doing weird and bad things to me. I hope she won't be mad at me or think that I did something wrong. I worry that she might.

She is in her bedroom, so I walk in and sit down on the edge of her bed. "Mom, there's something that I need to talk to you about."

She sits down next to me and says, "What is it, Abby?"

"Dad has been touching me."

"What are you talking about? What do you mean?"

"He's been touching me down there," I say, pointing to my private parts.

"Your dad wouldn't do that. That's not him. He's your dad. I don't want to talk about this anymore, Abby. That's enough about it. Don't talk about it anymore."

My mom's face never shifts. Looking at her, it's as though I didn't tell her anything at all. Feeling unsure about what just happened between us, I walk out of her bedroom.

My mom doesn't even believe me. She isn't going to do anything about it. She acts like what he did to me never even happened. I don't understand. Will this just keep happening to me over and over again? It's not right. Why doesn't anybody care? Why doesn't my mom want to stop it? Why doesn't she go yell at him and tell him not to do it to me anymore?

Most of the time things are good here. Everybody else probably thinks so. We have a nice home. We have nice things. I have nice clothes and a pretty room. They always feed us, make sure we go to school, and my mom sits down with us at the dining room table to help us with our homework. But I feel all alone, like nobody really cares about me. If somebody did care about me, then these bad things wouldn't be happening to me. *I don't have anybody to listen to me. Nobody to protect me. There is nobody to care.* I just get to live here and pretend to be happy. I get to pretend that everything is normal, until it's just my dad and me. Until it happens the next time, the unspoken bad thing. Over and over again. I don't think he is ever going to stop.

He always waits until I am alone when nobody else is home. That is when he does it. He touches me. He acts like there's nothing wrong with it. He tells me not to tell anyone. "Don't say anything to your mom. Remember, this is just between us, Abby." And I feel alone, and dirty, and bad because of what he does to me. Even after it's over, it's like I can't really get rid of it all the way. Like the things he does to me somehow become a part of me. Kind of like smearing black dirt across a white towel until it changes the color. I am stained.

ABIGAIL

AGE 13

The Move

Today, Mom and Dad call us all down to the living room and tell us that we are going to leave Hawaii and will be moving to Houston, Texas. I'm sad about leaving. We've lived here for four years. Who would want to leave this paradise?

My mom said that my dad isn't planning to come with us. He has to stay behind to "take care of some things," so just my mom, my sister, my two brothers and I will be going. That part is the best news I've ever heard! I don't want to be around my dad. Since he won't be coming with us, at least I know he can't bother me anymore. Hopefully, he won't ever do it again. Maybe it will stop. I wonder if my mom is making him stay behind because of what he did to me—to punish him or something. I'm not sure. Maybe his actions have nothing to do with why we are moving, but I sure am glad to be away from him no matter what the reason.

My mom is a good mom, but she doesn't believe me about my dad. This makes me so angry, like if she was really a good mom, she would do something about it.

We move to my mom's sister's house in Houston, Texas, that she shares with her husband and their kids. It's a brick house that's all one level with four bedrooms. We have new cousins to play with now, which is pretty cool. Our new aunt and uncle seem nice, like they are happy for us to be living here with them. There is a big back yard.

At this point, I'm not feeling nervous about starting a new school here. I feel like I've already started school at so many different places that I'm kind of used to it. I don't really like being the new kid because I'm shy, but it is what it is. I just have to deal with it—again. I don't really see the point of making new friends. We just end up having to leave them behind. That happened when we left San Antonio where we lived with Real Mom, and again when we left the shelter.

We walk to church with our new cousins every Sunday. We always have a family dinner afterward. I really like Sundays because of that. I look forward to the fried chicken, french fries, enchiladas, Mexican rice, and jambalaya my new aunt and uncle cook. Us kids like to run around the house and hang out outside all day. They have pet chickens and cats. We get to feed them and help take care of them.

At our new school, we have to wear stupid uniforms: khaki pants, tucked-in, navy collared shirts, with a brown belt and white or black shoes. We all look the same. I miss wearing whatever I want to wear to school. I guess the good thing about having a big family is that I don't really need any friends because there's always somebody around for me to hang out with. I earn mostly A's and B's at this school, but I sometimes get C's in subjects like math and reading. Those two are the worst. When I think about what I might like to be when I grow up, I think I'd like to become a teacher one day. That would be a pretty cool job.

The really good thing about living with my aunt and uncle is that my dad is still living in Hawaii. That means that he can't bother me here. I am so happy about that. I thank God every night for keeping him away from me. I hope it stays this way, but I know that eventually he will move back in with us.

After about a year living with our aunt and uncle, my mom tells us that we are moving out on our own, to a three-bedroom house in Houston. My dad is going to join us there. *Oh no. I don't want him to come. I don't want him to live with us. I don't want him to be anywhere near me. That means that it may start again. The things he does. But maybe he got better since we've been away. Maybe he's not going to do that anymore.*

I don't wonder if it's wrong now—the things that he does to me. I *know* that it is wrong. And that he must be sick in the head to do it. There is something wrong with him to want to touch me the way that he does. This isn't normal. It's not right. I know that now.

And I fear him moving here with us because of it.

ABIGAIL

AGE 13
Houston, Texas

Dad Returns

My dad got a job as a maintenance worker at a hospital in Houston. He flew here and we all live together again in a three-bedroom house now. It is back to our "normal" family life here. But it is only "normal" for me until my dad walks into my bedroom at night or finds me in the living room alone when everyone else is away. He is a sick, sick man. I wish I never had to see him again. Living with him is the worst. I have learned that it is impossible to stay away from your own dad when he lives in the same house as you. He can always get to me. He finds a way. I guess he's not in the Army anymore. That's why he had to get a job at the hospital here.

After that house, the next place we move into—there are a lot of them—is a three-bedroom apartment in Houston. And that means another new school. *I am so sick of changing schools. Why can't we ever just stay in one place?*

Since my dad moved back in with us, the abuse has gotten worse. He is touching me more often now—almost every day—like I am his new bad habit. One that he can't seem to stop.

I am afraid to be alone with him. I am afraid when it's time to go to sleep now. I am fearful when I am lying in my bed at night. I am paranoid when I see everyone else leaving to go somewhere. I don't like being anywhere near him. I always worry about when it's going to happen again—the touching—because it always does happen again.

Yesterday, I met a girl at the apartments who quickly became my new best friend here. That is the only good thing about our latest move. I met her outside our building one day. We just started talking and hanging out, then I learned that she lives in the same building that we do.

New Best Friend and I hang out often. We're either outside or at her apartment, but rarely do we go to mine. I try to avoid being at mine for obvious reasons, mostly because of my dad. I like to stay away from him as much as possible.

My parents have always treated me differently than my siblings. My older sister, younger brother, and stepbrother get to be "normal" kids. They get to have friends, go outside anytime they want to during the day, go to fun places whenever they are invited, and they even get to spend the night at other kids' houses.

I get to do none of these things, with the exception of getting to play outside when New Best Friend rings the doorbell on occasion. I love it when she is on the other side of the door. She is my only escape. I ask her to come over to get me every single day, but she isn't always able to. My parents never let me go ask her to play. I am *so sick* of being treated differently than everybody else. And I'm not even the youngest kid—my brother is!

My parents like to say it's because of "traditional Mexican values." Over the years, I've learned to stop trying to argue with them about it. It doesn't really matter what I say, they won't listen to me anyway. I've tried to raise the point with them on multiple occasions.

"Why does my little brother get to go outside and have friends, but I can't?"

"Because he's a boy. He knows how to take care of himself, like a boy should. You're a girl."

"Then why does my sister get to go have friends and go do what she wants? She's a girl, too!"

"Well, that's because your sister is older."

"That's NOT fair!"

"Well, it doesn't really matter if you think it's fair or not, Abby. That's just the way it is and that's the way it is going to be."

Traditional Mexican values come with a lot of rules. Girls are raised differently. (I guess, unless you're my sister, anyway). Swearing is not allowed. (Well, that rule does apply to her, too.) You must do everything you are told. You do your chores, which mostly involves the women doing everything. My brother and stepbrother just have to take out the trash. Women (and girls) are expected to clean the whole house and do everything else: dishes, laundry, sweeping, cooking, scrubbing. Women aren't supposed to have tattoos. They are the caretakers of their family. The man is the head of the household and the one in charge. Women are to be protected by their male family members. One day, a woman marries someone her father likes and approves of, and that is when she moves out of her family's home. But these values only seem to apply to me, not to my sister. I feel like it's not based on logic at all, but they like to hide behind their "traditional Mexican values" as the reason why I basically get treated like a prisoner wherever we live.

I think the *real* reason is because my dad gets jealous over me. He worries about me meeting boys, being a regular girl my age with friends, or having any kind of a normal life. So, I don't get to have a life at all. I just sit here, in this stupid apartment, to secretly be his. And my mom lets it happen. She pretends nothing weird is going on. But I told her about it when it first started. She knows—at least *she should* know. But knowing about it and caring about it are two different things. There's no point in telling her anything about it anymore. She doesn't care. It continues to happen.

I don't think my dad touches my sister the way that he touches me. She would completely freak out on him. She would probably fight him. She would scratch his face, kick him, and bite him, and she would tell everyone. He couldn't get away with doing that stuff to her the way he does to me. Part of me wishes that I could be more like her. That I could be more of a fighter, to kick, claw, and punch him, yell mean things, and tell the world about what he's doing. I wish that I could have a life, and friends, and go places to hang out, and have a regular dad who doesn't abuse me. But in some small way, a part of me is okay with taking the abuse if my sister doesn't have to. At least it's just happening to one of us, and if it has to be one of us—why shouldn't it be me?

There is a boy who I have a crush on who also lives in our apartment complex. I've seen him playing basketball with my younger brother sometimes. He is really cute. He's Hispanic, like me. He's kind of tall and has a stocky build with black hair, light brown eyes, and an air of coolness about him. Whenever I see him, I feel excited. It's hard for me not to keep staring at him because I like looking at him. I really like this boy.

One day, I go to the park, and I see that Cute Boy is there. We walk up to one another and start talking. We then walk over to the playground equipment and sit inside this large plastic tube thing on the playground, when all of a sudden, he leans across the space between us to kiss me. I let him. And I kiss him back. I feel really excited and nervous, like there are tiny butterflies fluttering in my belly. It feels nice to kiss him and to feel Cute Boy's soft lips on mine, so gentle. I've never been kissed by a boy before. I've only been kissed by my dad. (That's pretty sick, I know. But it's true.) I guess you could say that this was my first kiss *by choice*. I like this boy. He likes me. And we are kissing because we want to—because *I want to*. I feel nervous about it, but I like it.

All of a sudden, I hear the loud voice of a girl saying, "Ummmm, you're gonna be in trouble!" I look up and see one of my girl cousins standing at the edge of the playground. "I totally saw you! I'm gonna go tell your mom and dad what you're out here doing." She and her mom and dad—my aunt and uncle—and her siblings had come to visit and hang out with us at our apartment for the day. I didn't know she was outside. I had no idea anyone else was at the playground or

I never would have kissed Cute Boy. *Oh no. Oh no. Oh my God. Please don't tell on me. Please, no.* I shout, "Please don't say anything!" as she takes off running toward our apartment. *I am going to be in so much trouble. This is really, really bad. So bad.*

I tell Cute Boy I have to go, then I dart as fast as I can after the little snitch—my new enemy—toward our apartment. I am embarrassed for getting caught. But I'm more scared about what's going to happen to me when I get there. Terrified.

I walk in. I close the front door behind me. I walk into the living room. I can tell by the look on the face of everyone in the room that I'm in big time trouble. My dad is so angry. He runs in my direction as he reaches to start pulling off his belt. I can tell he's going to try to hit me with it. I frantically try to get away. We run in half circles back and forth around the living room. My mom says, "STOP RUNNING AND PUT YOUR HANDS ON THE COUCH, ABBY. WE ARE GOING TO SPANK YOU FOR WHAT YOU'VE DONE."

I scream like I am being murdered, and shield my body with my hands. He swings the belt through the air at me, attempting to hit me with the leather strap. I am still trying my darndest to get away, but with two of them trying to get me, my darting in different directions across the small room doesn't last long. My dad hits me with the belt across my butt and the back of my legs. I scream. "Please don't hit me! Please stop hitting me!" The whole family watches—with my sister, brother, and traitor cousin standing by with wide eyes like onlookers who don't want to watch, but can't seem to turn away.

Mom says, "THIS IS SO Y'ALL KNOW [WHACK] NOT TO BE DOING THINGS WHEN YOU AREN'T SUPPOSED TO BE DOING THINGS," in the direction of the other kids. Another smack stings my skin. WHACK. He hits my hands as I struggle to get away. WHACK. They try to pin my hands down on the back of the couch. WHACK. My dad and mom take turns beating me with the belt. WHACK, WHACK, WHACK, WHACK. I don't think they are ever going to stop. WHACK. Finally, I can tell my sister feels sorry for me, because she pipes up, "That's enough. You've taught her a lesson. Stop hitting her." My mom replies, "DO YOU WANT ONE, TOO?" So, my sister stops defending me. By the time they are done hitting me, I've probably taken seven or eight whacks of dad's leather belt across my backside, my face is streaked with lines of streaming tears, and I can't walk right. I limp toward my bedroom. I've never been hit by them before. My skin is hurting. It's burning really bad and tingling. It's red and there are lines of pink welts across my lower back, butt, and legs. *I hate them! I really, really hate them!* They don't just leave welts as punishment for my first kiss with Cute Boy. They leave bruises. And I hate them for it.

The worst part for me is realizing that this didn't really happen to me just because I kissed a boy, like any normal girl my age might accidentally get caught doing. It is because I kissed a boy when I'm supposed to be just my dad's to kiss and to touch. Because something is very wrong with him.

Speaking of that, my dad still tries to get me alone all the time. He's been touching me ever since we moved into this apartment with him, after he moved back here from Hawaii to be with us. My brothers and sister get to play with their friends and be outside all the time. I'm not allowed to leave, unless New Best Friend comes looking for me. Only then do I get to go outside to play for a while. She is my only relief.

My dad usually bothers me when my siblings are outside playing or when they are gone. They are having fun out there, while I get stuck in this apartment—with him—touching me in a way he shouldn't be. But still, he does it anyway.

After living in in this apartment in Houston for a few months, I decide that I'm going to tell New Best Friend about what Dad has been doing to me. The only person I ever told about it was my mom and she didn't believe me. I'm not sure what to expect. I think my secret hope floating in the back of my mind is that once I tell her, I'll be able to live with her and her mom.

New Best Friend and I are sitting outside one day, when I begin to tell her about what my life is *really* like. "It's kind of embarrassing to tell you about this, but you're my best friend. You're the only person I feel like I can really tell. I get abused at home. It's—my dad. He sneaks into my room and he touches me in a sexual way. He does it when nobody else is around. There is something wrong with him. I can't take it anymore. I really can't." Tears stream down my cheeks. I feel ashamed and embarrassed to say the words aloud.

New Best Friend takes in every word I say. The look on her face makes it clear that she feels sorry for me. "Abby, that's wrong. He shouldn't be doing that. You need to tell someone."

"I know, I'm telling *you*. I tried to tell my mom about it, but she doesn't believe me."

"I mean—you need to tell *someone who can help*. I can tell my mom and maybe she can help you?"

"No. Oh my God, no. Please don't tell anyone. Pleeeeease. Don't tell your mom about this. I am begging you not to say *anything* to *anyone* about this, *not even your mom*. I need this to stay between us. I just had to tell someone."

"I won't tell anybody, Abby. I'm glad you told me. I'm your best friend. You can always tell me anything."

Her promise to me turned out to not be a promise kept. I can't say that I blame her.

Two days later, a report was filed with Child Protective Services by New Best Friend's mom alleging my dad's sexual abuse against me. A CPS worker visited our apartment and came to talk to all of us and look around.

We immediately packed up our entire apartment and left the same night.

ABIGAIL

AGE 13
Laredo, Texas

The Coyote

We move to Laredo, Texas—me, mom, dad, and my siblings. We now live in a big, white house with our new "grandma"—my dad's stepmom. She's a stranger to us. We just met her. She is a short Hispanic lady who is slightly pudgy and has short, black, curly hair. She's not very pretty and kind of has a scary look about her, like she's not someone you'd want to mess with. She lives in the nicest house I've ever seen. There are big statutes outside and it has a gate all around it. It looks like a rich person's house, like a mansion. I can't believe we actually get to stay at a place this nice. It looks like a place you would only see on TV.

We are just going to stay at her house for a while, until my parents find us a new house. We are all going to sleep in the family room on blow up mattresses. Our "grandma" sleeps in her bedroom upstairs. I like being here, at her house, because anytime that we all have to sleep in one room together, it means that I am safe. My dad can't try to touch me here with other people around. He is sneaky, so he still sometimes finds a way to do bad things to me, but at least it's not all the time anymore.

Our grandma is a coyote. I bet you probably are wondering what that means. A "coyote" is a person who helps people cross the border illegally from Mexico to Texas. Not like a human trafficker or anything. She just helps people who want to come to America for a better life or a good job. Her first language is Spanish. She sounds funny to us whenever she speaks English because she has a thick accent. She's really nice though. And she pays us if we help her to move people across the border! She says, "Do you kids want to go help me to move some people today?" To which we exclaim, "Yeeesss!! We'll go!"

We love to help her because she pays each of us $100-200 each time we go with her, then we get to spend the money on whatever we want. I usually spend mine on junk food or Barbie dolls. For us, it's big-time money. I guess our grandma must make big-time money to live in a mansion like she does and to pay us to help her.

Today, she needs us to help her take four immigrants across the border. "Okay guys, I need y'all to get in the truck," Grandma says.

"Why, Grandma?"

"We're gonna take a drive to San Antonio. I'm gonna give y'all $100 if y'all come with me."

"Okay!"

We all hop into her SUV. There's a driver and a passenger seat in it, but no middle seat. Three immigrants sit in the empty middle space. She then puts suitcases on top of them to cover them up. Afterward, we sit on top of the suitcase. It seems kind of weird to be sitting on people, but they have to hide to get across the border, so I guess they don't mind. I'm jealous because my sister gets to sit in the middle beside the fourth person, an immigrant sitting in the front passenger seat. Because my sister is in that seat and she is older, my grandma is going to pay her extra money for pretending to be the immigrant's girlfriend, if we get pulled over. She's lucky.

We think the immigrants sound funny when they talk because they only speak Spanish. We only speak English. We know certain Spanish words, but not very many, just the Spanish words we have heard our family members say. When they try to say words in English to us, they sound funny. They are always nice to us though. They seem really happy to be coming to America and glad that we are helping them. Still, it feels kind of weird to sit on top of people.

We drop the four of them off in San Antonio and then turn around to head back to Laredo. Our Coyote Grandma pays us the money and we hide it in the family room where we sleep.

The next day, The Coyote takes us shopping to spend our money. I buy a bunch of gum and candy, a bunch of coloring books, and a big box of crayons—the biggest one with *all* the colors and a built-in sharpener. Coloring makes me feel happy and it gives me something to do whenever I'm bored. My sister buys shoes and clothes. I don't know what my brother buys. I don't really pay attention. Probably new shoes. Hopped up on soda, candy, and new stuff, The Coyote drives us back home to her mansion.

Eventually, we—mom, dad, me, and my siblings—move out of The Coyote's house and into our new, big orange house that has four bedrooms. I am going to have my own room now. While I like the idea of decorating it any way I want to and having a place for only my things, I don't want to have my own room. That means that my dad can get to me easier now. I decorate my whole room with SpongeBob SquarePants. It looks like a happy room, but I know that it's not going to be one.

We have another new school here. I don't even care about it anymore. It's so hard to try to get good grades when we move all the time. Every school is different. We get different teachers who are teaching different stuff than what we were learning at our last school. It makes me feel stupid that I'm not good at reading and terrible at math. I still like art because I'm pretty good at it. I'm not going to try to make friends at this school. There's no point.

Since we moved out, The Coyote now brings immigrants over to spend the night at our new house. We do it to help her out. We hang out with them and they eat meals with us. It's kind of weird having strangers around, but they are always really nice, and I'm not afraid of them. Sometimes, they only stay a few hours. There are other times they will stay with us for a day, or even a week. The Coyote comes for them when she says it's "safe" to move them. Me and my sister sit and talk with them sometimes. We like to hear their funny accents and interesting stories. Some of them tell us about what it's like in Mexico and why they want to come here. They say things like, "You have it so good here." I think it's cool that The Coyote helps them. I wish I still made $100-200 for helping her move them from Laredo to San Antonio.

One day, there is a lady—an immigrant—sitting in my dad's car in the driveway of our house. Apparently, he was trying to have sex with the lady outside and my mom caught him, so they begin to argue. Things get loud and ugly really fast. They both scream at each other. My mom shrieks at my dad, "You want to be with HER? You want to be with someone else? I'M GOING TO LEAVE YOU."

My dad walks out of the house. A few moments later, he walks back in holding a gas can. Me, my siblings, and my mom are all in the living room, as my dad starts to pour gasoline all over himself. He then starts dousing everything in the room—the curtains, carpet, and the furniture. It stinks. The smell starts to burn the inside of my nose. My dad takes out a lighter and is acting like he's going to light himself on fire. Right here, right now, in this room, with us. *If that's what he wants to do, let him do it. I hope he does*, I think to myself.

He flicks the lighter, but it does not spark. *Why isn't it sparking? Why can't he just actually do it?* My mom screams, "DON'T do it. IT'S OKAY. It's okay. Don't do it." She is trying to calm him down. I think it might be working. My mom then turns to my older sister and says, "Come and help me to clean up this gasoline." *Why are they stopping him? Why are they cleaning up the gasoline? Why didn't that stupid lighter just spark? Why couldn't he just set himself on fire? Why?*

When I lie down in my bed to sleep later that night, I think about how my dad has never done anything *that* crazy before. He must really be losing it. And I know he was trying to have sex with that immigrant lady in the car. That's what started it all. *That means he was trying to touch someone else besides just me. I wonder if there are other people that he has tried to do that to? I bet he has. He needs help. He is crazy.*

ABIGAIL

AGE 13

The Abuse Worsens

I fear nighttime now. The lights are out. Everything is still. The house is quiet. Everyone is in bed, except for him. I lie in my bed. I stare at that crack in the door.

I know that he is going to walk through it. He always does now. He visits my room every night since we moved into this house. Every. Single. Night.

All I can do is wait. And worry. And feel sick to my stomach. And try not to cry. I want to pretend that it's not going to happen again, but it always does. There is always a next time.

It's gotten worse now. He still touches me over my panties and all over everywhere else. But now, he makes me touch him, too. He hisses, "touch me," and puts my hand on his private part over his clothes. It is so disgusting. Having him lying in my bed, looking at me in a way that he shouldn't be, and me having to touch him is the grossest thing I have ever done. I don't want to do it at all. But I don't really have much choice. He is here. And this is what is going to happen. Again.

There are times when touching is all that happens. There are times when it gets worse.

One night, he walks into my room. He unzips his pants, pulls them down to his knees, and gets into the bed beside me. He is wearing only his boxers. I am the most scared that I have ever been.

I'm not sure what is going to happen, but this feels different, darker, like it might get worse. If I don't want to do something that he tells me to do, he says, "Do it, or you're gonna GET IT WORSE." When he says that, I know that he will find a way to punish me more *while* he is doing it. Not that I can imagine anything being worse, but he seems to always find a way to make it worse. He is rougher. He slams his fingers—and more of them—into my body harder. He pins my body down more forcefully. He does what he can to try to hurt me more, when the things he is doing to me already hurt me so much. I hate this. I hate him. I hate living here.

ABIGAIL

AGE 13

The Rape

One evening, as the sun is setting, my mom and all my siblings leave to go to the grocery store. "You just stay here, Abby. They'll be back soon. You don't need to go," my dad says. My stomach swirls with sickness and dread.

I am at home alone with my dad. I am in my bedroom, sitting on my bed, wearing my favorite SpongeBob SquarePants pajamas. My dad walks into my bedroom and says to me, "Undress." It is a demand, not a request.

"No."

"No?"

He is wearing jeans, a plain white tee shirt and dirty socks. He strides over to where I am sitting on the bed, and aggressively grabs at the waistband of my pajama pants. I attempt to back away from him, lifting my butt and trying to scoot backwards, but his tight grip on the fabric waistband holds me in place. I cannot escape him. He attempts to pull my pajama pants down. I try to pull them back up, but he is stronger than me. It is no use. I can't stop him. This time, I know something is going to be different, that it is going to be worse than all the other times. It is in his aggressive movements, the commanding tone of his voice, and the sick glint in his eyes. I am standing next to the bed, still fighting with him as he yanks my pajama pants down, exposing me.

"Get on the bed."

"No."

He pushes me down onto the bed. There is nothing I can do about it. He pins my arms at my sides to the mattress on either side of me. I cannot get away. I scream. "No, no, no, don't touch me. No. Please don't do this!" I scream, but is no one here to hear it. I keep trying to stand up—to fight him off. My efforts get me nowhere. He pins me down with the full weight of his body. I cannot move now. I cannot try to stand up. I cannot get away. I am stuck here, on this bed, with him. This is going to happen. I can't do anything to stop it. "GET OFF OF ME!"

My words and attempts to move away from him do nothing to alter my fate. I am lying on my back on the bed, restrained beneath his weight, pant-less, exposed.

He unzips his jeans. He pulls down his boxers. I am terrified. He is still pinning me down onto the bed. I cannot move. Tears are freely streaming down my cheeks. "No, please don't do this. Pleeeease. No. Don't . . ." He then pushes his hard penis inside me. Down there. To have sex with me. All I can do is lie on the bed, crying and pleading as I try to wiggle my hands loose from his tight-fingered grip. Breathing broken breaths and squirming beneath his body, I am still trying to find a way out.

He looks down at me like I am his girlfriend or a lover as he pushes in and out of me. In and out of my body. In and out. Aching, burning, tearing. Slamming into me. *I am going to fight him off. I have to fight.* I begin to scream, "NO, GET OFF OF ME! GET OFF OF ME!" In one swift movement, he flips me face down onto the bed and shoves my head down into the pillow in front of me to muffle my screams. "NOOoooo. DOoooon't." He now stands behind me, forcing me down harder as his whole weight pounds into me from behind. Hurting. It hurts. I am crying. I try to buck my body up into the air to get him off me. It doesn't work. He is still there. In and out. In and out. It is no use. The more I try to fight him, the harder he pushes himself into me and the more painful it feels.

In and out. In and out. It feels like my skin down there is ripping. It is burning. It hurts. I stare at the wall in my bedroom. I am focusing on the SpongeBob SquarePants design on my sheets. The walls that are the color of the ocean—light blue on top and darker blue on bottom, covered in SpongeBob wall decals. SpongeBob looks happy, but this room is no longer a happy place. I notice that the less that I fight, the softer he pushes himself inside of me. *I just want this to be over. I just want this to be over. Please just let this be over. SpongeBob sheets. Blue walls. Light blue on top. Dark blue on the bottom. Ocean-colored walls.* My pillow is wet from my tears—and my screams—spilling into it. *Please let this be over. Please let this just be over. Pleeeease.*

When he is finished, I feel his body jerk a bit, then he stills for a moment. His tight grip around my wrists finally loosens and I feel the weight of his body lift from mine. His eyes reflect nothing. Dark brown. Flat. Cold. He pulls up his jeans, zips his fly, and buckles his belt. He then turns around and walks out of the room.

I can't move. I don't even want to move. I pull the covers up around me. I am left alone, sobbing, in pain, my breaths coming in waves, lying on the bed curled up on my side and tucked into myself, feeling the most alone that I have *ever* felt. I feel dirty and disgusting. I feel used up and thrown away, like human trash. Like I am what gets left behind. There is a spot of wetness between my legs now. I hurt down there. I feel the deepest sadness that I have ever felt. It is mixed with the shame of what just happened to me—what my dad just did to me. The salty tears spilling from my eyes mix with the snot that is running from my nose, joined together and sliding down the side of my face lying on my bed, like a river of shame. My shame.

I hate him. I really hate him. What did I ever do to deserve this? I didn't even get in any trouble today. Why is it worse today? Why did he do THIS? He is so disgusting. He is so, so disgusting. I can't believe this happened to me. Not this.

I cannot deal with this. This is too much. I keep thinking about the way he looked at me while he was pushing himself in and out of me while I fought him. The thought of it makes me want to throw up.

I don't want anything like this to ever happen to me again. Something like *this* should never happen to *anyone*.

I don't think that I am going to be able to put *this* into an invisible box in the back of my mind. The one where I will learn to keep all the bad and dirty things. All the secrets and lies. The box that holds it all, where I tuck it away.

Not this. *This is too much.*

This was another "first" my dad would take from me. My first sexual experience. My virginity. My innocence. Another choice torn from me as though it was never one that I held in the first place—control over my own body. Another piece of my identity stripped away from me. Another lie that I am forced to tell.

ABIGAIL

AGE 13

After the Rape

*W*hen I am finally able to pull myself together enough to move, I head straight to the bathroom to turn on the shower. I pull off my SpongeBob pajamas—my favorite ones, that I now hate—leaving them in a heap on the floor as I step into the bathtub. I stand there, in shock, as the water pours over my head and down my body. I cry softly, trying to suck in my next breath, with my arms protectively wrapped around my body, as the hot water darts down onto my skin. At first using only my hands, and later a washcloth that is lathered with soap, I scrub at my skin, especially my legs and my belly. I feel dirty. Like what he did to me is now on me, it is a part of me. I scrub until my skin is pink with marks and burning when I rub the washcloth across it. I hurt so bad down there that I can only rub the washcloth across myself gently. I scrub my body until I have no more tears left to mix with the shower water, as I attempt to clean away the dirtiness, the ugliness, the shame. Deep breaths. A broken heart. Tattered flesh. More tears.

I finally turn off the water, step out, dry off with a towel, being careful not to rub across myself too hard down there because it is sore and aching, and pull on some new pajamas—different ones. Plain ones. Not the ones with SpongeBob SquarePants' happy face all over them. I hurry back to my bedroom and pull the door closed, sitting in the room where everything happened, while I wait on the rest of my family to get home from the store. Then, I'll know that I am safe.

When my mom and siblings walk in and start hauling in the groceries to put them away, it's as though nothing has changed. Just another day at home. It's like nothing happened at all. I am more quiet than usual. I am keeping to myself. No one seems to notice. I give only short answers when spoken to. I feel like I am 3,000 miles away from them, tucked way deep down inside myself. They probably just think I'm in a bad mood. That I had a bad day.

My mom prepares a meal for us and we all sit down at the table to eat dinner together as a family. I can't pay attention to what anyone around me is saying. I don't care. About their stories. About their day. About what happened at the store. About the jokes they tell. I don't care about anything anymore. How could I?

My dad is sitting at the head of the table acting totally normal, like nothing happened. Like he didn't just pin me down on my bed and shove my face into my pillow while I screamed. Like he didn't just force himself inside of me. Like he didn't just strip out a part of me that wasn't his to take. I hold my fork. I choke down a bite. I stare at my plate. I pick at the food. I don't care about the food. I am not hungry. I'm not really much of anything, anymore. Just here. Just sitting. Just chewing occasionally. Just existing. I feel numb. Confused. Used. Dirty. Broken. Gross. I take another bite of food that I can't really taste. That I don't really want. I swallow it down. Just like the events of this day.

Nothing matters. I hear them talking. Laughing. My dad is talking to them. My mom and my siblings are talking to him. Just another day. Everything is normal for all of them. But nothing is normal for me. I don't think that anything will ever be normal again.

My dad raped me. In my bedroom. Today. Just a few hours ago.

All the scrubbing in the world will never remove the stain of what he did to me. It's on my skin. It's in my mind. It is all around me.

After dinner, I slink back to my bedroom. I don't really want to be in here with them. I don't want to be in this house. And I definitely don't want to be around him. *I could tell my mom, but she wouldn't believe me. She didn't believe me before when I told her about him touching me. She definitely wouldn't want to believe this. She'd probably be mad. I'm not sure if she'd be mad at him, or mad at me, probably mad at both of us. But I know that she wouldn't do anything about it. She doesn't want to believe that he would do these things to me.*

In my SpongeBob themed bedroom with ocean blue walls, wearing plain pajamas, lying in my bed, as tears stream down my face in long wet lines, I sob into my pillow. This time, freely.

ABIGAIL

AGE 34
Present Day

Reflecting Back

I wish I could tell you that it only happened the one time—my dad raping me as a child. But that wouldn't be true.

Having my own bedroom at our house in Laredo gave my dad easy access to me. He would wait until he thought everyone else in the house was asleep, including his wife—my mom—and he would sneak down the hall to my open doorway. (We all slept with our doors open.) He would walk into my room. I always knew what was going to happen next.

His hands. His body on mine. Him doing things to me that a father should *never* do. The type of things any man should never do to a child. Yet he—my adopted dad and uncle—did those things to me.

Night after night. Through the darkness he would enter. He would climb into my bed in my seemingly beautiful, childlike bedroom. Beneath the covers next to me he would lie down, beside my fear, and next to my shame. To take pieces of me that I could never get back. Stripping away pieces of my innocence, my youth, my vulnerability, my body, my soul. Tearing away at my feelings of self-worth—my confidence, my identity, my sense of self. Bit by bit. Day by day. Rape by rape.

When I was in the seventh grade, my stepbrother—Aunt Laura's son—was in the hospital battling leukemia. My mom was at the hospital with him a lot during that time. That left me at home often with my dad. It was common for him to pick me up from school to have sex with me. Afterward, he would make me take a shower, then he would drop me back off at school to finish out my day.

The rapes would happen again.

And again.

And again.

My dad raped me nearly every single night that we lived in that house in Laredo. Every. Single. Night. It always happened. The darkness cued his next unwelcomed arrival into both my bedroom *and* my body.

I found myself fearing nighttime. Dreading bedtime in a different way than most kids did. Worrying in the darkness. Clinging to my fear. Breathing in my impending reality. Him appearing in the doorway. The shape of a man in the dark. Climbing into my thoughts the same way he climbed into my bed. Unwelcomed. Night after night.

I always found myself wondering how no one else in our house seemed to notice this or realize that it was happening. *How did they not know? How did they not hear? Did they not see him enter my room? Why did my mom not believe me about him touching me when I told her before? Why didn't she watch him more closely? Did she know? Did she just not stop it? Why didn't my sister or brother seem to notice? How did they not know? Why didn't anyone notice this and try to help me?*

The questions consumed my mind and chipped away at me in the darkness, just as they haunted me in the daylight. They were the questions to which there would never be answers.

It was just me, lying in my dark bedroom, with the door wide open, staring at the doorway—almost unblinkingly—waiting for him to appear. Waiting for him to invade my private space. My body. Too terrified to fall asleep. Breathing. Staring at the doorway. Waiting.

Heart racing. Stomach sinking. Knowing that it was going to happen. Because it was. He was going to appear. Waiting. Watching. Until he would appear. He would walk into my bedroom, quietly stride across the dark room, climb into my bed—where he didn't belong—to force himself inside of my body, where he also didn't belong.

TRUTHS:

Age thirteen. First kiss? Dad.

No longer a virgin. First lover? Also, Dad.

Number of times? More than I could possibly count.

I was marred by what my dad did to me. Diminished by it.

The thought of it made me want to hurl. It made me feel dirty, like I was less than, like I had lost things that I could never get back.

No choices. No decisions. No regular boys. No normal "first" times of any kind for me. Every should-have-been-special moment in my life had been encroached by his vile deeds.

That was my reality.

Night by night.

Day after day.

Walking through life.

Always watching.

Always waiting . . .

Darkness. His body next to mine. The intrusion. Me wanting it to end.

Trying to scrub out his disgusting sins from my flesh in swirls of soap and water down the shower drain. Trying to remove his filth from my body. Trying to erase his constant presence from the stream of thoughts that ran through my mind.

At war in my own flesh. Embroiled in a battle in my own mind. All the while walking through each day of my life pretending like everything was normal. Like my family was normal. Like I was normal. Like everything was fine. Like I was fine.

When *nothing* about my life was normal.

My dad was a perverted, sicko rapist.

And I was *so far* from fine.

ABIGAIL

AGE 15

The Truths I Hide

I know you may be wondering why I don't try to tell someone at school or another parent about the disgusting things that my dad has been doing to me. Well, that's pretty simple. If my own mom won't believe me, why would a stranger? Plus, any time somebody does report it, CPS comes to visit our house—wherever we are living—and then we pack up our things and move to the next place that same night. It's pointless. I'm stuck here.

This abuse has become my life. I hardly ever leave home, never get to do things with my friends, and I'm stuck inside this house nearly every day. That is my reality. I see only two ways out of this: I can run away or I can kill myself. There is no other way out.

My dad is a pig. He's a sick, disgusting man who isn't right in the head. He couldn't be normal to do the things he does. And no one around us sees it. He blends in well. He wears an invisible mask of decency. Everyone likes him. They think he's a good husband, a good dad, a good provider. But they couldn't be more wrong.

In Hawaii, he used to touch me one or two times a week. Since we moved to Laredo, it is something that happens every single night. I close my eyes and pretend that it isn't happening to me the entire time that it is. I wish CPS had never taken me away from Real Mom. If I was still with her, none of this would have ever happened. At least that's what I tell myself. But they did take me away. And I am *his*.

I don't know if my sister even realizes the things that are happening to me here. I've never told her about any of it because my dad warned me "not to tell *anyone*." If mom couldn't or wouldn't help me—what could my sister do about it? It seems pointless to tell her, but I'm not sure if she already knows. If she does know, she has never asked me anything about it or mentioned it to me.

School—whichever one we happen to be attending—is my safe place. It's the only time I know that nothing bad is going to happen to me. It is a place where I can put away the nastiness, if only for a short while. He can't get to me there. I try to shove the abuse down deep inside of myself. I try not to think about it. I try not to dwell on it. And above all, I try not to allow it to sicken me and make me feel dirty. But some days, that is impossible. It consumes me. His sickness. The gross sex acts that he has with me as a kid. I wish I had never met him. I think I would have been better off anywhere else, even with a stranger or one of the "fake parent" couples from the shelter.

It is difficult when I stop to think about how I'm the only one in our whole family who seems to have this terrible life. My sister, brother, and stepbrother are perfectly fine. They are happy. They get to have a normal life and do normal things. They have friends. They go places. Dad is only obsessed with me.

I already feel like I miss out on so many things. There is no way that I could ever talk to a boy. Whenever I see a couple my age in the hallway at school, I feel sadness and jealousy. I wish that I could have that thing that they have. That I could choose who I want to be friends with or talk to, the same way I chose to kiss Cute Boy. I wish that one day, I will be able to walk down the hallway and hold hands with someone if I want to. That I could actually have a boy call our house to ask for me. But I likely will never get to have these things. That much is already clear. I am my dad's property. His and only his. I am the niece-turned-daughter who has become his obsession. He watches me. He glances at me in a not-normal-way. He sneaks into my room. He touches me. He is an evil, manipulative man. I hate him.

I have no idea how he can walk out of my bedroom after doing disgusting things to me and then talk to me two minutes later as though nothing gross happened between us. "Abby, do you want to go to the store with me?" *I don't want to go anywhere with him, ever.*

So, I shove all the abuse—the glances, the words, the touches—into that invisible box deep in my mind. And I shut the lid tight.

ABIGAIL

AGE 14
8th Grade

The Dance

The eighth-grade dance at my school is a big deal. I am going tonight. I am so excited! They go all out with decorations and everybody dresses up. It's pretty much a middle school version of a prom.

When I initially mentioned going to the dance, my dad said I wasn't allowed to go, but my mom talked him into it. She said, "If Abby's younger brother gets to go, then she gets to go. He can watch over her." The idea of my little brother—a seventh grader—*watching over me* at the dance is so ridiculous. I should be the one watching him! But it's always been like this. It is something that I just have to deal with.

My mom takes me shopping for a dress. I try on a hot pink one that is strapless. It is so beautiful. The top half is covered in tons of tiny beads, like rhinestones, that sparkle when the light hits them. It is tight across the top and then flares out at my waist, like a fancy wedding dress. I feel so pretty in it.

We sit in the living room. I am wearing my pretty pink dress. My mom pulls half of my hair up and then grabs a strand and twirls it through the rod of a hot curling iron. It turns my dark, straight strands into big, beautiful, bouncy curls. I'm not wearing any makeup because I don't really like to. My mom seems excited to help me get ready, like she is happy that I get to go.

My dad walks into the living room and sits down on the couch across from where I am sitting. He lifts a can of Bud Light up to his mouth and takes a big swig. He is wearing jeans, a plain black tee shirt, and a mean glare. I can tell that he has been drinking for a while. His eyes look slanted. His expression is angry. My mom curls another strand of my hair. My dad glares over at me, before he begins to spew hurtful words at me. "YOU'RE A SLUT! YOU'RE A BITCH. YOU'RE A WHORE! You're ugly, even in that pretty dress."

My mom continues curling my hair. My lip begins to tremble. I am holding my breath and trying really hard not to cry. *I won't let him see me cry. I won't let him see me cry. He is just trying to ruin this for me. I won't let him.* That's when my mom says to him, "That's enough! You're being ugly to her."

"Well, I don't give a fuck. I don't want her to go."

My little brother is sitting in the room. He shows no reaction to any of this. He is probably just glad my dad's anger is always directed at me, not him. He is also probably used to it. This is nothing new.

My mom finishes curling my hair. It looks so beautiful. I see kindness in her eyes when she looks at me, like she feels sorry for me that my dad is treating me this way and said those nasty things to me. *I don't know why he has to be like this. I know that he's just mad that I'm all dressed up and going to the dance. That, for once, I am actually getting out of this house to go do something fun with my friends, even if my brother is supposed to act as my keeper. I should be the one watching him!* I feel sad about how my dad talked to me, but I also feel angry. I just want to go to the dance. To have fun. To laugh. To forget. To feel pretty. To spin around in this pretty pink dress.

My brother and I walk out to my mom's dark green van and we climb in. She drives us to the dance hall. We walk in. It is so beautifully decorated. My brother walks straight over to his friends to hang out with them. I find a few of my friends. We talk, and we laugh, and we dance. The dance lasts about three or four hours. It's the best three to four hours of my life! I am exhausted in the best way. Until finally, they turn the lights on to indicate that the dance is over. People say goodbye to their friends and begin to shuffle out the exit doors.

My brother and I walk outside to find my mom waiting for us, standing beside her van. She slides the door open and my dad stumbles out. He is drunk. He is tripping over his own feet and can barely stand. He is slurring his words. I see that he is holding a bouquet of orange and yellow flowers wrapped in fancy paper.

He staggers over to where I am standing, hands me the flowers, and mumbles, "I'm sooorryyyy. You are so BEAU-ti-ful." The words were uttered on a broken whisper, chased by a sour wisp of beer breath. There are people all around, walking across the parking lot to get to their parents' cars. I am afraid they might see him. Drunk. Stumbling around. Being embarrassing. But I am happy that he is apologizing for being so mean to me.

I am still glowing with excitement about the time that I got to spend at the dance. We all climb into the van and my mom drives us home. Once we get inside, my dad is so drunk that he passes out right away. Thankfully. (I guess there is some benefit to him being so drunk.)

I head to my room to take off the pretty pink dress. I pull on pajamas and crawl into my bed—so happy. I really do feel like it was the best night of my life! The one time that I finally got to actually go do something. The one night that I was able to escape this place and everything that it holds.

I fall asleep to flashes of sparkles twinkling in the light, music thumping through speakers, and memories of me in a swirling pink dress, hair pinned in curls, dancing like a fool, and smiling—the biggest smile that I have ever had—with my head thrown back in laughter, giddy, grateful, and so freaking happy—until I was the best kind of exhausted that a girl could be. And the happiest that I have ever been.

ABIGAIL

AGE 15
9th Grade

Mission/The Valley

When I'm a freshman in high school, we move to Mission, Texas, which is often referred to as "The Valley." I have lost count of the number of schools I've attended or homes that I have lived in up to this point. The homes and schools don't even matter anymore. They are like pieces of furniture in a dollhouse: non-descript, unimportant, and totally interchangeable. We never stay anywhere for long. Whether it's to flee random reports made by people to Child Protective Services out of concern for us over the years, because maybe my parents can't afford to pay the rent, or perhaps for other reasons I know nothing about, we wander on to the next place. There is *always* a next place.

Our latest house in Mission is a white one-story with a fairly big backyard that has huge cement pillars and solid gates around it. You can't see through them, or over them. For that reason, it kind of feels like a fortress. As far as moves go, this one felt more normal than some of the others, maybe because it didn't come on the heels of a social worker's visit and didn't occur in the middle of the night as though we are fleeing, like some of our past moves did. The thing that wasn't so normal about this move is the fact that my sister didn't join us here. She stayed behind in Laredo, Texas, where we used to live. She now lives with her boyfriend. She wanted to finish high school there. That part sucks for me—her being gone.

It's just me and my two brothers now—and THEM. I have my own room here. (You know what that means.) I may be one of the only teenagers in all of America who instinctively fears having her own bedroom. I'd rather share a room with two-dozen people, where I am uncomfortable, but also, untouchable, literally.

I am sitting in my room one day, when I hear my mom say, "Abby—Come here for a minute," so I walk into my mom and dad's bedroom, where I find both of them lying on the bed. My mom looks at me standing in the doorway and says, "Come over here, sit down. We want to talk to you." I take a seat on the corner of their bed. I have no idea what they want to talk about.

My mom continues, "Since me and your dad can't have kids, you're gonna be our surrogate for us. You are going to have babies for us." She says it in a matter-of-fact tone, like she's telling me something normal, like what we're having for dinner.

"Have babies for you? No."

"Yes, you are."

"No, I'm not. I'm not doing that."

"Yes. *You are.* You *don't* have a choice, Abby. You are going to do it."

She said the words as a declaration, a final verdict, as though I had no say in the matter. As though telling me that I was going to have their babies was the most normal thing in the world. The messed up words that she didn't say which were inferred right along with the others were that: (1) I would be having sex with my dad—her husband—not only with her permission, but with her encouragement; (2) I would get pregnant by my dad (the rapist) *on purpose*; and (3) I would have a baby while I am still in high school—and then I would let my mom and dad pretend that *my* baby is actually *their* baby. *Oh my God.*

They are freaking crazy! Completely crazy. I haven't even finished school yet. Why would a 15-year-old have a baby on purpose when they are still in high school—much less by their own dad, and with their mom's permission?

But by this point, I know all too well that I have no control over my own body, my personal choices, or what happens in my life. It isn't really mine to live. My body and my life are things *they* control, and they came up with this sick, twisted, ridiculously crazy plan together. It doesn't matter that I don't want to do it. Just like my mom told me, "You don't really have a choice." *How can I not have a choice about this? This is too much. This is crazy.*

Lifting my eyes from the spot that I have been staring a hole through on their gray bedspread, I rise to my feet, saying nothing. No acceptance. No further denial of my perceived fate.

I walk out of their room cloaked in worry and stifled by panic. I find myself wondering if my mom knew that her husband—my dad—has been touching me and raping me *for years*. She knew. She totally knew. I told her about the touching when it first happened. She did *nothing*. She told me to stop talking about it. She knew. She had to. And now, she is not only allowing it to happen, but she is actually encouraging it to happen, welcoming it, maybe even participating in it, and freely willing me to get pregnant by her own husband. *Sick. She is sick. They are both sick, deranged freaks who are literally crazy. Mentally messed up. And I am stuck here—with them.*

Not long after my mom's declaration, she buys a paper calendar to hang on the wall in my bedroom. Each month features a picture of an island at the top. The pictures in it are beautiful. The purpose behind it is utterly repulsive. My mom then uses it to track when I get my period each month. Either she or I circle that date on the calendar, so my mom will then be able to tell when I am most likely to get pregnant and will use that date as an anchor for the next month, so she can see if I do get pregnant—by her husband—my dad. It is disturbing—unthinkable, really. Yet, here we stand, in my room, circling dates on the island calendar each month, all the while my mom hopes to herself and prays to God that I get pregnant. All the while, I hope and pray that I don't.

ABIGAIL

AGE 15
9th Grade

The Threesome

I don't even know how to find the words to describe what happens next.

The first time my "parents" call me into their bedroom to draw them baths and massage them, I instinctively already know what will ensue, despite being unaware of how utterly repulsive and filled with angst it would leave me. The sex acts involving both my dad and mom annihilated any shred of trust that I still unwittingly possessed. For my dad to rape me and physically hurt me is one thing. While it may sound messed up, I've become accustomed to it. I still hate it, but I know how to better survive it. But to now have my mom standing in the bedroom is almost too much to bear.

The first time it happens, my mom and dad both lie down on the bed and start to have sex with one another as they force me to watch. I have no idea what reaction they expect from me, but the whole thing is so messed up that I just keep closing my eyes to block out the images of the two of them, the pounding bodies, the gasps, my mom trying to act sexy. My eyes fly open when my mom angrily bellows, "OPEN YOUR EYES, Abby. WATCH US."

I would rather be anywhere else in the world right now than here, in this bedroom, as my two psychotic parents look on. Then, it escalates to involve me and my body. Whenever I am involved, my dad seems to moan more. His sounds make me cringe. The two of them are the worst people that I have ever met. I hate my mom for this. She touches my breasts. She plays with herself. The two of them force me down onto my back on the bed. My mom calls out, "Stick it in her, as she rubs on herself. She then grabs my right breast, continuing, "Make sure you come inside of her." The two of them have me pinned down so there is no way for me get away. The idea of getting pregnant in this way makes my stomach turn.

The second time there is a threesome, it is made clear to me that they expect me to give oral sex to my mom. The sweaty rolls of her body. The stench of her body ever-so-slightly masked by cheap, fruity body spray. The beardlike patch of tiny black hairs that she never plucks beneath her chin. Her round face contorted by pleasure. Her dark eyes staring at me—watching me. Her moaning. Her not only acting like this is "okay," but commanding it. The thought of it repulses me. The actual act of it makes me want to die inside. I think a part of me actually does—die on the inside. Again, I close my eyes to block them out. I close my eyes during all of these group rapes as much as I can get away with it without them yelling at me to open my eyes.

Following the group rapes, I am filled with bone-deep hatred, soul-consuming anger, and disdain. I'm so filled with rage, I'm not sure how I can make it through another day in their house. I can't believe that my mom would allow this to happen, and not just as a person who stands by and allows it to happen—as she always has— but as an encourager and an eager, active participant in my undoing. I hate her to the core of my being, deep down to the essence of who I am.

Hatred rattles in my bones, fury rolls through my blood, and when I'm not feeling the pent-up anger, I'm beyond distraught at all that has occurred. All that being said, I never allow them to see me cry during the group rapes. I hold it in and take what I must. But when I retreat to my bedroom in the aftermath, I fall completely apart. I am a girl spiraling in sorrow, tainted by emotionally torturous sexual acts, and I am coming undone from the inside, out.

I feel like less of a human now—doing this—with them. Like I am garbage. The lowest of the low.

The physical acts are bad enough. But seeing the way they look at one another during the sex acts—their eyes glazed over with lust, is all too much to take. I hate them both with every fiber of my being. I do not want to be the "plaything" in the middle of them as a couple, or a point of interest in their completely twisted sex life.

I burn to tell someone, but who would I tell? I wouldn't want to inflict this confession upon anyone. It's too dark and terrible. Too disgusting. Too humiliating. I don't want this to be what other people think about when they think of me. *If* they believed me. And who would believe me?

No one.

ABIGAIL

AGE 15
9th Grade

Cross-Country Running

I'm on the cross-country team at my "new" school in The Valley. The latest one. I've lost count at this point. I'm pretty good at running. It makes me feel strong. I prefer long distance running, which is usually three or four miles. We don't run on a track, but more in nature, up over a hill, beside a ditch, along the grass. On the trails, I feel free. It's about the only time I feel that way. I like being away from home. I like to feel the sun on my face and the wind in my hair. I like to not have anything to think about except for taking my next step. Birds chirping. Tiny pebbles crunching beneath my sneakers. Beads of sweat clinging to my shirt. Nothing and no one to bother me out here. That's why I love it.

There's a block that we always run around by our school to get ready for our upcoming meets. The whole team runs four laps around the building. Our coach says it helps to "build our endurance." That basically just means you just run until you're tired. And then you do it again the next time. I don't mind it though. There are both boys and girls on our team. While my dad and mom supported me trying out for volleyball and taking a ballet class, they aren't very pleased with the fact that there are boys on my cross-county team. They don't want me around boys. My dad gets jealous.

Today, we are running our four laps around the block. I pace myself near a few girls that I am friends with on the team. We are running and talking a bit here and there, not about much of anything really, just trying to make the time go by faster.

I see my dad's pickup truck off to my right. He is following along closely behind us. *Oh no.* He is driving super slowly, at about the same speed as we are running, to keep up with us. He is a short distance behind us now. Creeping along. Following us. Drawing attention to me. Making me feel embarrassed. Making himself look like a weirdo. Being jealous over me. One of my friends notices him lurking behind us.

"Who is that?"

"That's my dad."

"Why is he driving beside us, like that?"

"Oh, you know, he's probably just trying to watch out for me because there are some bad people out there."

"Oh."

What I don't say aloud is that *my dad is crazy.* I know he's just following along behind us around the block because he's worried that one of the boys on our cross-country team may try to talk to me. One might think that I'm nice or that I'm pretty. He doesn't want me talking to any boys or being anywhere around them.

I am tired of having to make up stories to explain things to others to try to make my life seem normal. There isn't anything normal about the things my dad does to me.

One of our track meets is at a different school. The whole team is going to ride together on a school bus today. My dad isn't too happy about that. He doesn't like me hanging out with my teammates, especially the boys on our team, but there's not really much he can do about it, since the whole team is expected to ride on a bus with our coach.

I am secretly interested in a boy on our cross-country team. We have been talking whenever we can at school for the past month and a half. We obviously don't get to talk much because we only see each other at school or during our practices. It's not like he can call my house or I can call him, or we can ever hang out, but I still consider him to be my "boyfriend." At this point, he's the closest that I'll ever get to having one. We sit together any time we can on the bus whenever we travel places together as a team, like we are today. He's cute and he always smells good, plus, he is nice to me, and we both enjoy running.

I climb up the steps onto the bus and make my way down the aisle toward the back. My boyfriend is sitting next to the window and says, "Abby! Come sit beside me." So, I plop myself into the seat beside him. This trip will take a few hours because the school we are headed to for our cross-country meet is far away.

I spend the entire trip to the track meet feeling happy to be near my boyfriend, but a bit upset because of the way things have to be for me in my life. I wish I could sit with a boy, just like this, and that I could formally claim him as my boyfriend to my family. I wish that I could choose to hang out with, or talk to a boy, like all the other girls around me do, so freely and normally. I wish that we could talk on the phone sometimes, or walk while holding hands in the hall, or go over to each other's house for dinner, or to watch a movie. But that is never going to happen. It feels nice to sit beside my secret boyfriend and hang out with my teammates all together though, just talking and laughing, like everyone else in high school gets to do.

We finally arrive at the meet, where we run our hearts out. Afterward, we get back onto the bus to make the trip back to our school, where our parents will come to pick us up.

The bus eventually pulls into the school parking lot and eases into a parking spot before coming to a stop. We all stand up and begin to file off the bus, one by one, to meet our parents and head home. I am toward the middle of the pack. I step back and let my secret boyfriend go in front of me as we make our way toward the front of the bus to exit, so he steps off of the bus just before I do. As soon as his sneakers hit the concrete, I hear my dad's voice hiss in a threatening tone, "If you EVER touch or talk to my daughter AGAIN, I'll beat your ass myself." He doesn't yell the words, his voice in a low and ominous whisper as he glares at my boyfriend in the form of a not-so-subtle warning.

My secret boyfriend nervously stammers, "No—uh, nothing happened. We just sat together. That's all."

I step off the bus, standing off to the side with my shoulders slumped and head down, immersed in an invisible cloak of embarrassment, humiliation, and shame. I fear that my boyfriend, and maybe even my teammates, will think that my dad is a psycho. He is one. But I don't really want them to know that. I don't want anyone to know our thinly veiled secret. *My boyfriend will think he's just being protective over me. He'll believe that. I'll say that's why he acted that way.*

I try my best to play off my dad's verbal attack on my not-so-secret boyfriend as if nothing is wrong. Inside, I am reeling. Shrinking. Yet again. I excel in the fake life we have fabricated to portray a normal outward appearance to those around us.

At this point, I could win an Emmy for the mistruths about my life that I must sell to others in order to hide my shame. And the award for "Best Actress in Hiding Sexual Abuse goes to . . . Abigail Castillo, for playing . . . herself . . . in her own messed up life." There would be no clapping. Just more kids climbing off the bus behind us, quickly dispersing into tiny clusters of walking, talking teammates in search of their parents, as I slink away behind my dad attempting to shake off the sting of lingering humiliation. The realization sets in that this relationship with my not-so-secret boyfriend is now officially over.

My dad and I shuffle toward the car. He is fuming with anger and deadly silent. He doesn't speak a word to me the entire ride home. I know that I am in trouble. He knows that I was sitting with a guy. I sit quietly, worrying about what is going to happen when we get home. As we walk into the house, he quickly turns on his heels to finally address me. "YOU KNOW THE RULES ON TALKING TO GUYS, Abby. YOU KNOW."

To which I replied, "I don't care about your rules."

"You don't care about the RULES? I'm going to SHOW YOU that you're GONNA CARE."

And I know that he has his terrible ways to make me care. Fearing what may happen next, I lower my head, say nothing in response, and head to my bedroom. It is a silent acceptance of what he has told me—no guys are allowed in my life. Not this one. Not any others. There's not really much I can do about it.

My dad is always around. Always watching. He makes sure that I don't get to do normal things. Ever. I should have known this thing with my secret boyfriend couldn't possibly last. I don't know what I was thinking to even attempt it. I just wanted to have a normal life *so* badly.

I am a girl who deeply *longs* to be normal, trapped in a life where she knows that she will never get to be.

ABIGAIL

PRESENT DAY
Reflecting Back To Age 15

The Lies They Tell

*Y*ou are nothing. You are nobody. You are never going to amount to anything, Abby. Nobody is ever gonna believe you. You are worthless. You have no value. You are nothing.

I internalized these words that were uttered to me by Chevo and Laura on a regular basis, if not daily, beginning at the age of 15. Their words—emotional weapons thrown like barbs at a shy, brown-eyed, dark-haired young girl, who happened to be me. For a long time, I believed them—the words. I swallowed down their lies, like a thick venomous bile lingering inside me on its way down.

Each hatred-filled word was a grenade, thrust strategically toward me to dismantle my confidence and erode my identity. My self-esteem quickly crumbled, like a wobbling wall—leaving a heap of rubble at my feet. My self-worth diffused through the air like particles of dust—carrying away small bits of me with each verbal assault, each taunt thrown, each lie bought. *Worthless. Nothing. No one. No value. Useless.* Each word etched into my soul, embedded into my flesh, like an invisible marker of who I *really* was, a shell of a girl who didn't feel like she was worth much of anything.

Maybe I really am nothing? Maybe I really don't matter? Maybe nobody really does care about what happens to me? It seems to be true.

I have no way out. I'm stuck here—with them. No one seems to care. "*You are nothing. You are nobody. You are never going to amount to anything, Abby. Nobody is ever going to believe you. You are worthless. You have no value. You are nothing. Besides, even if they did believe you, you would go to jail, too, for letting it happen.*"

The words thrown like daggers danced like faint echoes through my mind, stabbing me into perpetual compliance, even when they weren't around. *Nothing. No one. That's who you are, Abby. Nothing. Someone who doesn't matter. Someone who doesn't count.* That became my new identity. No longer my own person. I became theirs.

A couple's plaything.

A teenage girl taken apart, then rebuilt using evil words strung together by lies.

The girl Chevo and Laura victimized day-by-day, word-by-word, vile act upon vile act.

The girl they took apart bit by bit.

ABIGAIL

AGE 16

Number One

O ne year after I was forced into becoming my parents' sex slave, I wake up feeling sick. I realize that it has been more than a month since I had my last period. I fear that I may be pregnant—by him. I hope and pray that I am wrong. I do not want to look at the island calendar to check the anticipated date.

I do not want to be pregnant.

I do not want to carry "their" baby.

I do not want to walk the halls of my high school as a pregnant sophomore for mistakes that I did not have the opportunity to make.

I want to pretend that this isn't happening, but I can't. I know my mom will look at the sick ass island calendar where we track my periods as a family. Each month, she always bombards me with questions, "Did you get your period? Did you start yet? Are you bleeding yet? Let me go look at the calendar to see when you're supposed to start. Do you feel like you're about to start?"

When she asks me this time if I have started my period, I say, "no." A glimmer of excitement fills her eyes. There is a hollowness behind mine. I feel dead inside. Sad. Worried. Scared. I feel disgusted by the entire situation. *This cannot be happening. Please don't let this be happening. No way can this be happening.*

"Oh, this is *so exciting*, Abby! I bet you are pregnant!"

I am not excited. Pregnant is the last thing I want to be.

My mom drives to the store to buy a test and returns home with it. "Come here, Abby. I got a pregnancy test. You need to pee on this stick."

I do not want to pee on the stick. I want to pretend this isn't happening.

"Make sure you hold it right in the stream as you pee."

Please don't be pregnant. Please don't be pregnant. Please don't be pregnant. Pleeeease let this be negative. Let me just be late.

With my mom looking on, I hover over the toilet to pee on the stick . . . and await my fate.

"Give that to me." My mom perches over the stick like it is the world's greatest prize, staring down at it as though she is enthusiastically willing it to develop two pink lines, while I sit praying for the opposite.

"Oh my God! We are PREGNANT!" She is so happy that she starts to cry. Tears of exhilaration stream down her smiling face.

I feel gutted. Empty. Reeling. I want to puke.

My mom and dad are both so happy. They are celebrating.

I feel like a part of me just died.

How am I supposed to deal with this? How am I supposed to explain this? How could this possibly be okay?

Of course, my mom has a story in mind to cover the truth. "Abby, you just need to tell everyone that you got pregnant by a guy you knew at your last school. It's simple. They will believe that. That's what you need to tell everyone—your teachers, kids at school, everybody."

I don't want to tell anyone *anything*. I don't want to deal with this at all. *Pregnant? By my dad? And they are going to pretend that it's theirs?* No way. I cannot survive something like this. It's too much.

I then walk through the next several months of my life pretending that this isn't, in fact, actually happening—that I'm not pregnant. I do so, until I can't pretend anymore. In my own mind, I come up with a story to make my situation more tolerable. I met a guy. We fell in love. He is so good looking. He is so excited that I am pregnant with his baby. We are going to get married and be a real family. We will have a beautiful home. We are going to be so happy. All lies, but I certainly learned from the best when it comes to telling them.

The fake story I tell myself seems to help me to pretend that my situation isn't as messed up as it is. I can't fit this whole thing—being pregnant with my dad's baby after group sex with my mom and dad—into "the box." The box has no room for this. This is too much. Too dark. Too crazy. It is absolutely warped and thirty thousand steps removed from any normal sense of reality. I pretend to be happy. I pretend to be in love. I pretend to have a fake boyfriend and an entirely different life to keep myself from dying on the inside. Because I truly do feel like I might be—dying on the inside.

ABIGAIL

AGE 17
10th Grade

Baby One

*I*n the early morning of November 16, 2005, the contractions begin. I feel my stomach seizing up in a debilitating cramp and realize that I am in labor. This baby is coming whether I want it to or not. I am scared. I wish I didn't have to go through whatever comes next. I have no idea what to expect. We all climb into the van—my mom, my dad, and me—to head to the hospital. On the way, my mom keeps coaching me on what to say.

"Abby, remember, when they ask you who the baby's father is, say that it's some guy from Laredo—a one-night stand type of thing."

In a half-whisper, I reply, "Okay." But it's not okay.

"Just remember—this is OUR baby. We're gonna be her mom and dad. You're gonna call her your 'sister.'"

This baby doesn't even feel like a real baby to me right now. Up to this point, it's just something that has been growing in my belly because they wanted to put it there. Still, their words bother me, probably because they are all lies and because this was never my choice.

I don't want to go to the hospital. I do not want to have this baby that is *his*. And I do not want to then hand this baby over to *them* to raise it as their own when it is *not*. But it doesn't matter what I want. It never has. I'm just supposed to stay quiet, whisper the lies, push this baby out of my body, and do what they tell me to do afterward—whatever that is.

I hear my mom exclaim, "I am so excited! I can't wait to see the baby."

My dad follows with, "She is going to be beautiful."

Hearing the excitement in their voices makes me want to puke.

Once we arrive at the hospital, they place me in a wheelchair, and wheel me down several long hallways, until we finally arrive at my room—the one where I will give birth to this baby that I have pretended I am not having. "Here you go. Put on this gown and someone will be in to check on you shortly," the nurse says.

I step out of my clothes and pull on the hospital gown as my mom and dad look on. There is no point in hiding my naked body from them. They are no strangers to it. I then sit down on the bed, which is inclined in an upright position. My mom and dad could both win an award for the level at which they each are able to convincingly play their roles as my doting parents. It's despicable and laughable, all at the same time.

To the nurses and doctors at this hospital, we probably appear to be a normal family. They probably believe that my parents are good, caring parents, who are here to support me through a difficult situation, and eager to meet their first grandbaby. They probably judge me for being a teenage mom, knocked up by some random guy who couldn't even bother to show up at the hospital. I am forced to carry that entirely unearned, unjustified judgment. If anyone here should learn the truth of the situation, I am going to be in major trouble. We will probably all go to jail and the baby will go to a shelter where she will be raised by strangers. That's what my mom has always told me. "You're in on this, too, Abby. You took part in it. That means that you'd be in trouble, too." I must do my best to play along with the story and spew the lies.

After pushing through contractions until I didn't think that I could push anymore, with one last push, I finally give birth to *my baby*. They hand her to me, so I can hold her, *since I am her mother*. I look down at her tiny, beautiful face that she keeps scrunching up as she makes the faintest grunting sounds. I can't help but notice how pretty she is—so tiny, so perfect. I had no idea how I'd feel holding her. Now, I do know. She truly is beautiful. She has a full head of black hair and dark eyes, like mine. *I have a beautiful daughter.* Behind that thought, all I feel is numb and freaked out. I am now here, with a baby—*my baby*—and they are going to take her away from me and pretend that she is *their* baby. Any time a nurse or doctor is in my room, my mom and dad act like she is my baby and allow me to do everything for her, but any time we are alone, which is most of the time—they make it clear that she is theirs. The only time I get to feed her, burp her, or change her diaper is when a nurse comes to visit me. The hospital will only allow one person to spend the night, so my mom stays with me at the hospital. My dad heads out to drive home once the visiting hours are over. He kisses my mom and *my baby* goodbye. "I'll be back tomorrow." When he glances at me with a look of admiration and longing, I feel nothing but disgust.

Once we are alone in the room, my mom again reminds me of how things are going to go. "I am going to do everything for her, Abby. I will be the one to take care of her. I am her mom."

I look over at my mom, who is sitting in a chair, holding my pretend sister—lovingly looking down at her. "Hello there, little one. I'm your mom. You are so beautiful."

When it is time to name my baby, my mom takes over. I do not get to choose her name. The birth certificate bears my name as her mother, and no identity for her supposedly-dead-beat-one-night-stand father. (You know, the one I never met.) Along with the name they chose for my stolen daughter—the one I would have named Anastasia.

I hate them. I hate their lies. I hate this. She is not theirs. She is mine. She grew inside *my* belly. *I am* the one who pushed her into this world. She has *my* jet-black hair, the same domed nose as me, and dark eyes. *She is mine.*

ABIGAIL

AGE 18
11th Grade

The Declaration

Today, I learned that my dad got a job working as a janitor at my high school. *Unbelievable.* My mom acted happy about it, like she thinks it's great, but there isn't anything *great* about it, at least not for me. My response to learning this terrible news was a simple, "oh" punctuated by a long, heavy silence and an intense surge of anger that I did not dare to share. I know *exactly* why he did this—it is so he can keep a close eye on me every single day. While he is carrying a broom or pushing a garbage can through the hallways of my high school, he is going to watch me. He is going to see whether I chat with anybody while making my way to classes, or when I visit my locker, and especially—specifically—whether he can catch me talking to any guys.

I find ways to work around his constant presence at school. I now sit in the back of my classes intentionally because there is no way for him to see me through the slit of a window in the classroom door if I'm seated in the back of the room. I also try to learn where he is lurking, and when, so I can either rush to my next class, or take a different route to get there. School used to be the only place where I felt relaxed, like I didn't have to worry about him watching me, or bothering me, but that safe place is no longer "safe." Not anymore. The halls of my high school have become a watching ground and I am the stalked prey. I now feel on edge at every passing period. I feel angry and disgusted every time I see him here. I feel jealous of all the other girls with "normal" dads.

My dad tries to control what I wear to school. Some mornings, he has told me, "Go change. You look like a slut." In reality, anything I try to wear to school isn't any different than what all the other girls wear. There is nothing wrong with the clothes. There is only something wrong with *him*—and with the way he views me to be a piece of property that is *his*.

On one hot morning, I decide that there is no way I'm wearing jeans to school and that I'm going to wear a skirt. I pull a blue jean skirt from my drawer and pull on a black shirt that has flowers on it. My dad didn't see me or my outfit before school that day, so I wear the outfit to school.

While on my way to my next class, a guy I know was walking beside me—talking to me. My dad watches for a second, then walks straight up to us. I am dying on the inside. I have no idea what he's going to do, or what he may say. I don't have to wait long to find out.

"If I see you *with her* again, I'm going to have *someone kick your ass*." He whisper-hisses the last four words, pinning the guy with a hate-filled glare. The guy looks stunned and starts apologizing with a frightened stutter. My dad then turns his hateful glare my way. I immediately start crying and I walk away, feeling humiliated, angry, and so entirely sick of this—so tired of dealing with him. I end up driving myself home in my dad's car right after that because he let me. I was so upset that he was probably worried that it would draw attention.

The next day, I see the guy in the hall in passing and tell him, "I'm so sorry about yesterday—about my dad. He's just one of those 'Mexican dads.'" And I give him a look that matches my words, the *it-is-so-annoying-having-one-of-those-kind-of-dads* look.

I wish that is all that he was. That he was just an annoying, overprotective "Mexican dad," but he is *so* much more than that. He is my uncle. My dad. The father of my child. And my abuser.

ABIGAIL

AGE 18

Football Guy

*E*arlier this morning, I noticed a really cute guy who lives across the street from us. He has dark eyes, short black hair, is fairly tall, and has a stocky build. He is on the football team at my school, so I'll just refer to him as "Football Guy." From my window, I sometimes see him outside hanging out with his family in their front yard and I can't help but notice him. I feel like a bit of a stalker watching him from my window like this, but I try not to be obvious about it. I don't think he's noticed.

Not long after my perched admiration from the window, Football Guy walks up to me in the hall at school to ask, "Are you the sister of [my brother's name]." I reply, "Yeah, that's my brother," with a big smile and flirty eyes. I feel a flutter of butterflies take flight in my stomach. I honestly think he just used my brother as an excuse to have something to say to me. I sure am glad that he did. I may be shy, but I'm not blind, and he is *so* good looking. I can't believe he walked up and started talking to me. Not only is he cute, but he also dresses well, and seems to be a nice guy. I am thrilled to get to talk to him and have the opportunity to maybe get to know him better.

Ever since that day in the hall at school, Football Guy sometimes stops by our house to talk to me, either in the morning, or right after school, of course, only at times when my parents aren't home.

He is one of the only guys my age that I actually get to hang around with sometimes, since he lives right across the street. He knows that I can't see him at all if my parents are home. I warned him, "my dad is one of those 'Traditional Mexican' dads." That's all I had to say for him to understand that my dad is strict and over-protective of me. It's a buffer. And it's bullshit. But I use this excuse to explain my dad's behavior as normal. No way could I tell him the truth of my situation.

After we start talking at school and during the occasional yard or house visit, Football Guy begins to hang out with my brother every now and then. It gives him a reason to come over to our house under my parents' noses under the guise of being my brother's friend. They usually play video games and sometimes shoot hoops outside. Since my brother is present, it allows me to be around Football Guy with undetected motives. For once, my "little" brother seems like a blessing to my benefit, rather than his usual annoying position as my one-year-younger-overseer.

I try to be around Football Guy as much as I can whenever he is hanging out with my brother. I'm not sure if my brother has taken notice of it, but he probably has. I'm not sure what he thinks about it, but I honestly don't care. He probably just believes Football Guy thinks he is cool and wants to hang out with him.

I'm happy to have such a cute guy living across the street who has taken an interest in me. His close proximity to our house—and to my brother—buys me a bit more time with him.

I cling to slivers of stolen moments at the bus stop, brief encounters in the hall at school (if my dad isn't around), and hanging out with him and my brother sometimes when he comes to hang out at our house. We are friends who flirt—that's a good way to put it. I get to pretend that I have a "real" boyfriend, even if that is something that I am pretty sure that I will *never* have.

ABIGAIL

AGE 19
12th Grade
2008

Number Two

*T*his morning, as I crack a few eggs into a skillet for breakfast, I realize that the smell of eggs makes me want to gag. That's when I know that I am pregnant. Again.

This baby wasn't "planned," but it's not like my mom or dad did anything to prevent it. I don't need to consult the stupid island calendar to look at the date. I don't really even need to pee on the stupid stick. I know it deep down, in my twisted gut, that I am carrying baby number two—my dad's baby. I can't stand the thought of it.

My mom notices me turning my nose up at the smell of the eggs and asks, "Did you start your period, Abby?"

"No, I didn't. The smell of the eggs is really grossing me out."

"Oh my God! I bet you are pregnant again! This is truly a miracle, Abby! A miracle! It was meant to be for us to have another baby."

My mom spends the next few moments being "so grateful to God." I am reeling. *I cannot do this again. I already did this once. I did what they wanted. I survived that. Not again. I seriously cannot do it again.* I head to my bedroom to lie down on my bed in a heavy blanket of cotton and denial.

Why am I pregnant again? Why? Why would God allow this to happen?

I don't want to be here anymore. I don't want to live if this is what my life is going to be. If I do this again, then this HAS to be the last one. No more. This is it. They need to be happy with two. That is all they are going to get—two babies. I can't do this again. And I won't.

In the days that follow this one, I flit between two alternating states of existence: complete and total denial of my situation and the soul-deep conviction that this is going to be *the last baby* that I will *ever* carry for them. This is it.

I. Am. Done.

ABIGAIL

AGE 19

2008

Carrying Baby Two

M e being pregnant with "their" second baby seems to lend me some small sense of currency with them, some increased form of value. They try to keep me happy since they want to claim this baby, just like my first one.

"Abby, you're going to tell everyone that this one was some random guy you met at the movies—no name or anything. Just tell them it was a guy you didn't really know at all. A one-night stand. You were only with him just the one time."

Lies. More lies to choke down and swallow. More lies to create a story to make it seem like I am sleeping with random guys, while my dad hides beneath a cold mask of indifference and the reality of what he has done—what they *both* have done. I am left to carry the lies across my lips to sell their latest carefully crafted deception. Lies that will make Football Guy think badly of me, since we have been talking the past few months and things are going good between us.

I hate them for it. I'm starting to hate myself, too, for playing along with it, but I don't have much choice. This is their world. And in that world, I am merely a pawn, a human plaything to spice up their twisted marriage, a means to an end. I am a possession of theirs, nothing more. I am a sex slave and human incubator for two evil people.

Any time I spew the lies to explain my "situation" to others, I see pity in their eyes with a glint of judgment. Judgment for the make-believe story I tell them about the things that never even happened. I feel the shame of the story, but its burden is light against the weight of the all-consuming shame I feel about my life. I didn't sleep with a random guy. I never even had the chance to meet a random guy. There was no fun meet up at a movie theater followed by lust-filled sex in his bedroom. There were no fast-beating hearts, rapid breaths, and fumbling hands guided by teenage lust. There was only my dad forcing himself inside my body—one more time—while my mom, a captive onlooker, participated in the touching, taunting, teasing, holding down, and raping of her own adopted daughter.

I think she does this to keep him—my dad. I'm pretty sure of it. Them including me in their bedroom time and sex acts has livened up their sex life, as though we are all willing participants engaged in consensual acts. These are the lies they probably tell themselves. I will never swallow down those lies, not fully.

There was never consent. There never COULD be. There was never a choice. I had none. I was only a child then. And now, I am a 19-year-old mother of one baby with a second on the way—one who is pregnant and trapped.

Since I got pregnant with Baby Two, the group rapes only happen about twice a week. My dad is a bit gentler with me now. They are afraid that something could happen to the baby, so at least the sex doesn't occur as often, and it isn't as rough.

The thing I crave most right now is hot, crispy french fries from McDonald's. My mom and dad willingly make trips through the drive-thru to pick fries up for me when I say that I am craving them, which is often. They also don't make me perform the housework, like I normally do. I still have to clean the house and do all the chores, but they bargain with me on the timing now.

My mom says, "Okay, we're letting you slide on the housework right now, but tomorrow it better be clean." I am happy to have the break. These are the few advantages I get for carrying "their" baby.

It is nice to be able to sit on the couch and relax for once, rather than mopping floors, vacuuming carpet, dusting furniture, cooking breakfast, cooking lunch, cooking dinner, washing dishes, scrubbing counters, taking care of my daugh—my "sister," and doing everything else around here, like drawing their baths and massaging their tired, nasty, sweaty bodies until my fingers cramp up each night. I'll take the french fries and the couch to my regular life any day of the week.

I don't feel as scared as I did with my first pregnancy. I had no idea what was going to happen to me, or what labor would be like. With this one, I kind of know what to expect. Don't get me wrong, I'm still a bit scared that something could go wrong this time around, but I know what it's like to go to the hospital, how they handle things there, and how to push the baby out of me. I know to expect that it is *not* really going to be *my baby* at all. The only time I will get to be her mother is while we are at the hospital. That's it. Then I will assume my role as babysitter, house slave, and fake "sister." No part of my life is just my own. I live my life fulfilling their needs, their wants, and their sick desires.

I have no voice, no choice, and there is no way out.

ABIGAIL

AGE 19
12ᵗʰ Grade
2008

The Senior Prom

I didn't think there was any way that they'd allow me to attend my senior prom. I am no longer held captive by the delusion that I can lead a normal life. Not anymore. I am the daughter of a psychopathic rapist. The carrier of his babies. The sex slave to my parents. A person held captive in my own life. My life is starkly different than that of my siblings. It is darker, far more dysfunctional, and utterly blurred at the edges to the point it is unrecognizable from the life I thought I would get to have back when we first moved to Hawaii. There is no happy family here.

All a person would need to know to realize the depth of our dysfunction is that *it is my father's baby* that grows inside my womb. And that it is *the second time* my rapist father has impregnated me. There is no scenario under which this is actually acceptable or tolerable, much less okay. They are sociopaths. And I am theirs.

My mom has spent several days trying to talk my dad into letting me go to the prom. I've gotta give it to her that there are times when she stands up for me. I think she feels bad for me sometimes. Clearly, they aren't the times when it would matter the most—like when her husband is raping me—but she does throw a favor or courtesy my way every now and again.

"Chevo, she's graduating this year. It's her last thing she can do as a kid. It doesn't matter if she goes with [Football Guy] or not, she's pregnant anyway."

Yep, pregnant. She said that last part in an ordinary tone, deceptively normal, as though there's nothing wrong with the present situation at all. She left off the part about the baby inside me being her husband's child. The one she wanted him to put there.

Finally, my dad reluctantly says I get to go to the prom with Football Guy. He knows that Football Guy and my brother are friends, and has met him when he came over to "hang out with my brother" at our house. He seems to think he is an upstanding guy. I'm so excited to get to go on a real date, even if it is under my current circumstance.

Football Guy believes that I'm pregnant by a guy from my last school. "It was with a guy I really liked. We only did it the one time and I got pregnant." That's what I told him. I tried to make the lies sound a bit prettier and a little less pathetic.

In reality, I wanted to save myself for marriage, but it was a choice that was never mine to make. At a minimum, I would have been with somebody I loved and who loved me back. But that facade gets us around the ugly truth. The bitter reality that stands behind the palatable lie.

His.

Raped.

Seven months pregnant.

Baby number two. *His.*

Broken by life.

I am wearing a red dress tonight. It is a baby doll style dress with spaghetti straps and has a ribbon below my bust that ties in the back, flows down across my pregnant belly, and stops at my knees. It is beautiful, as far as dresses on big pregnant bellies go.

Football Guy walks across the street to our house looking all handsome in his black tux, white shirt, and a red tie that matches my dress. He hands me a beautiful corsage of two red roses with tiny white flowers for my wrist. He is wearing a single red rose on his chest. We truly do look like a normal couple going to prom. I feel elated to be doing something special, like this, with him. And for my family to know about it. (Although, they don't know the *whole* truth.) This is gonna be my night. Nobody is going to ruin it. I look pretty in my red dress and, for the first time ever, I have a *real* date.

My dad is pissed. He sits on the couch with his arms crossed and an ugly sneer pasted on his face, looking at both of us—pretending he's not looking at both of us—quietly basking in his disdain and stewing in anger. I'm just glad he's not saying anything ugly. Thankfully, we leave to head to the prom. My mom drives us there and drops us off, promising to return later that evening to pick us up.

The prom is held in a beautiful dance hall that is covered with black and silver balloons. It is stunning. We take a seat at a table with Football Guy's friends and their dates. A few of my friends are there hanging out with us, too. There is music playing faintly in the background. We all sit around the table and talk, with our forks and knives downturned onto plates filled with baked chicken and green beans. I feel so happy to be here, with them, enjoying this night.

After dinner, they start to play more lively party music and people walk out onto the dance floor. The lights are dim, with a strobe light reflecting colors of pink and blue around the room. Everyone is dancing and having a good time. Since I'm seven months pregnant, the dancing isn't the easiest thing for me to do, so I mostly sit at the table watching everybody else having a good time. Football Guy dances with his friends for a while, then walks back to where I'm seated to get me to dance with him. I do. I then head back over to the table to sit down and catch my breath while he remains out on the dance floor with his friends.

My cell phone pings with an incoming text. I look down at it to see what it says.

"You're a slut."

Ping.

"You're a ho."

Ping.

"You're probably somewhere hiding with him and giving him a blow job."

It is my dad. Oh my God. He is such an asshole.

I set my phone back down and try to ignore the bile, now mixed with panic, that is creeping up my throat. I try to focus on the music. I look around at the black and silver balloons and spinning prisms of light. I watch Football Guy dancing with our friends. The song *Low* by Flo Rida blares through the speakers and fills the room with the thrum of bass. I get up and walk back out onto the dance floor to dance with Football Guy. I certainly can't go all the way down low in my present condition, but I go as far down as I can to the floor, then ask Football Guy to help me get back up. He does. We are having such a great time dancing together. Once the song ends, they get ready to announce the Prom King and Prom Queen. We go back to our seats to watch and listen.

Ping.

"I'm waiting outside for you, slut."

Ping.

"If you don't come out right now, I'm going to come in there and drag you out."

Why—why does he *always* do this to me? Why would he come here? It's not that I'm surprised by his texts. I'm just so *sick* of it, so sick of him. I'm completely over the way he acts and the things he does to ruin my life and humiliate me.

I lean over Football Guy, "I have to go."

"Why? What's going on?"

It's not like I can tell him the real reason. After all, he thinks I'm pregnant by some random guy from my old school. He has no idea what is really going on—how messed up my life really is.

"I'm just not feeling very good. I just want to go home."

Lies. All lies. I feel fine and want to be here more than anything in the world. I just can't be.

Football Guy responds, "Oh, okay. I understand. Will you be mad if I stay behind?"

"No. I want you to stay. I want you to have fun. I'll be fine."

"Okay."

I get up and walk out toward my fate in the form of a pissed off dad who is waiting for me outside the building with a hate-filled sneer on his face. He says nothing. Tears begin to spill down my cheeks because I have accepted that my night is ruined. My mom pulls up to where we are standing in her van and my jealous, possessive, psychopath dad and me both climb in.

He starts to run his mouth at me again.

"You're a bitch. A slut. I *can't believe* you ended up going."

A torrent of tears run down my face, streaming down onto my neck, before spilling onto the red satin fabric of my dress. I am sobbing—and attempting to do so quietly, privately.

I hate him. I really, truly hate him. I hate him so much. I am so sick of this.

We drive the rest of the way home with an ominous silence settling around us. Nothing about this night is normal. Nothing about it is fair. It shouldn't be like this. It doesn't have to be. Yet this is exactly how it is—my life. He couldn't even allow me just one good night. Not even one.

Once inside my bedroom, I strip off the red dress and kick my shoes into the corner. I pull on pajamas and throw myself down onto my bed to process what happened as I try to shake off the ugly reality that clings to me. I assume my dad must've passed out after we got home because he never visits my room—*thank God!* I lie in my bed on my side, my skin against the cotton sheets, thinking about the time I spent dancing with Football Guy and talking with friends, as I cry myself to sleep.

No more strobe lights. No more silver and black balloons. No more laughing. No more dancing. No more fun.

Just tears.

A hand across my pregnant belly . . .

Tucked between the paralyzing sting of the secrets we keep.

And a crushing tsunami of the lies we tell.

ABIGAIL

AGE 19
2008

Hello, Graduate

Graduation day comes, finally*!* I am proud of myself for finishing school, especially after all that I have endured at this point in my life. It was a lot to go through—to not only carry two babies during my high school years, but to do so while shouldering household chores and tending to every whim of my mom and dad by day—and *by far* too many nights.

My mom and dad pushed me to graduate from high school. They wanted this for me. My mom always made sure I got out of bed to go to school, even on the days that I felt too exhausted from being pregnant and had no desire to go. She always made sure I turned in my homework and was making decent enough grades to pass the semester. "You are going to finish school, Abby. You aren't going to use these babies as an excuse to drop out. You are going to go to school and get your diploma, so you can be somebody one day," she'd say.

This always confused me. I think their idea of me being "somebody" and my idea of "being somebody" look nothing alike. I exist as "their somebody." I am not my own. But I'm proud of myself, and I'm grateful that I at least have this.

At the ceremony, I walk across the stage seven months pregnant. My round belly silhouette cannot be hidden by my dress or royal blue cape. As I step into the spotlight, I am handed my diploma: the one I earned, even though I changed schools *so many* times. Football Guy is graduating today, too. I am happy that this is something that we get to do together. Now, we can both "be somebodies."

Hopefully, together.

ABIGAIL

AGE 20

Delivery of Baby Two

*C*arrying Baby Two was a little easier for me from an emotional perspective because of Football Guy's presence in my life. Having a real boyfriend makes it a lot easier for me to pretend this baby was created by choice and out of love, from a stable foundation upon which a family could grow. Football Guy always tells me, "I love you and I'm going to be there for you. You and the kids." I am so lucky that he still wants to be with me, even though I already have a little girl and a new baby on the way.

I pretend that this baby that I am carrying is his. That we have our own family—Baby One and now Baby Two. It makes the emotional burden a bit lighter for me to carry as this baby grows inside my belly, although the soul-crushing weight of my family's secret suffocates me.

The day my contractions start—on July 11, 2008—my parents and I head to the hospital. Only this time, Football Guy meets us there. On a few occasions, I catch my dad giving Football Guy an evil glare, but my parents recognize that Football Guy's presence helps to convincingly perpetuate our lies. The nurses assume that Football Guy is my baby's father. The nurses have no idea that the child belongs to my dad. I am relieved that they don't ask us many questions this time, though I'm sure they make assumptions. I begin to feel the familiar fear that if they find out, we will all go to jail for what we have done, and that both babies will grow up without a family. While I don't like this situation, jail and losing the babies sounds far worse. At least this way, I can watch over both of them and they will have a family, albeit one built upon my abuse and all our lies.

In reality, I know that this birth will unfold the same as the last. I will not get to name my daughter. I will only get to pretend to be her mother when the nurses are in the room. I will basically be my mom's assistant with her care. There will be no father listed on her birth certificate, only my name as her mother. I know and fully comprehend the reality of my situation.

They will claim her.

She will be theirs.

They will take her over. I will not get to be this baby's mom. She will never even get to know that she is my daughter. I will become her fake older sister. My presence in her life is simply to help them carry the reward of their evil acts. There will never be a colorful card or handmade craft made for me by my child on Mother's Day. Those will go to my mom. Each time I hear my mom claim herself as my child's mother when she publicly introduces us, my soul will cringe, and a piece of me will die on the inside.

Our true identities do not matter.

I am nothing.

I am no one.

I do not matter.

My mom and dad determine my fate, consume my days, and steer my future.

ABIGAIL

AGE 20

The House Servant

I hate being at home now. The pride that I felt as a high school graduate took a sharp dive into damnation just days after my graduation ceremony. Attending school each day used to be my safe place. It gave me a full day's shield of protection from the abuse that I suffered at home. There is no safety now.

My days are an endless loop in service to my parents, this house, and taking care of *my* babies whenever my mom—my daughters' *fake* mom—isn't around. I wake up early to cook them a hot breakfast each day. I crack eggs into a skillet and fry bacon. I prepare buttered slices of toast. Sometimes, I make pancakes. I make coffee and pour it into mugs. I do all the dishes, sweep our carpet, mop our floors, and dust and clean every surface in our house. I take out the garbage. I cut the grass and I take care of our yard to keep it looking nice. I wash, dry, fold, and put away all the laundry for all of us. I then cook lunch and clean the dishes from each meal. Lunch is when the days get darker.

Every day, around noon, I hear the crunching of gravel. I hear the slam of a car door in our driveway. I know my dad will walk in any second now. He is here to eat lunch. But that is not the real reason he is here. The only person here besides us right now is the baby. He walks up behind me and wraps his arms around me to cage me in, trapped between the counter and his body. He rubs a hand across one of my breasts and squeezes it until I wince. He yanks down my pajama pants and panties in one quick tug. Then he shoves his hard dick inside me. He pounds into me from behind, over, and over again. I hate every moment of it, but I do not scream. I do not claw. I do not fight. It's pointless. I know that now.

My soul lurches as he hammers into my body as though it is an extension of his own. I have no voice, no choice, and no power here. When my dad has finished raping me in front of the kitchen sink, he pulls up his pants, slaps my ass cheek once, and heads out the door to go back to work. I finish washing the dishes. I cry on most days. I shove my shame and sorrow into "the box." Then I continue on with my household chores. The sweeping. The vacuuming. The laundry. I feed my baby and change her diaper throughout the day. She is the only happiness that I know here. In the late afternoon, I usually sit on the couch to watch TV for a while before the chores that come next.

The evening chores are more demanding. I prepare a meal, set the table, and serve my family dinner. I fill their plates with food and place them in front of the two of them as though Chevo is a king and Laura is a queen. When we finish eating, I wash our dishes and wipe down the counters. Then, my nightly post-dinner duties—the ones I loathe doing—begin.

I draw a bath for my mom. Undressing, her clothes fall into a heap on the bathroom floor as she steps into the bathtub. Squatting on my knees, I take my position beside the tub. I soak a washrag with warm water, swipe it with a bar of soap, and I begin to wash her body. Once her skin is scrubbed clean, I wet her hair. Once I lather the shampoo into a thick layer of foamy bubbles across her scalp, I rinse the shampoo. Then I condition her hair. When my mom finally stands and steps out of the bathtub, I hand her a towel to dry her body. If she needs her fingernails or toenails clipped, I clip them. Then I rub lotion across the folds of fat on her body. I rub the lotion in large white swirls until it soaks in.

Next, I do the exact same thing with my dad, with a few additions. I draw his bath. I lather his body with soap. I squirt shampoo into the palm of my hand and rub it into his hair until it is clean, then I apply conditioner to it. I lather his face with a thin layer of shaving cream and I shave him. (I debate pushing the blade hard into his neck.) I then scrub at the thick callouses lining the bottom of his nasty feet. It makes me want to throw up. After my dad gets out of the tub, I trim his nasty toenails and fingernails if he needs me to. Then I rub lotion all over his body, the one which—disturbingly—I know all too well. The one I wish I never had to see or feel—ever again.

Sated by sudsy water and relaxed, they go lie down on their bed, where each eagerly awaits a full-body massage. I spend an hour-and-a-half each night massaging each of them, rubbing down their disgusting, greedy, needy, gross bodies. My fingers begin to cramp up after about twenty minutes and I know that it is going to be a *long* three hours. When I am done, my hands feel numb and I can barely move them.

When either of them prompts, "rub my feet," I know what comes next. The foot rub is their way of initiating the group sex that I am forced to partake in with the two of them. They take what they want from me. They leave behind all that I have left—it is not much. I am merely a body to fuck. A body to clean and to cook. One who serves. A person to wash, trim, and massage them. The girl who was forced to deliver and care for "their" babies. I am choking on the helpless feeling that accompanies each day and suffocating in the gut-wrenching sex acts that stain me in the night. This is all that I am good for. Just this. This is all that I am ever going to be—their house servant, their sex slave, their surrogate mother, their caretaker. I am their property. It does not help to wish for a different life, so I've stopped doing it.

Tomorrow will be the same. And the next day after that. Each day bleeds into the next. This is my life. The cooking. The cleaning. The lunchtime rape. More cooking. More cleaning. The baths. The washing. The trimming of nails. The shaving of a whisker-covered throat that I'd like to cut. The trimming of hair. The massaging. "Rub my feet." I know what comes next . . .

ABIGAIL

AGE 20

Over It

*M*y newborn baby is crying, so I warm up a bottle to feed her, while gently rocking her back and forth in my arms. I change her soiled diaper and re-button her onesie. She is innocent, so pure, so beautiful, and she will be brought up cloaked in tightly wrapped cover stories that they have woven all around her. Lies that are suffocating me slowly from the inside out.

When my mom is around, she takes my baby away from me. She feeds her and changes her diapers. My mom holds her, soothes her, looks down at her with a loving look on her face while cooing, "That's right, I'm your mom. You are such a beautiful baby—my beautiful, perfect baby. My little angel."

My throat constricts, anger surges within me, and I am consumed by hatred for this entire messed up situation that I am in. I am cloaked in a thick, invisible blanket of hopelessness for being forced to play along with their twisted plans. I fucking hate them—both of them—my rapist father, and my complicit, abusive, repulsive mother—more now than I thought I could ever hate another living being.

"Abby, isn't your baby sister so beautiful?"

I dare not respond, as the truth thrums in my bones.

She is beautiful, but she is not your daughter. She will never be your daughter.

I am so sick of being trapped in this house and working in service to these horrible people all day and night. For a few months, they were high on the new baby, and I didn't have to do as much around the house—and when I say "as much"—I basically mean that my entire life was not dedicated in service to them. There were breaks in our routine. Over time, things slipped back to how they used to be.

About two months after the birth of Baby Two, the group rapes start up again. My dad still pulls into the driveway each day at lunchtime to violate me—sometimes in the kitchen, sometimes in one of our beds, and sometimes on the couch. At this point, I am so disconnected from the act that I can almost remove myself (at least mentally) from the room. In the evening, there is almost always forced group sex between me and my parents. If that doesn't happen, then my dad finds his way into my room. Yet again. The more I fight, the deeper the bruises in places where they can't be seen and the rougher the rapes become.

There is no longer an escape from the things I endure here. After I am raped and it is over, I don't have time to put that dirty, ugly thing into the box to seek some separation from it—to pretend that it didn't just happen—again. It consumes me, body, heart, mind, and soul. I am raped twice a day now. There is rarely a day that goes by when I am not raped. That's a whole lot of ugly things that I cannot fit into the box, so I can hide them. It's a whole lot of stained flesh, tattered soul, and vile sex acts to try to shove into an invisible box and compartmentalize.

I hate each day.

I loathe each night.

I hate being me.

I hate my life.

I cook, I clean, I sweep, I wash dishes and launder clothes, I take care of "my sisters" and then host the elaborate day spa experience for my parents each night.

I don't want to be here anymore. I cannot continue living like this. I don't think I can stand being raped by him one more time. *Is killing myself the answer?* I think that it is probably my only way out. *But I can't leave my babies behind—not with them.*

So, I drudge through each day fulfilling chores and am utterly repulsed by two sets of evil hands rubbing across my body each night. It's just too much. *Can't they just leave me alone? How can they get away with this? Why doesn't anybody see what's happening? This can't be my entire life.*

But as much as I want to end my pain, I will not leave my beautiful daughters behind with these sadistic people. No way. So, as a hollowed-out shell of a person, I walk through my days and somehow, I survive my nights.

I start to sneak alcohol when they aren't around. It helps to numb my pain. The cold swigs of beer help to anchor all that is dirty, untethered, ugly, and messed up inside of me to a place where it doesn't wound me quite as deeply. It allows me to hide those unlovable parts of me from myself, even if only for an hour or two. The more beer I drink, the better I feel. It certainly doesn't change anything about my situation, but at least it dulls the emotional ache that accompanies the permanent stain embedded in my flesh.

I have to get out of this. Football Guy and I have to move in together. That's it. We need to go. If we don't, I might kill myself. I can't stand this anymore.

I can't and I won't leave my babies behind. But I can't stay.

ABIGAIL

AGE 20

The Runaway

I can't live here any longer. Not one more day. Two months after the birth of Baby Two, I'm done. As soon as my mom and dad leave to go to work, I tell Football Guy that I'm leaving to go to my sister's house. I then pick up the phone to call my sister, who is still living in Laredo with her boyfriend. I spoke to her late last night, so we could come up with a plan. She understands that I am ready to leave this house, *finally*.

"Hi. I need you to come pick me up."

"Hi Abby. Okay, I'll leave in a minute."

"Okay. I'll see you soon."

After hearing the exchange between us, Football Guy says, "Well, if you're leaving, I'm coming with you. I love you. I want to be with you. I want to help you take care of the kids."

I reply, "Okay, if you want to come with us, get ready. She'll be here soon."

I head to my room to pack a bag. I grab a few outfits for me, along with a few outfits for Baby One, and Baby Two. *We are finally getting the hell out of here.*

My sister pulls up, I get the kids strapped into the car, and she drives us to her house. As we put more distance between the House from Hell and here, I feel glad to be leaving. But lingering directly behind that relief is a heavy dose of worry mixed with fear. *They are going to find us. They are going to come after us. There is no way they are just going to let me leave like this. They are probably going to hurt us.* But there is no turning back now.

We decompress at my sister's house for several hours before my cell phone rings later that afternoon. It is my stepbrother on the line, "Abby, where are you? Mom overdosed. She tried to kill herself."

"She—what?"

"She tried to kill herself. She took a bunch of pills. Where are you?"

"What? Oh my gosh. I'm at my sister's house."

Not long after his call, there is a knock on the door. My sister opens the door to see my mom standing there. My mom looks different, terrible, like she isn't well. As I step out onto the front stoop, my sister and Football Guy follow me out. My dad walks over to where we are standing and stops a few feet away. He bears a look of concern without anger and, for once, is keeping a bit of distance. *Interesting.* I feel nervous and scared. I have no idea what they are going to say to me, but I'm pretty sure they are going to try to make us come back home.

Wearing a smile, they each greet us politely. My dad looks directly at me—his face marred by a look of distress—and he is the first to speak. "When your mom got home from work today and saw that all of you were gone—that you had left and taken the girls with you—she freaked out. She took a bunch of pills, Abby. I had to call an ambulance. Your mom actually died. She died, and the paramedics, they brought her back to life."

"She did? Is she going to be okay now?"

My mom feebly replies, "I'm fine now, Abby. They pumped my stomach at the hospital. I'm okay now."

She continues, "I was so worried when I got home, and you guys weren't there—that you ran away. We are a family, Abby—all of us. We just want all of us to be together. I need you to come back home, Abby. I need you to help take care of me. No one else is going to be able to help me. I *need* you."

I feel sick. And confused. I wanted to get out of there—to leave them. I was finally able to get out and to be free of them. We got away. *Should I go back?*

"Your dad and I talked about it and we've agreed that [Football Guy] is going to move in with us. You guys can get married. You can be together—make a beautiful life together. Everything is going to be perfect. You just need to come back home. It is going to be a beautiful life, Abby. You can get married and have the life that you always wanted."

I am consumed by a wave of soul crushing guilt. *It's my fault that this happened to her. I am the reason that she did this. She almost died, because of me. If I wouldn't have left, this wouldn't have happened. I am the only one who can take care of her and help her now.*

"So, if I come back home, we can live together—we can be together—and get married?"

"Yes, that's what we want to have happen. That's what we wanted to come tell you."

My dad chimes in, "Yes, we will allow you to be together. Just come home."

I turn to Football Guy, "Do you hear what they're saying? What do you think?"

Football guy replies, "I want us to be together. Let's do it!"

After a long pause, I reply, "Okay. I'll come back."

As the words leave my mouth, I realize that Football Guy is clueless about my abuse, the true father of my daughters, and everything that has happened to me. He probably thinks this is an ordinary family feud.

We all pile into the van—the kids, Football Guy, my parents and I—and we make the drive from Laredo back "home" to The Valley.

ABIGAIL

AGE 20
Mission, Texas

Football Guy Moves In

*T*his is now our third home in Mission, Texas, a small white house with yellow trim. I am so happy that Football Guy gets to live with us now. They even allow him to sleep in my room, just like they promised. I feel so happy to finally have what feels like a-kind-of-normal life.

As messed up as it sounds, running away has shifted the household power dynamics a bit. My parents now make an effort to keep me somewhat happy. They buy me soda, pickles, or more coloring books and crayons (my only pastime within these walls) to keep me busy at home. That's also the *real reason* Football Guy gets to live with us, to keep me happy, and to keep us here.

They want to keep my babies. That is the only reason why Football Guy is allowed to exist within these walls as my "boyfriend," much less sleep in my bed. I love sharing a bedroom with him, not only because I love him, but because he unknowingly acts as a protective shield against the future rapes and threesomes with my mom and dad.

Sick, I know, but it's true. Football Guy knows nothing about the truth of my life. I keep the shame and secrets buried deep inside. Besides, he probably couldn't handle the truth. I don't want him to know the ugly things about my life.

Football Guy being my bedmate only lasts about three months, because my dad isn't pleased at all with our current sleeping arrangement. If my dad had his way, my boyfriend never would have been allowed to move in with us in the first place, but in the wake of my mom's attempted suicide, he didn't really have much of a choice. It became the card that he was forced to play in order to get me and their fake kids back here with them. I often see my dad glaring at Football Guy, especially when he sees us holding hands or hugging one another. The venom in his eyes leads me to believe he'd have no trouble committing murder to bring an end to our affection. I fear that could actually happen at some point. He is evil. And he is obsessed.

On the heels of my dad's displeasure for our new arrangement, one afternoon, my mom and dad drag another bed into my bedroom for Football Guy to sleep on, to get him out of mine. This is my dad's way of putting more distance between the two of us. There's not really much I can do about it. *Of course, they lied. They always lie. He hates him. He hates this.* I guess I'm just glad my dad still can't walk into my bedroom in the middle of the night to bother me as long as Football Guy still sleeps in my room.

My bedroom security would be short-lived. About three months after the addition of the second bed in our bedroom, my mom and dad tell us that Football Guy needs to move into a separate bedroom altogether.

I'm totally pissed. They said that he could live here, be here, in my bed, with me! That's what they told me to get me to come back here! Why would they let him move in with us, let him sleep in my bed, then change things? I'm *so* sick of them, their bullshit lies and manipulation, the disgusting things they do, and their stupid rules. The ones they intentionally tuck, twist, and weave so tightly around their abuse.

Fast forward another three months, and they tell us that "we need to talk." Football Guy and I are seated on a couch in the living room with my parents standing there, looking at us. My dad says, "Y'all are moving too fast. I don't like him living under the same roof as you."

My mom tacks on, "Y'all are gonna end up getting married too soon. It's not appropriate right now because you really don't know each other."

My dad says, "I agree with her."

I reply, "But y'all said we can get married and be together."

My mom jumps in, "Y'all are . . . he just can't live here."

My dad adds, "I agree with what she said."

Tears begin to stream down my cheek. I am so upset and angry. *This isn't how things were supposed to go. They promised me. They told us.*

My mom says, "We aren't going to argue with you about this. This is done. It is decided. He's going to move out."

We resign ourselves to the unfair verdict.

Football Guy says, "Okay. *I'll go.*"

He walks into his bedroom, grabs his stuff, stops to say "goodbye" to me, and walks out the door, leaving me behind with Baby One, Baby Two, and my parental captors.

ABIGAIL

AGE 21

The Abuse Resumes

E ven though my parents made Football Guy move out of our house, we are still technically "together," but with him gone, the abuse starts up again. My parents work each weekday. I am left at home to clean, do dishes, wash all our laundry, cook all our meals, care for the two babies during the day, until the evening round of chores begins my hell in the form of the nighttime ritual.

Every day is the same routine. The cleaning of floors and wiping of counters; the cooking of meals; the washing of dishes; the washing, drying, folding, and hanging of laundry; the washing of bodies; the massaging of naked bodies; and the group rape. Each day bleeds into the next. They like to wound me with their well-placed, sharply edged words.

"You are nothing. You are nobody. You are worth nothing. You have no value. This is all you're good for, right here—cleaning and fucking. Laying on your back. You are never going to amount to ANYTHING, Abby. You are NOTHING."

My dad still drives home during his lunch breaks nearly every day to rape me. If I am washing dishes, he sidles up behind me, breathes into my hair, presses his unwelcomed body into my backside, grabs my hips in his meaty hands, and glides them all over my withering body. It always ends the same, with him inside me. And me floating outside of myself to survive it. There is no point in fighting anymore.

I am nothing.
I am no one.
I will never amount to anything.
They take what they want.
There is nothing left.
And all that I am—*is theirs.*

ABIGAIL

AGE 21

Telling Football Guy

*F*ootball Guy returned to live at his mom's house, which is about a ten-minute drive from our house in The Valley. We still see one another when my parents are at work and I'm at home with my girls. He borrows his mom's car during the day and drives over, parks in the back alley—where his car won't be seen—and comes into the house to spend time with me. I make sure that he is never at our house at lunchtime for obvious reasons. He comes to see me almost every day. This is all we have now—these stolen moments between us.

My mom and dad know that we are still dating, but they are just happy to have him out of our house. I've now been dating Football Guy for about a year and a half. He is my one true person. The only person who truly cares about me, the only person who loves me. He is my only way out. I thought I was almost free, until my mom and dad revoked their promise for us to get married and have that beautiful life that they dangled. Throw one more lie upon the invisible heap.

One morning, Football Guy comes over to visit me. We are sitting on my bed in my room when I decide to question him on where things stand between us.

I ask him, "Will you marry me?"

"Yes, you know I want to. I have a ring already."

"We have to get married *now*," I insist. "Why wait?"

He throws a weird look my way. "Why are you in a rush to get married?"

"There's a lot you don't know about me and that you don't understand." *How can I begin to explain my life over the past ten years?*

"Well, try me."

My stomach drops, my heart is beating fast in my chest, and I feel myself shaking. *Should I tell him? Should I tell him? What will happen if I actually tell him?*

"I can't tell you." I don't even know where to start. My hands are clammy. My entire body is vibrating to the core and I can barely breathe. I know that I am standing at the crossroads between ugly truths and safe lies. I'm not sure what to do. *Will he believe me? What is he gonna think? What is he gonna do? Is he gonna save us?*

He sighs, "Well, if we're gonna get married, you need to trust me."

I take a deep breath, then much like falling off a cliff, I utter, "The girls' dads aren't who I said that they were. They aren't from random boyfriends of mine."

His face is plastered with a look of confusion.

"The girls are Chevo's. That's their dad."

His brow furrows, like he isn't sure he heard me right.

"Don't look at me like that. *Please*," I beg. "I told you that you wouldn't understand. But Laura and Chevo told me I was gonna have their kids. I told them no, but there was no way of getting out of it."

He gets up from the bed. "I can't do this."

He steps away from the bed and moves toward the doorway.

"Don't leave me. I still love you. Please don't leave me."

"I can't deal with this shit."

He turns his back to me and walks out the door.

Sitting on my bed, I feel jarred by shame, regret, and a broken heart. I am consumed by the soul-crushing sting of betrayal that accompanies the unacceptable truths that I carry. The ones that I just spilled out.

He is gone.

I am alone.

In case you are wondering if this was truly the end of our relationship—it was. If you are wondering if I left anything out about how my revelation of truths between us took place—I did not. Harsh, cold words and his back retreating through my doorway was the end of it. It was the end of us.

ABIGAIL

AGE 21

San Antonio

Not long after Football Guy walked out on me, my parents move us to San Antonio into a white, four-bedroom house with yellow trim. My last memory of him—now permanently etched into my mind—is the lash of his cold, sharp words, "I can't deal with this shit," illustrated by the burning image of his back as he walked out of my doorway for the last time. It plays over and over again in my mind for days, weeks, and months.

It's difficult to explain the shame. I carry it like invisible bags that are tethered to me, filled with lofty weighted undetectable bricks of memories, stories of abuse, spilled tears, and the burden of all that has been done to me up to this point. Though I try to move forward, my body buckles beneath the heavy bricks of horror everywhere I go. Nobody else can see them—the bricks of shame—*my* shame. But that doesn't make them any less of a burden to carry. Maybe, I deserve to carry the shame.

I am so exhausted. My situation is hopeless. There is no way out. I used to believe that marriage is the one thing that would set me free from this hell hole. I have no one now. Marriage is now a million miles away. It might as well be impossible.

I can't fucking stand being here. I hate them. They hold all the power. I hold nothing. I am trapped by their bodies. I am being smothered by their lies. I am tortured to the core by what I have become for being dirtied by their hands.

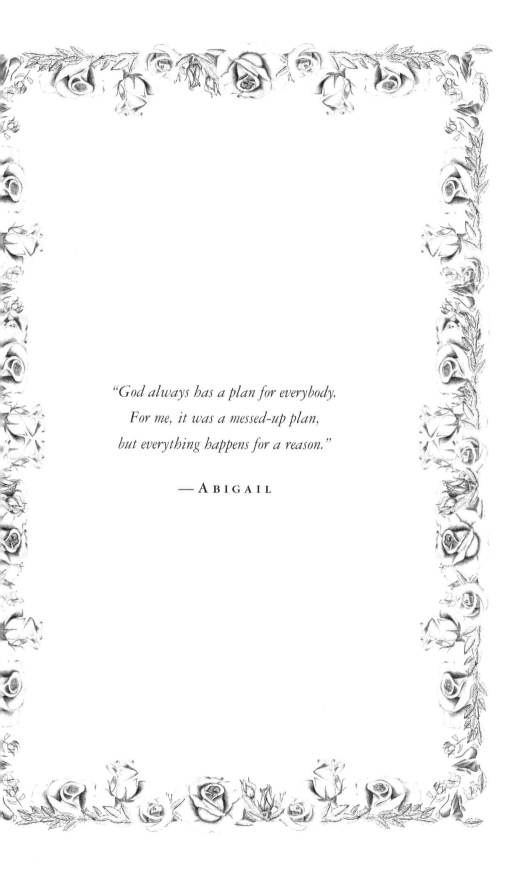

"God always has a plan for everybody.
For me, it was a messed-up plan,
but everything happens for a reason."

—ABIGAIL

ABIGAIL

AGE 22
2010-2011

Number Three

*T*hey always say God never gives you more than you can handle.
I think He either misjudged me or perhaps, He misjudged what would happen to me after I came to live with *them*. There is another baby growing inside my belly—my dad's baby. My third baby. *His* third baby. I cannot do this again. I just can't. I won't.

There is no way that I will ever survive this.

Not again.

My frustration and helplessness are at an all-time high. I don't have to *wonder* what will happen when this baby is born. I've seen it play out twice now—the robbery of my children. I know that I won't get to name my son, just as I didn't get to name my two little girls. They are born of me, created inside of me, an extension of me, a piece of my own heart and my own soul, but it will all be stripped away with smiles and fake stories. *Abby the whore. Abby who gets pregnant over and over again by random guys she barely knows. Abby whose mom and dad step in to parent her children, as though it is a kind gesture and not a deliberate hijacking.*

I cry myself to sleep most nights. I carry this baby inside of me the same way I did the others, but my reality is only despair now. There is no hope.

On April 12, 2011, my third baby—*my son*—is born. He is delivered with my two captors—parents—in the room to secretly claim him. I love him immediately, at first sight, just as I did my other two. So perfect, so precious, so tiny.

And just about as quickly, I swallow back the tears that spill from deep within me knowing that the same thing will happen with this baby as with *my* last—they will steal him in plain sight and claim him as their own. I feel as though I am rotting away on the inside, but no one knows. It is a feeling that only intensifies, it never fades. I feel stupid for allowing this to happen again, but I see no way out of it. My mom's excitement over my "new baby brother" makes me want to punch her in the face. I'd like to castrate my dad. My thoughts have turned dark and I feel as though I am being pulled into a black hole of anger and despair.

About two months after Baby Three is born, I began to snort small white lines of cocaine up my nose to numb the pain. Not just the pain of losing my third born while he was still right in front of me, but also to quiet the silent screams inside me, and help me to endure daily rapes by my dad, all the while living in this twisted pretend-family world.

I hate them both. And I hate myself even more for still being here, for allowing this to happen to me. Again. And again. And again.

ABBY

AGE 24
2012

Be Mine

*I*n 2012, my mom, who had always struggled with bouts of pain and exhaustion, is diagnosed with Lupus. She is in rough shape and things are not going well for her. A lot of days, she can't make it out of bed, much less actually do anything. Since all the work around the house is already my job, that part doesn't matter much. But she is now having a hard time just making it through life in the day-to-day. My dad and I don't think that she is going to live long if things stay the way that they are.

One afternoon, my dad and I are sitting in the living room, when he looks over at me and says, "Once she's gone, it's just gonna be me and you." He then starts talking about her hypothetical funeral. I sit quietly and try not to react. I want to throw up.

"Abby, we already have our kids. I'll be your husband. You'll be my wife."

Listening to this line of absolute nonsense, I am dumbfounded. *What in the heck is he thinking? Is he serious with this? No freaking way.* This is wrong on so many levels that I can't even process it. He is married to my mom, who is still alive. I am his adopted daughter, his niece. My kids were born of rape. No way would we ever be married. I absolutely fucking hate him.

He drones on, "We can have more kids. I'm going to buy rings for us and everything."

I have no words for the deep disgust that I feel. There are no words to describe how deranged he truly is. No way is this ever going to happen. I would kill myself first.

Later that night, my mind vividly flashes to a memory from my childhood.

I'm five or six. I'm with my mom, Aunt Laura, and Uncle Chevo. My brother and sister are there, too. We are swimming at a pool at the Holiday Inn in El Paso. We are having fun together as a family. Uncle Chevo and Laura seem nice. My mom just left to walk my brother and sister back to their hotel room. We are still in the water together, just Uncle Chevo and me. He looks over at me and says, "One day, I am going to marry you . . ."

I'm not sure what he means, or why he says this to me. He's my uncle. I'm just a girl. I'm not sure if I ever want to get married. Maybe one day, when I'm a grown up. But he's my uncle. I don't think I would ever marry my own uncle. That would be weird. I don't even think that is allowed. Plus, why would he even want to marry me? He already is married—to Laura. He's a grown up. I'm just a kid. I don't understand . . .

Consumed by disgust and reeling from the disturbing memory, it is in this moment that I realize that he has *always* been obsessed with me and his eyes were always fixed upon me from the time I was a little girl—an innocent five-year-old swimming in a pool with her uncle. The little girl I used to be, before him and his disgusting acts, before all of this.

I am his dream come true.

And he is my nightmare.

ABIGAIL

AGE 22
2013

Creation of the Chapel

$\mathcal{W}$e move into our fourth house in San Antonio. This one is a small, white ranch style house with bright, sea-foam green trim, a generous front porch, and a large yard for the kids to run around in and play. There is a tiny white house behind the main house that is also ours.

The moves never seem to stop. I catalog each temporary house in my mind by the street's name. There was Woodlawn, then The Coyote's house on South Central, and our latest house on McLaughlin Street.

Since I graduated from high school, the moves don't affect me as much as they used to, but the moves now affect my eldest daughter who is in elementary school. I hate that for my children, that they are constantly being shuffled around to live in random houses the same way I always was. It's hard to feel like you ever truly have a "home," when that home is constantly changing like seasonal clothing. Each "home" is short-lived and fleeting. That is the one constant—the moving.

Ever since we moved into this house, my parents have suddenly become super religious. Growing up, they only took us to church on holidays and on rare occasion on a random Sunday.

Them embracing their religion apparently stemmed back to an incident that took place when my eldest sis—I mean, my eldest daughter—was three months old.

On that day, Baby One was lying in her bassinette and my mom was lying on her bed. All of a sudden, my mom saw someone standing in the doorway—her dad, who was deceased, like an apparition. He said to her, "Look at the baby. Look at her." My mom was terror-stricken that he had appeared to her in that way and immediately got up to check on the baby.

Standing over the bassinette, she looked down and realized that the baby had blue lips and wasn't breathing. My mom immediately leaned down into the bassinette and began to perform CPR on her. Baby One began breathing again. My mom had brought her back to life because of the vision she had of her dead dad telling her to check on the baby. From that moment on, my mom dubbed her "the miracle baby."

When my eldest daughter—the "miracle baby"—was around age six or seven, my mom started telling my daughter that she was a "miracle baby" and that she could heal people, that she had always been gifted. Reflecting back, I was obviously happy that my mom was able to resuscitate my baby the day she suddenly stopped breathing in her bassinette, but whether that meant she was capable of healing people was another story.

I never saw any proof of that between the day that my daughter nearly died and the time that my mom started planting the seed in my daughter's head that she could heal people. It was a bit bizarre to me. Not just the way it all happened, but the fact that my parents, who rarely attended church, became devout "believers" randomly overnight.

Anyway, one thing led to the next and before I know it, my suddenly religious parents decided that she was "The Miracle Girl" and that they were going to start their own chapel in the back yard for people in need of blessings, prayers, and healing, so they can come to visit her. While I do believe that some people have the ability to heal others, I don't know that I believed my young daughter to be one of them.

On the heels of their spontaneous spiritual epiphany, my parents converted the tiny home in our back yard into the St. Peregrine Chapel—a Mexican National Catholic Church of the Holy Rosary—ran by Bishop John Parnell and the future healing hub of my daughter, "The Miracle Girl." My mom tells others that my daughter is "God's vessel." Saint Peregrine, after whom the chapel was named, is known as the saint for cancer patients.

My parents launched a Facebook page for the chapel to promote it online. It didn't take long before the word of mouth began to spread about the eight-year-old "Miracle Girl" at the St. Peregrine Chapel who could heal people.

My parents bought a bunch of folding chairs for the chapel—the house out back converted into a makeshift church space. I know this may sound a bit odd to those who aren't Mexican Catholic, but makeshift churches like this one are very common in Texas, especially within Hispanic communities in San Antonio.

They bought several stands to place throughout the room in various spots to hold Bibles. They dressed my daughter in a long white gown with a beautiful white lace veil that covered her face, so she would truly look the part of "The Miracle Girl." People—namely Hispanics who were devout Mexican Catholics—began to flock to the chapel every Sunday to attend the mass and have my daughter's hands laid upon them to bless or heal them.

My daughter had to stand up there donning her lacey veil—at the front of the chapel outside during masses—while holding an intricate silver bowl filled with "Holy water" that she would dip her pointer finger into so that she could draw an invisible cross on each person's forehead and pray over them. Many of the people who visited her were afflicted with cancer and drawn to it due to its namesake, Saint Peregrine. A few claimed that she had taken away their pain for several hours after she prayed over them. (And she truly did put her all into praying over them.)

For an eight-year-old little girl, this was both, physically exhausting, mentally daunting, and it took a lot out of her. She prayed over people and laid her hands upon them to bless them. They then placed money into the basket when it was passed. My parents basked in the donations. Word of mouth continued to spread, right along with the Facebook posts, and people flocked by the hundreds to see her.

Fast forward one year, and "The Miracle Girl" hit the local news channels in San Antonio. Reporters traveled to the chapel to report on the story. My mom told people that my daughter was able to channel Our Lady of Guadalupe (the Virgin Mary) and that she possessed special abilities to help or heal people with cancer. My parents loved the publicity. They knew that the news coverage would bring even more people to the chapel. And more people coming to the chapel meant that there would be more money in the basket when it was passed on Sundays.

My daughter's blessings and prayers became a major stream of revenue for my parents. One that my daughter paid the price for every single Sunday. On many occasions, she would tell them, "I don't want to do it. I'm not going to do it. I don't want to do it anymore."

Whenever she objected, they would bribe her. She could get anything she wanted—candy, Barbies, soda—if she would agree to show up and lay hands.

So, like any little girl that age would—she took the bribe. She laid the hands. They could usually still get her to wear the lace veil, but there were times when she'd be wearing a lime green tee shirt and shorts or whatever she happened to feel like wearing at the time. She'd stand at the front of the chapel to wear herself out, yet again, in an effort to please "our" greedy parents and get that golden ticket to the treasure bounty.

I hated seeing the toll this took on my daughter each Sunday. I hated seeing my parents' smiling faces as the basket was filled with donations from good, honest, hard-working folks who came in search of healing, a blessing, or even a miracle. I truly hope they got what they came for. Some certainly claimed that she had helped or healed them. My daughter truly did pray over these people and try to help them. But to me, it all felt like a scam and a money-grab on the part of my greedy parents who wanted to fill their pockets. I found it despicable and felt bad for being in any way associated with it. It was just one more thing for me to hate them for.

It is also kind of ironic that my all-of-a-sudden-devoutly-religious-parents-and-founders-of-that-makeshift-chapel-of-miracles were still continuing to rape me on a regular basis. As others passed their donations basket, they passed me between the two of them at night. My dad certainly didn't look anything like a devout Catholic man while shoving himself inside of me as my devout Catholic mom looked on and partook, playing her role in the human triangle of sex acts and shame.

If only people knew the truth about them. But no one did—no one except me.

Evil can clean up nice on Sundays to hide in the daylight.

Upon first glance—unnoticed.
Some enter our lives.
As saviors.
Angels walking upon earth.
Footprints in the dirt.
Light on the path.
When fate steps in . . .

—JAMIE COLLINS
(For Abigail)

RUDY

AGE 39
Present Day

Introduction

*M*y name is Raul Fidencio Alvarado. But everybody calls me "Rudy." I grew up in San Antonio, Texas, the second youngest of four siblings—with an older brother, older sister, and a younger sister. My mom was one of those traditional Hispanic moms, a devout Mexican Catholic who always had a meal waiting on the table for us in our humble three-bedroom apartment, its walls adorned by traditional Mexican artwork. My mom loved us and took care of us, but we were exposed to a lot of things we never should have seen as kids. She was around, but never really on top of us as far as what we were doing: when we went to bed, what time we woke up, whether we went to school, if we did our homework, where we were, who we hung around with, or what we did. We pretty much did our own thing and she did hers. In a way, it was nice not having anybody bossing me around all the time. But in other ways, I wished for something different.

Basketball was the only thing outside of family that I ever loved. I've always had a "don't fuck with me" attitude. I can't stand bullies. I hate assholes. And any man who hits a woman deserves to have his ass beat. I don't have many memories of my childhood prior to the age of ten—weird, I know. I guess my mind somehow blocked out a lot of what happened during those years.

That said, I do vividly recall that I flunked the first grade. (Not at all my fault. For real.) My mom inadvertently checked the box for "bilingual" on my application for elementary school, so I found myself seated in a first-grade classroom with a teacher who spoke only

Spanish. The other kids also spoke Spanish. Let me be clear that I only spoke English and knew just a handful of Spanish words that I'd heard my mother routinely utter over the years. I had no idea what was going on in that class for about 18 weeks straight. I didn't know what the hell the teacher was saying, much less what the other students were saying. I just sat there, looking dumb, understanding nothing, and feeling confused as hell sitting at my desk. The teacher thought that I was "pretending" not to understand her. And I thought she was pretending that I actually spoke Spanish. So, let's just say my whole first grade year turned into a debacle. Then, the first grade "flunkee" thing became one of those things from my past that I will *never* live down amongst family members.

I remember one day when I was ten, the summer of my fourth-grade year, my cousins came over to visit one day, and us kids were all playing outside together. We were hanging out, when I left to use the bathroom for a bit and returned to find everybody gone. I walked around and the apartment complex and ended up finding them near the outer perimeter of it. I found them just in time to hear a kid from outside of the apartment complex talking shit to my cousins. They grew up poor and didn't have the best clothes, so the kid was making fun of them.

My sister, who was with us, ran off to go tell my mom about what was happening. Once I saw her leave, I started to act all big and bad, taunting the kid, like I wanted to fight him. That's when my mom showed up.

She looked me in the eyes and in a stern voice, said, "Mijo, you better KICK HIS ASS, or I AM gonna whoop YOURS." So, I told the kid, "Me and you, one-on-one—nobody else steps in." Dude agreed, so we squared up. The dude took a karate stance. I took a boxer's stance. Dude attempted to karate kick me and I knocked him down. That happened twice. The third time it happened, I got on top of him and started to pummel him in the face with my fists.

My mom—who didn't realize that I actually knew how to fight—ended up pulling me off of him. Before walking away, I glanced down at him and said, "Don't be bringing that karate shit to the streets."

That is one of the earliest memories I have of standing up for myself and not allowing somebody to punk me or anyone close to me. I guess that's what happens when you are raised by a strong woman and you grow up in the hood. She makes sure you can hold your own.

I grew up in a rough neighborhood surrounded by gang-filled streets with a bad neighborhood on both sides of the fence of the apartment complex where we lived. Back then, the gangs were running San Antonio. They'd taken the area over, much the same way the mafia took over New York City back in the day. The police couldn't really do much to control it. The gangs were running things. Their power was real. Beat downs and dead bodies were commonplace. The most lethal gang in the area at the time was known as the "Land Syndicate." People were targeted in drive by shootings, beat down on the sidewalk, or taken out in gang-style hits with their dead bodies left lying in a ditch on the regular. I know, because I saw the underbelly of these things growing up in that neighborhood.

In middle school, my best friend's brother was a leader of the gang. I liked hanging around my best friend, so that meant I'd often find myself surrounded by gang members, more by association than choice. They'd all meet up at this house that everybody called "the dead end house," which was located just past the fence of the apartment complex where we lived. The Dead End House was next door to my best friend's house, and also the gathering place for the gang. They laid claim to the turf and about 30 to 40 of them would congregate there to sit around and talk shit, drink, smoke, and fight.

Hanging out with my best friend pulled me into the middle of a lot of shit. The Land Syndicate members would gather in a circle on the grass with two people in the middle to fight. I was often one of them—the fighters. I was a lot younger than the gang members were. I was also a lot smaller. For that reason, I'd get my ass handed to me in those boxing circles. But I wasn't gonna get punked, and I couldn't back down from stepping into that circle. I didn't feel like I really had a choice.

The gang member fighting me would land a few hard blows to my face and I'd fall down onto the grass. But I always got back up. Every. Single. Time. They nicknamed me "Little Man." I'd be lying on the grass, face swollen, heart pounding, starting to feel the pain spreading through my face, after getting my ass beat down at the Dead End House, still—I would pull myself up onto my feet again.

The guy would land another hard blow to my jaw, and I'd find myself down on the grass again. And again, I would get back up. It would get to the point that some of the gang members would eventually start to shout, "Just stay down, Little Man. Stay down. Don't get back up . . ." And, of course, my dumb ass would get up— one more time. For that reason, the gang members all knew me by association as "Little Man."

I guess you could say that I was semi-willingly beaten into some bizarre street-form of acceptance. I wasn't in the gang but being known by 'em for my courage (or maybe, more like my stupidity) offered me some level of protection within the gang's territory, which was pretty much everywhere I went.

I remember one day three guys ran up on me when I was walking down the sidewalk. I was prepared to fight, until one pulled a Glock and forced me onto the grass on my knees. He pointed the barrel of the gun right at my head and taunted, "Do you know who the fuck I am?"

I replied, "I don't fucking care."

In that moment, I remember thinking it was a cool looking gun. That was my initial thought. Maybe I was about to die. Maybe I was a bit scared. Maybe I didn't really give a damn about much of anything. All of a sudden, I hear a guy shout, "Hey, that's Little Man—LEAVE HIM ALONE!"

Their eyes got wide with acknowledgement of what they'd just heard and they let me back onto my feet. Then the one with the gun said, "Oh shit, so you're Little Man. We were just fucking with you. Cool. You are [so and so's] friend. We heard about you."

The gang member walked up to where we were standing and said, "Yo, you don't want to mess with him, man—not him—that's Little Man."

"Oh . . . that's Little Man?! Aw, shit, I didn't know." Upon learning my street name, he acted like we were cool, walking up and giving me a fist bump. He walked away impressed with a newfound understanding of who I was. I walked away pissed as hell, hoping that I would one day be able to take revenge for what he did to me.

My mom said I took all the anger and hate that I carried inside me—probably from all the bullshit that I saw as a kid, both inside and outside of our house—and that I "walked it." I guess she saw it in the way that I carried myself. I didn't mess with anybody, but I sure as hell didn't want them to mess with me, either. It wasn't an easy area to grow up in. If people respected me, I respected them back. If they didn't, then we'd have a problem. I learned that people would treat you the way that you allowed them to. While those "boxing" matches at the Dead End House beat me down, as a young boy living in the hood, they also saved me.

When my dad was around, he was an asshole. That's exactly how I thought of him back then. He used to beat my mom. I hated him for it. And when he hit her, I don't mean slaps or light taps, he would full-on punch her in the face with a loud "thunk, thunk" of his clenched fist while staring down at her with his face twisted in disgust, anger, and hatred. One of the only memories I have, around the age of six, was of me hearing them arguing one night. I had walked out of my bedroom to see that asshole beating my mom with his cowboy boot. He'd taken it off his foot, was holding it in his hand and lifting it way up into the air, then bringing it down and striking her with the steel toed part, pounding her with it over and over again.

With no hesitation, I ran straight toward him, "Stop hitting my mooommm." I jumped on his back with everything I had and put small arms around him in a childlike version of a chokehold. He began to laugh like a psycho, "You little motherfucker. You want to hit ME? You think you're brave?" He grabbed me from around his neck, holding me pinned and cradled in his arms, then he slammed my back down onto his knee forcefully like that move they call a "backbreaker," then walked me out to the balcony railing. He hoisted me up like he was about to throw me over it. I knew if he threw me off the balcony, I was going to die. All at once, my older brother—who was seven years older than me—came charging at him and tackled him around the knees, knocking us both onto the ground.

It was the only time I ever remember my brother intervening into the bullshit between that Asshole and my mom. The one and only time. He was the older one, the bigger one. Yet I was always the one who was stepping in. I was the one stepping up to run my mouth or try to help her. I was the one trying to save her. I was glad he stepped in that day.

The Asshole eventually left us one day and I was glad when he did. I hated him. We were better off without him. At least I knew my mom would no longer be his whipping post any longer, or so I thought at the time.

He would be replaced by another Hispanic guy my mom met—a smooth talker—who would become our new stepdad. He moved in with us. He seemed nice enough at first. He tried to talk to us, get to know us, and show interest in us, as her kids. Interestingly, he never worked a day in his life, but he *always* had money. He had a brother who would show up dressed in fancy clothes, looking like a true Mexican cowboy wearing a Western-style button down shirt with embroidery, tight jeans, dark cowboy boots, a large, flashy, gold belt buckle, and a wide brimmed hat. His brother stood about 5' 10" and weighed about 160 pounds with a stocky build.

The first time I ever saw him wearing those tight-ass jeans, I remember thinking, "Damn bro, *no way* can your nuts breathe in those." He would pull up in his fancy sports car like he was the shit. Just like Stepdad, the Cowboy also didn't "work," yet he reeked of money and status, and had an air of power that lingered around him. The word was that they both sold drugs and were in the Mexican Mafia. I think they were Sicario—mafia soldiers who beat people down and carried out hits. They never spoke about this, or brought any aspects of it into our daily lives, but it was something that we all just kind of knew about that my mom had pretty much confirmed on occasion.

I would come to learn that my stepdad was no better than that Asshole that came before him. He started to abuse my mom. Only, Stepdad was way slicker about it. He would hit her in places where we couldn't see the bruises or marks. He would do it when we weren't around. There were times when she would stay locked in her room for days, so that we wouldn't see her battered face and bruised body. When we became worried about her because we hadn't seen her for a while, me and my sisters would step in, especially my feisty older sister. If my mom had been locked in her room and too much time had passed, me and my sisters would demand to see her, refuse to leave her bedroom door until we did see her, or barge our way into her room so we could confirm that she was, in fact, okay.

But nothing about that entire situation was "okay." Maybe that's why I don't remember a lot about my childhood, because of the violence. But that violence was always directed at my mom, never at us. Still, it affected me deeply. I sensed her panic, despised the way she feared him, and felt her pain as if it was my own.

We knew what was going on and that it wasn't right. This asshole was no better than the last one. My mom sure knew how to pick 'em. We lived through six or seven years of him beating my mom. I couldn't stand it.

When I was 16, my mom told me, "Rudy, when your Stepdad comes home tonight, I want you to kick him out." He had been out drinking all day. She already had his shit packed in bags and sitting outside on the trunk of the car. She continued, "Mijo, you have always been the man of the house. The protector of the house. I'm asking YOU to do it." I remember standing there wondering why in the hell she was asking *me* to do it. I was just a 16-year-old boy, and she was asking me to kick out a grown-ass man. Again, I'd always wondered why my bigger, older brother wasn't the one jumping in to intervene, beat some ass, or put a stop to the bullshit, but it had always been me. I was always the one doing that. I guess it made sense that I would be the one doing this. When Stepdad finally pulled up, I walked out into the driveway, looked at him and said, "I've got bad news for you. See all these bags? All your shit is in there. You're never coming back in." "Why? What did I do?"

"What did you do? You mean—like today—where were you, you pendejo (dumbass)! You're out there cheating on mom, and we all know it."

He picked up his bags off the trunk of my mom's car, threw them into the backseat of his car, and pulled away. We would never see him again. When I walked back into our mobile home, my mom said, "You've always been the protector. You saved all of us, Mijo."

From middle school on, I learned to rely on myself and not depend on anyone. I was done dealing with grown-ups and their bullshit. I didn't need them. I didn't need anything from anybody. I didn't need my dad, my mom, my stepdad, or my teachers. I didn't need anyone besides me. I was the only person I knew that I could always count on. I would make my own way and it would be on my own terms.

After trying out for the basketball team my freshman year of high school and not making it, despite my level of skill and talent, I ended up dropping out of ninth grade. If I could practice for hours every single day and not make the team, which was the one thing that

I truly cared about, then what was the point of being there? To me, there was no point. I was over it. I planned to get my GED, but after flunking the math section by one point, I never tried again.

Not long after I dropped out of high school, my little sister got pregnant. Since I was home during the day anyway, I told her, "You need to go back to school. After you have your baby, I'll watch it, so you can go back to school." And that's exactly what we did. She returned to school after having my niece, and I watched her baby every day for about a year.

My mom and sister stepped in after that, and we all worked together to watch her child. My younger sister eventually graduated from high school.

I ended up getting a job at a mail processing facility on the second shift when I was 17. My older brother got me the job. He and my mom had both worked there for years. From that point on, I got up and went to work every day to make money and forge my own path.

One day, I met a girl and fell in love. We ended up having two daughters, the first was born when I was 20, the second when I was 28. I got up and went to work every day and she went to college to take general classes and later went on to enter the Sheriff's Academy. I worked to pay the bills and provide everything our family needed. We never got married, but we stayed together for 13 years. Over time, we just kind of grew apart, like couples often do.

When we broke up, it was my plan to stay single and to live my best life. I went out and bought myself a new dark gray Mustang. My mom said, "Rudy, you just need to stay single and find yourself, Mijo."

And that was my plan . . . until it wasn't.

RUDY

AGE 26
2009

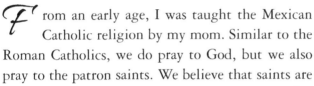

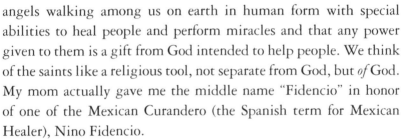

Mexican Catholic Religion and Healing

From an early age, I was taught the Mexican Catholic religion by my mom. Similar to the Roman Catholics, we do pray to God, but we also pray to the patron saints. We believe that saints are angels walking among us on earth in human form with special abilities to heal people and perform miracles and that any power given to them is a gift from God intended to help people. We think of the saints like a religious tool, not separate from God, but *of* God. My mom actually gave me the middle name "Fidencio" in honor of one of the Mexican Curandero (the Spanish term for Mexican Healer), Nino Fidencio.

One day, when my mom was pregnant with me, she fell down the stairs when she was home alone and landed hard on her belly. She was lying on the floor in a lot of pain and worried that she would miscarry me. She immediately began praying to Saint Nino Fidencio, "Please, Saint Nino Fidencio, I pray to you to protect my baby—please let him be okay. If he lives and is unharmed, I swear to you that I will honor you by naming him after you." Clearly, things worked out.

Anyway, when I was about 26, my interest in healing work piqued. I was curious and wanted to learn more about it. It was always a core belief system in my family, especially my mom, and it was something she spoke of freely throughout my childhood. She believed in the saints. She believed in miracles. And she also believed in healers. I know to some, it may sound weird or crazy, but in our Mexican Catholic faith, there isn't anything weird or crazy about it. It is simply a part of our religious heritage and a fundamental piece of the foundation of our religion. We don't just pray to the Padre (that's Father in Spanish), Jesus Cristo (Jesus Christ), or Our Lady of Guadalupe (the Virgin Mary), we also pray to the saints, and depending upon what our need is at that particular time, we pray to a specific saint to seek his or her help. Each saint is known for performing certain types of miracles or helping people in a certain area. You can think of it as customizing a prayer and sending it to one of God's focused helpers, who is an extension of God with the ability to assist Him.

Hispanic and Mexican homes often feature pictures of saints hanging on a wall, sitting on shelves or bookcases, and some people even build small shrines that they adorn with pictures, candles, flowers, and other objects, where they pray. It is kind of similar to what you'd see at a Catholic church, where people go to light a candle, recite the Rosary, and pray. People tend to gravitate toward certain saints and develop their own favorite ones to pray to, so when they eventually marry, a husband and wife often find themselves praying to both sets of saints—his and hers—as a couple. Like I said, it's a strong part of our heritage and religion and something that gets passed down through the generations.

My mom liked to visit a well-respected Healer named Alberto Salinas. He would pray over people, bestow blessings upon them, perform cleansings, and do other rituals to help them. They typically approached him with a specific problem or issue. He would also tell people what type of herbs to take or what kind of tea to drink to help them with their issues. The Healer always had two helpers present with him who would assist him with various things during his sessions.

My first visit to the Healer took place after a past break up with my ex, who had cheated on me. Back then we had one daughter together and any time I went to drop our daughter back off at my ex's place, my daughter would begin to cry hysterically. It crushed me.

After the split, I was having trouble sleeping, couldn't keep down any food I ate, and because of it, I'd lost 20 pounds.

One day, my mom drives me to Edinburgh, Texas, to visit the Healer. We make the four-hour drive through a torrential Texas downpour with almost no visibility. It storms so hard that travel advisories get issued and we almost cancel the trip, but my mom feels so strongly that I need to visit the Healer that we go anyway. During the drive, she keeps saying things like, "See? Evil is trying to stop us from seeing Nino with all this rain, Mijo. But it's not going to happen. We are going. You need this." I feel so depressed. She is right to seek some form of intervention.

By the time we arrive, the rain has turned to a light drizzle as we pull into the lot outside his home. There are a lot of people here to meet Alberto Salinas. We see small shrines with pictures of Nino and candles set up in various spots, as well as a large wooden swinging chair that was crafted to look like the iconic one that Saint Nino used to sit on in Mexico. The chair was apparently built for the Healer as a tribute to Saint Nino. We walk into a building with two rooms. The exterior room holds the line of people waiting and the interior room is where Alberto Salina is. My mother and I stand in a line about twenty people long as we await our turn to see the Healer. I am anxious with a twinge of excitement and an edge of nerves. I have no idea what to expect. I feel so awful at this point in my life that I'll take whatever help I can get. I truly need it.

As the line dwindles down, it is finally our turn to see the Healer. Typically, only one person enters the room at a time, or one family, depending on what their needs are. Since the Healer speaks only Spanish, my mom goes in with me to translate for us. My hands feel clammy and my body is shaking as we walk into the fairly large room. Alberto Salinas—a man in his fifties or sixties with white hair, wearing a long white robe with a red cape and a flat, red square-shaped cap—is seated at the head of the room, with his eyes closed, and two female helpers standing on either side of him awaiting the next visitor. The helpers are clothed in white. I notice a small shrine in honor or Saint Nino that casts the glow of flickering candles upon various photographs of him. Everything in the room is white and red and the space elicits a sacred vibe.

Why are his eyes closed? What's going to happen? My mom and I take a few steps and approach him. His eyes remain closed. *For real, why doesn't he open his eyes?*

"Hola (hello)," he says.

I reply, "Hola."

He extends his hand and asks for mine, so I reach forward to place my hand on his. My legs are shaking so bad I think that they might go limp.

"Que puedo hacer por ti? Que ocurre?" (What can I do for you? What's wrong?)

With my mom translating for us, in English, I reply, "I'm not eating good, sir. I can't seem to keep food in my stomach. My girlfriend cheated on me and left. I'm lonely and it hurts to see my daughter cry—she's six years old. I'm very depressed and I get thoughts of suicide, but I know those are not *my* thoughts. I love life and I help people. I have a daughter—so *why* would I want to hurt myself?"

The Healer, still holding my hand, replies, "Who are you?"

"Rudy."

"Cual es tun ombre real?" (What is your real name?)

Glancing at my mom, I say, "Raul Fidencio."

The Healer sits there for a moment with his eyes still closed.

I stand there, waiting. *He's probably reading all my anger and hate right now. I don't belong here.*

"Te conozco. Me lo prometieron." (I know you. You were promised to me.)

I'm stunned. I can't even believe it. The Healer then opens his eyes to look at my mom and says, "Dimo lo que paso." (Tell me what happened.)

So, my mom tells him the story about her taking a hard fall down the stairs when she was pregnant with me and home alone and about her praying to Saint Nino to save me. The Healer listens intently to everything she has to say. He then closes his eyes before speaking again.

"Oh si. Eres mi hijo. Eres especial y dotado." (Oh yes. You are my son. You are special and gifted.)

With a look of confusion, I say, "No sir, you got it wrong."

"Aprenderás mis caminos y me ayudaras con mi trabajo. Empezaras a venir y ver a Alberto para apender y con el tiempo canalizare a través de ti." (You will learn my ways and help me with my work. You will start coming and see Alberto to learn and in time, I will channel through you.)

His voice is so soft and soothing. Basked in shock, tears begin streaming down my face. *This—this isn't why I came here.*

One of his helpers grabs a small branch of herbs and starts to perform some type of a cleansing ritual on me. She softly taps the herbs against my body in various places. Thump. Thump. Thump. The Healer continues to pray over me in Spanish. I have no idea what he is saying, but I slowly feel the veil of darkness over me being lifted. The more he prays and the more she gently thumps my body with the herbs, I feel lighter, freer, weightless, as though the darkness is being lifted and pulled from me. *Please work. I want my life back. Lord, please help me. I am sorry. I really want my life back.* He continues to pray over me, in Spanish, for a few more minutes.

After the cleansing ceremony, he tells us about certain teas that I should drink daily to help ease anxiety. He continues, "Bebe vino tinto todos los dias con frutas y rezame. Siempe estaré contigo cuando me llames. Nunco me apartare de tu lado." (Drink red wine daily with fruit and pray to me. I will always be there with you when you call upon me. I will never leave your side.)

"Cómpreme tres velas y ponga su foto en la parte inferior de las velas con una nota sobre lo que necesita. Coloque las tres velas en un triangulo con mi imagen mirando hacia el oeste." (Buy three candles of me and put your picture in the bottom of the candles with a note about what you need. Place the three candles in a triangle with my picture facing to the east.)

"Okay, I will. I promise."

"Gracias." (Thank you.)

"Gracias." (Thank you.)

Finally, he releases my hand. Then, mom grabs the Healer's hand to kiss it and I do the same, then we both turn and walk out. After we leave, I truly feel unburdened. It's difficult to explain, but I felt a lot different than when I walked in, like I've been touched by God.

Looking at my mom, I say, "I think it worked! I can't believe he knew about you praying to him to save me when you were pregnant with me and fell down the stairs. I felt better as soon as he began to pray over me." She replied, "I believe it did work, Mijo. That is why we came. He has healed you."

As we approach Dairy Queen my mom asks, "Are you hungry, Mijo?" Considering I hadn't kept any food down for nearly two weeks, I was starving, but I was worried that I still wouldn't be able to stomach eating. She pulls into the drive-thru and orders us a sack of burgers and fries. I take a bite of the double cheeseburger. The melty cheese and meat are so delicious. I shove the whole thing down in a few bites. I was worried that I wouldn't be able to keep it down, but for the first time in two weeks, everything is fine.

I am back. And this is my new beginning . . .

My ex and I got back together not long after my visit to the Healer. Our second baby girl was born a few years later in 2011. We tried our best to raise our daughters—who were eight years apart—together and to remain a happy family, but as time went on, we just kind of found ourselves growing apart. Over the years our interests and priorities changed. She cheated. I took her back. I didn't know if I could trust her anymore. I tried to. At times, I failed to. The passion left us. We ultimately ended up parting ways in 2013, when our girls were ten and two, but we remained good co-parents to our two beautiful daughters and on good terms with one another as we each walked down our own separate paths in life.

RUDY

AGE 30
September of 2013

The Chapel

M y mom and I visit the Healer on a few more occasions, to seek his help and learn more about how he does the healing work. His health is declining, so between that and the language barrier—with my mom always having to translate between us—I don't really learn much. I do get to assist him as much as I can during our visits though.

During one visit to the Healer, we run into Bishop John Parnell, who knows and sometimes works with the Healer.

"Hey, where y'all from?" the Bishop asks me.

I reply, "I'm from San Antonio."

"Wow, that's even further up than us. I made y'all drive. I'm gonna be working in San Antonio tomorrow at a chapel. It's my chapel, owned by St. Peregrine Church."

"Really? That's tight!"

"I have two people running it. You could help me with the mass and the people?"

"Oh, really? I'd love to come help you."

"And there's a little girl there that can talk to the Virgin of Guadalupe. She can see her and talk to her. She does healing. She's almost a saint. She's been taking on a lot of work. You could go over there and help her."

"Yeah, I'd love to do that."

"Come over tomorrow morning."

"Okay. I'll see you then."

The next morning, I wake up, shower, and dress myself in the type of clothing my mom would approve of for this type of a healing event, consisting of a white button-down shirt, the nicest pair of jeans I own, shiny white dress shoes, and a black belt with a freshly shaved face, and a clean haircut. Since Alberto Salinas always wears white, it's something that my mom has instilled in me as being the proper healing work attire. I definitely want to look presentable in case the Bishop introduces me to people.

I hop into my gray two-door Mustang and drive to the chapel. I pull up to the curb on a street lined with cars, where I see a large green and white flag that says, "St. Peregrine." *This is it. This is the place.*

I feel excited to be here, to do this, but my stomach lurches with anxiety, as I walk up to the little white chapel. The gravel crunches beneath my shoe with each step I take. The closer I get, the more nervous I feel. I see a long line of people—a flock of about 50— already gathered outside. They must all be here to see the little girl. The chapel is unimpressive at first glance, a basic structure of one large room with a door and two windows. I don't see the Bishop yet. I don't know anyone here. *Am I at the right place? Are these the right people?*

Inside the chapel, there is a large, open center aisle that is lined by rows of folding chairs that flank both sides of it. I'm guessing there are probably about 30 people seated in the chairs. Looking around the room, this is the most basic looking chapel that I have ever been in. They don't even have pews, just folding chairs with some wooden stands randomly placed to hold the bibles. *This place looks so makeshift, so plain, like trash.* I mean, I know it doesn't matter where a person worships, but this place really has me rethinking that belief. It feels weird to be worshipping in a dilapidated place like this that looks like a small wooden shack that was thrown together. As I glance around the room, I see pictures of saints accompanied by flickering candles.

It's not at all what I expected it to be, but I'm just here to do a job and help out. That's it. But you best believe if this becomes a regular thing, I'm gonna see about helping them to fix this place up. I see the Bishop standing in the back of the chapel. He's the only person I know here. I walk over to him.

"Rudy, welcome. I'm glad you came today. I'd like to introduce you to some people. This is Chevo and Laura."

Chevo—who barely glances up at me—shakes my hand abruptly, says nothing more, and walks off. *This guy is either too busy to be bothered or he's an asshole—not sure which.*

Laura says, "Your name is what—Rudy?"

"Yes, it's Rudy."

"Where are you from?"

"I'm from here—San Antonio."

Getting closer to me and somewhat invading my personal space, she says, "What saint do you pray to?"

"Saint Nino," I reply, while taking a step back to put a bit of space between us.

"Okay, well, it was nice to meet you. Go ahead and sit down."

"It was nice meeting you, too."

Dang, between that lady's tone and the way she was pressing all up on me, that felt like an interrogation. I don't know what I thought the chapel owners would be like, but that wasn't it.

The Bishop walks up to me and asks, "At the end of the mass, is it okay if I tell people who you are and that you'll be working with me at the chapel in the future?"

"Yeah, that's fine."

I make my way toward a seat in the third aisle from the front to listen to the mass.

I'm not sure what to think of Laura. While nothing she said was rude or wrong, her aggressive tone and pushy demeanor seemed off-putting and uncalled for.

The Bishop leads the mass and prayers. People eventually get up and form a line to take communion of wine and bread. Some of the older ladies around me are moved to tears and crying. Looking around, I notice that it's almost all women and children inside the chapel. The men are all outside, including that guy Chevo that the

Bishop introduced me to earlier. I saw Chevo walk in once earlier to pass out some bottles of water, but that's it. *That's weird. I wonder why the men aren't in here?*

People make their way up to the front of the chapel to meet the Miracle Girl and have her pray over them. Chevo is standing near her. When the Miracle Girl prays over some of the people, they fall over, as if the experience has overcome them. When that happens, Chevo and another man help them back up on their feet.

I see a younger woman go to the front to take her communion. She is Hispanic with really short dark brown hair and dark brown eyes. She is wearing black shorts and a white tee shirt, but she's one of those girls who is naturally beautiful without even trying to be. I can't help but notice her. When it's her turn to take communion, she takes a sip of the wine, eats the bit of bread, the Miracle Girl prays over her, then she totally collapses onto the floor, falling hard onto the ground right next to me. I take a step closer to where she is lying on the ground, and on a bent knee with an outstretched arm, attempt to help her get back on her feet. But Chevo rushes up to her and helps her stand, basically cutting off my act of chivalry. I notice the other guy doesn't help Chevo lift the woman, like he did with all the other people who fell over. Chevo seems really protective of her. Don't get me wrong—to me, her fall was comical looking, like it was too much. But that didn't deter me from stepping in to try to help her.

During the service, I can't help but notice a Latina lady with curly black hair who sits in the aisle across from me. She is wearing a short tight dress that reveals a large tattoo on her left thigh. I find myself staring at it. While the Latina definitely looks good in that hot ass dress, it's the other girl who is holding my attention right now—the one in the plain black shorts and white shirt. The one who isn't even trying. I can't help but notice the stark difference between the two of them, not any more than I can deny the pull that I feel toward the more natural looking one.

Weird. I'm just here to pray and help people out, man. I'm sitting in a chapel right now. Why am I even thinking about this? But I'm a single guy who isn't blind. Not my fault. I find myself glancing over at the naturally pretty girl. *Will she look over at me?* It's like something about her grabbed me and won't let go. I want her attention, but I'm not getting it.

As people take their communion and begin to filter out of the chapel, I notice the naturally pretty girl walk out of the chapel. A few others exit the chapel behind her. I casually follow her. She walks into the house that is located on the same property as the chapel and comes back out holding a stack of plastic cups in her arms. I just stand by the chapel hoping that I'll get the chance to talk to her. Three little kids—the little girl who is a healer, a younger girl, and a little boy—come running up to her as she walks back toward the chapel. She opens her arms to greet them. Then they run out into the yard. I approach her.

"So, you're Laura and Chevo's daughter?"

"Yeah."

"What's your name?"

"Abby," she replies quietly, looking down at the ground.

"I'm Rudy. You work here?"

"Yeah, we run the chapel." She looks into my eyes, then scans the area around us. *She seems nervous.*

"Are those your kids?"

"No, they're my mom and dad's kids," she replies, making no eye contact with me whatsoever. *What? They aren't hers? They look like hers.*

I notice that she keeps turning her head to look toward the chapel door as though she's looking for someone, waiting for someone to walk through it, or maybe doesn't want to be seen talking to me. *Who is she looking for? What is she worried about?*

Then she blurts out, "I gotta go——" and walks back toward the house.

"Okay, it was nice meeting you," I reply to her as she leaves.

Well, that was weird. Maybe she just didn't like me or didn't want to talk to me or something.

The entire drive home I can't stop thinking about her. I would have *sworn* those kids were hers when I saw them. I couldn't help but notice she had a tiny belly, like my ex did after she had our girls. Laura seems too old to have kids that age. Laura also seems too ugly to have kids that beautiful. Just sayin'. I guess I was just wrong about it, but it all seems a bit weird, like the pieces don't quite fit together. While I can't seem to make sense of my interaction with her, the kids, or the situation in general, I do know that I most definitely want to see her—*naturally pretty, not-trying-too-hard Abby*—again. And soon.

ABIGAIL

AGE 25

Meeting Rudy

I wake up earlier than usual because we have mass today. I walk out to the chapel to start setting out folding chairs for the parishioners who will be arriving soon. I sit down on one of the creaky chairs and place a big stack of fliers onto the chair beside me so I can fold them. This is something I do every Sunday to help my parents out. Once I'm finished folding all the church fliers, I take my spot beside the entryway door of the chapel to greet people as they enter.

"Hello, how are you today? Welcome to the chapel!"

I hand them fliers.

There are already a lot of people here and more continue to make their way in. It is going to be a larger service today. I notice a younger guy wearing a dressy white button-down shirt, dark jeans, and shiny white shoes walking up the gravel driveway toward the chapel, where I now stand gawking at him while trying to appear like I am not.

That said, I am totally gawking at him. I can't help it. *Look at this guy with everything matching. Clean cut. He probably thinks he's all that.* That's what I think to myself. Guys his age normally don't make an effort like this guy did to look respectable for church, especially with those glossy white shoes that look freshly polished and shiny. The closer he gets, the more I notice how attractive he is. He has a smooth, freshly-shaved face, his hair is faded on the sides and short on top, black in color, with masculine features and a square jawline with large dark brown eyes, and a chiseled chin. I can't help but take notice of him because I never see any guys my age anymore, especially ones that look like him.

Ever since I graduated high school, I never see guys anymore, unless we're out in public and even then it's only in passing. He walks up to the doorway where I am standing. I feel nervous. I manage to say, "Hi. How are you today?"

He replies, "I'm good. How are you?"

I respond, "I'm good."

It's weird because I feel as though I am immediately drawn to him. I'm not sure why, but I feel a pull, a connection.

I hand him a church flier, he takes it, pauses to briefly pin his dark brown eyes upon mine, then he walks past me into the chapel. *Yep. He thinks he's all that for sure.*

Once mass starts, I can't help but to glance back to where he is sitting in the chapel. Admittedly, I'm still gawking. Trying to check him out. I try to do so discretely, like I'm looking around the entire chapel at *all* of the people, not just at *him*, but in reality, that's exactly what I'm doing. I don't think he notices me looking. We never make eye contact.

When it's time for us to take communion, I walk across our row of folding chairs and up the aisle to make my way toward the Bishop. I eat the bit of bread. I drink the grape juice. The Bishop touches my forehead. The next thing I know, I wake up on the floor and realize that I must have passed out during communion. I have no idea who caught me. My dad is standing beside me, like he *always* is, with a loose grip on my arm. To others, it probably appears like a normal and loving gesture, but I know better. It is a possessive grip. A subtle way of claiming his ownership of me—that I am *his*.

Sitting on the folding chair in the makeshift pew, I recite the same prayer in my mind that I always do when I'm here.

Father, please send me help. Why do You allow this to happen to me? Why do You allow these supposedly Catholic people to do this to me? Please send me help. Please get me out of this.

Our Father, Who art in heaven, hallowed be Thy name; Thy Kingdom come, Thy will be done on earth as it is in heaven. Give us this day our daily bread; and forgive us our trespasses as we forgive those who trespass against us; and lead us not into temptation, but deliver us from evil. Hail Mary, full of grace.

Being shaped by the Mexican Catholic religion my entire life anchors my belief in God at the core of who I am. Still, I have a hard time reconciling why He allows this to happen to me. I question Him constantly. I pray to God begging for help. I pray that He will one day deliver me from their evil. My situation has not shaken the core of my faith, but it has definitely forced me to question it on countless occasions.

If I am a good person, why is this happening to me? If they are good people, how can they do this to me? But they aren't good people, not really. I come here, to this chapel, and listen to the Bishop preach about how various demographics of people are going to Hell for their life choices. I sit beside my parents—the owners of this little chapel—who seem to have the whole world fooled about who it is they truly are as people. They hide their evil behind their smiles, the Miracle Girl, and rosary beads. *Are they actually Catholic? If they are, then how can they be this way? How can they do these things to me?*

These questions run on a loop in my mind any time I'm in this chapel, or praying to God, but I never receive any answers to these questions. I'm still trapped here. I know that God has a plan for everything. But I'm not sure what that plan could possibly be for *me.*

Toward the end of communion—but with some people still waiting their turn—my mom leans over to me and asks, "Abby, can you go grab some more cups?" I walk out of the chapel and into the house. I grab a stack of plastic cups from the kitchen. When I walk back outside, I see that the cute guy is standing a few feet away from the chapel not too far from the chapel's doorway. *Oh my God, it's him.*

My heart is thumping unusually fast in my chest. I take a deep breath to try to calm my nerves, but it doesn't really help. I am so nervous.

"Hi," he says to me.

"Hi."

"So, you're Laura and Chevo's daughter?"

"Yeah."

"What's your name?"

"Abby." My eyes dart down to the ground. I have a hard time looking directly into his warm brown eyes. *If my dad sees me, he is going to flip out.*

"I'm Rudy. You work here?"

"Yeah, we run the chapel." I keep looking at the chapel doors, afraid that my dad is going to walk through them any minute. *Please don't let him walk out here right now.*

"Are those your kids?"

After a slight pause, I reply, "No, they're my mom and dad's kids," while nervously staring at the open doorway, hoping my dad doesn't walk through it. For some reason, I almost felt like I wanted to tell him the truth—that, yes, they are my kids. But I can never tell anyone that.

I'm so nervous. I keep glancing down at the ground. With each breath I take, I get more nervous. I am afraid that my dad might catch him talking to me and freak out, but I want to talk to him.

He is so good looking and friendly and has a bit of swagger to him. Just enough to be confident, not cocky. He's not at all like I thought he would be when I first saw him. I thought he'd be the player type, but he seems like a good guy.

Another lady exits the chapel doors and walks past us. Rudy looks at her and says, "Have a good day, ma'am."

Afraid that I am going to get caught out here talking to Rudy, I blurt out, "I gotta go—" and start to walk back into the chapel.

"Okay, it was nice meeting you," Rudy calls out to me.

Once I step inside the chapel, I attempt to catch my breath. My heart is thumping fast in my chest—thump, thump, thump. I'm so glad that I didn't get caught talking to him. No one knows. My dad could have walked out at any time and flipped the hell out. *Rudy is really good looking, nice, and he actually had manners. I don't know what he thought of me. I know I always act really shy around new people. I didn't really say much of anything. He probably thinks I'm shy, or weird, or both.*

Once the service is over and everyone leaves the chapel, I walk back into the house to start on my daily post-church routine which consists of the usual slate of household chores, the cooking of meals, and, of course, the pampering of my demanding, greedy parents.

My mind occasionally wanders back to my brief conversation with Rudy and his warm, expressive dark eyes—that instant feeling of connection that I felt. But I know that I'm probably never going to see him again.

RUDY

September of 2013

Researching the Chapel

*A*bout a week after I visited the chapel, I logged onto Facebook to see what I could find out about its background. I came across a Facebook page for the church, along with some posts about the Miracle Girl. I sent St. Peregrine Church a friend request, so I could follow its future posts and learn more about the work that its members were doing. I also sent a "friend" request to Laura, since she seemed to be the one in charge of it. I didn't friend Chevo because I got a bad vibe when I met him. He walked around like a wanna-be-tough-guy or something, like he thought he was the shit. Not my style. I don't think much of guys who carry themselves like that.

A few weeks later, I looked up Abby on Facebook. There wasn't much on her profile aside from some pictures. There were selfies without a smile, pictures of her with the kids, some images of just her with her dad, and some photos with of all of them together as a family. Looking at her Facebook wall, I got the feeling that Abby is sad.

Next, I came across a post of St. Peregrine Church that said that Bishop John Parnell was returning to the chapel in November. *Maybe I'll see Abby again if I go.*

I sent Abby a message on Facebook. Nothing big, just a "Hi, how are you doing" type of message. She responded a few hours later with "Hi, not much." The messaging between us stopped there.

In November, I returned to the chapel. I saw Abby while I was there, but we just said a basic "hi" and "how are you doing" in passing. It wasn't much.

Then our Facebook messaging resumed. Kind of.

"Hi Abby I was there tonight."

"Yeah, I saw you."

"We didn't really get to talk though."

"No, we didn't."

"What are you up to?"

"Finishing up at the chapel."

"I want to go to the chapel more, so I can see you."

"Yeah."

"Maybe next time we can talk?"

"I gotta go. I'm busy."

These basic ass messages aren't really getting me anywhere. Maybe this chick just isn't into me—for real. She doesn't give me much to work with and gives almost nothing back. It's almost like I'm talking to myself. What the fuck, man. What the fuck am I doing? Is this worth my time? Why am I doing this? Why?

Me going to the chapel to learn more about the chapel—or maybe more about her—is one thing, but why in the hell am I throwing myself at this chick?

But here's the thing—thinking back on the day that I met her, I felt like there was something that was a bit off about the situation. It was just a gut feeling that I had—nothing more. It wasn't something that I could really explain. It was in the way that she carried herself— or more accurately, the way she seemed to hide in a crowded room full of people like she was all alone, as though she was tucked somewhere deep inside herself, hiding in plain sight.

It was like Abby was a grown-ass woman sitting in that chapel but one who acted like she couldn't talk to or interact with anyone around her, besides her parents. It was bizarre. I only saw her talk to Laura, Chevo, and the three kids that day, aside from that short conversation that I managed to strike up with her outside the chapel. She's either super shy, or she's so damn religious to the point that she's not allowed to talk to or see anyone because she's into it so deep. I'm not sure which it is.

With the way things seem to be going, I may never find out . . .

RUDY

Hello, Facebook

*T*hree days later, I send another message to Abby on Facebook. "Hey, what're you doing?"

"Just sitting here in my room coloring to pass the time."

"Aw cool. Me and my daughter always like to draw and color together. What kind of music are you into?"

"R&B."

The next message pings. It's a song Abby sent me, "Lost in Love" by MC Magic. I recognize it, but I click in to listen to it anyway.

"That's cool. Yeah, I know that one. I like R&B."

Then I decide to send her back a song, "Hey There Delilah" by the Plain White T's. I assume she's listening to it. A few minutes later, another message pings.

"I gotta go."

"Okay. I'll talk to you later."

Well, so much for that. She cut me short again.

I want to get to know her better, but that seems hard to do. If she didn't like me at all, even as a friend, I don't think she'd respond to me at all. She does respond, but then she always cuts things off abruptly. I'm not sure what to make of it. It's 10 at night. *She's not in school anymore. What would she need to go do? Surely, she isn't going to bed this early. I guess maybe she had to go help out with one of the kids or something. Who knows? Maybe she's just really shy.* I definitely get that vibe from her in person.

I sit on the couch thinking about her. Why is she coloring in her room at 10 at night? Why can't she ever chat with me longer? I've only seen her talk to Chevo, Laura, the Bishop, and one other couple.

She doesn't move about the chapel to chat with people freely. I can't quite place what is off about the situation, but I sense that something is *off*. My stomach knots up thinking about it. What could it be? I have no idea. It's just something hitting my intuition. I can't ignore it, but I can't figure it out, either.

I guess maybe it's just their belief in the "traditional Mexican values," and her strict parents. It's probably nothing. I mean, her parents run the chapel, so surely, they are good people. I got a weird vibe from her dad, but that doesn't really mean anything. They probably just have strict rules. They don't like her talking to people and are worried that she'll get into trouble. They probably don't let her do much. I get it. Some people really do uphold those "traditional Mexican values." I'm probably thinking too deep into things. Her parents are strict. She's shy. And she probably had something that she had to do.

ABIGAIL

Communication Woes

I have a phone that my parents bought me. While I'm happy to have a phone of my own, it kind of feels more like a "fake" phone of my own. It's not much different than the calendar hanging on the wall of my bedroom where we used to track my periods. My parents made me tell them my passcode. They make it clear to me that they can get into my phone at any time. There are times when they approach me to command it. My mom walks up to me, sticks out her hand, and says, "Abby—Give me your phone." Then she plops down on the couch and goes through it like she is looking for something that shouldn't be there. I'm not sure what she expects to find. I have no friends. I have no life.

Rudy has messaged me a few times on Facebook. Usually, in the evenings, when I have a few minutes alone, I can see if he said something and message him back. I always delete the messages afterward. If my mom and dad saw that I was talking to a guy—to Rudy—they would flip out. Not because the messages say anything much—because they don't. They're really basic. But because they don't want me talking to anybody. They would take away my phone.

I'm so worried about getting caught that I'm barely able to message him. He probably thinks I don't like him or that I just don't want to talk to him. But I do like him, at least as a friend. I do want to talk to him. He seems nice. And I can't say he isn't cute, because he is. But I can't get caught messaging him, so I must be really careful.

I can't do it often, only when I'm alone, when they seem too busy watching TV to walk in and catch me. Considering I'm not allowed to close my door, I have little-to-no privacy here, and almost no alone time. We have only messaged back and forth maybe four times in the past two months. It's too risky. It's not like anything is going to come of it anyway. It just feels nice to have someone outside of this house to talk to.

RUDY

December of 2013

Back to the Chapel

One month later, in December, I return to the chapel to attend mass. I post on the chapel's Facebook page that I'm planning to attend the service.

I arrive early. Chevo is standing outside the chapel talking to a guy. He never looks at or acknowledges me. When I walk into the chapel, I see that there are only about ten people here so far, since it's still early. Upon entering, Laura sees me—she looks directly at me, but doesn't acknowledge me—then walks out of the chapel.

Admittedly, I'm still somewhat skeptical about the chapel based on its rundown condition and their claims that the Miracle Girl can channel the Mary of Guadalupe (the Virgin Mary). I don't feel like I've seen anything to confirm that—at least not yet.

When mass is over, people start to migrate from the chapel down the walkway to an adjoining second room of the chapel where the Miracle Girl stands ready to recite prayers over the parishioners and bless them. I remain inside the chapel, but at one point, I do glance into the other room to try to check out what's going on. I notice that Laura is also laying her hand on people's foreheads when they walk up to the Miracle Girl. I see that they even have the little boy, the Miracle Girl's brother, laying his hands on people. If the little girl is the one with the healing powers, what do they have to do with anything? Why are *they* laying their hands on people as though they are going to be the ones helping or healing them? I find it strange. I'm pretty much just chilling in the chapel now and watching as the line of people leading to the Miracle Girl dwindles down. Secretly, I'm hoping that I get to see Abby.

All at once, Laura comes rushing up to me. "Rudy—Rudy, you need to help me."

I follow her through the walkway and into the smaller adjoining room, where I see the Miracle Girl lying on a futon like she passed out.

Laura says, "Something is wrong with [Miracle Girl]. She's not breathing. Somebody call 911!!"

"Rudy—she was praying over people, and she's got something wrong with her, like she has an evil spirit on her."

I lean down to check whether she is breathing. She is. But she is unconscious, her body limp.

Laura barks out, "Rudy, I need you to say prayers and sage this room to cleanse it." I do as she asks, grabbing the bundle of sage from her, lighting it, and walking around the room reciting prayers. I have no idea if it will help, but if she wants me to do this, I'm happy to. It certainly couldn't hurt anything. Sage is known for its cleansing powers. Laura is panicking right now. Everybody in this room is concerned. I lift the sage. I say prayers. I walk around the room she is lying in, and then into the chapel. "Father, please let her be okay. Please lift her up and heal her from whatever is afflicting her. Please let this little girl be okay."

When I make my way back into the adjoining room, the Miracle Girl is sitting up on the futon. She looks a bit out of it, but far better than she was. A surge of relief floods through me. A bit later on I tell Laura, "This is dangerous—what you're doing. You having this little girl praying over all these people—their energy—when you don't know what's wrong with them."

"I know, but this is her gift."

I reply, "That's why you should ask me to come around more, to help out."

As I'm walking out of the chapel to leave, Abby walks up to me, "Thank you. Thank you for helping my sister. I appreciate it."

"I don't know that I really *did* anything, but I'm glad I was here to help out."

Before walking away, she softly says, "Write me."

"I will."

Later that night, I message Abby on Facebook, "It was good seeing you earlier. I hope you had a good day.

"I did. I hope you had a good day, too."

"My day was good. I hope your sister is alright."

"She's okay now. Thanks. I gotta go."

This would be one of my last visits to the chapel. But it wouldn't be my last visit with Abby. While our messages continued to be brief in substance, they picked up in frequency. And when it came to Abby—I always found myself wanting more. More time. More messages. More opportunities to get to know her better.

Around that time, my mom seemed to realize that I had taken a major interest in Abby on the heels of my break-up with my girls' mom. It was just a few weeks after it. My mom also knew that I planned to remain single for a while and to "have fun." I remember her telling me, "Mijo, you literally just came off a relationship and you're already *in love*. You are moving too fast. You barely know this girl."

"I'm not in love, Mom."

But I could not deny that I most definitely was in "like."

RUDY

AGE 30
December of 2013

The Fixer

$\mathcal{A}$bby and I have been messaging more often. She even messaged me her phone number. "Here's my number, but don't ever call or text me. I'll text you."

Um, okay. That's a bit weird, but whatever. I know she does have overprotective parents. At least I have her number now and can text her when she tells me she's available. We've even chatted in the afternoon a few times when she says that she can. She sends me a few brief messages in the afternoons and a few messages at night on most days, but never anything in between. It always seems to be around the same times and usually for no more than ten minutes at a time. I wish she could text me more often. It's kind of frustrating, like it always feels as though I'm being cut short. It's definitely better than the way it used to be, but it still bugs me. One night, I flat out ask her about it. "How come you can only text me or talk at certain times?"

"My mom and dad won't let me be on the phone much. It's their phone."

"Oh. Okay."

I'm tired of only being able to talk to Abby in limited pockets and for so little time each day. If this phone is the problem, there's a way to fix that. I go and add a second line to my cellular plan for $20 a month. Half of me wonders if I'm crazy to be doing this, but it's only $20. The doubt isn't enough to stop me. Neither is the cost. I buy a second phone. I even ask Abby what color she wants. Lime green is her favorite color. With a big ass smile on my face, I walk out of the phone store carrying a lime green phone that is going to be my new lifeline to Abby, or perhaps it will be her lifeline to me.

RUDY

AGE 30
January of 2014

The Lifeline

"*H*ey Abby, I got you a phone. I need to meet up with you to give it to you."

"Really? Okay."

"Do you want me to come to the chapel on Sunday and I can give it to you?"

"Why don't you come on Wednesday—we have mass. But be really careful. When you hand me the phone, make sure that it's just you and me in the room. Make sure my parents don't see."

"Okay. I can do that."

"Okay."

"I'll see you then. Bye, Abby."

I attend the mass on Wednesday, not so much as a parishioner, but more like a like-struck guy with a super-secret-lime-green-cell-phone in his pocket running undercover ops. It's equal parts thrilling and somewhat ridiculous. After all, she is a grown-ass woman. After mass, I linger. I try to act nonchalant and talk to people around me, so it doesn't seem obvious that I'm actually here for Abby. (Also, the entire reason that I am here today is 100% for Abby. I've got it bad for her. I have clearly checked my religious devotion at the door.)

At one point, Abby and I both find ourselves nonchalantly-but-entirely-on-purpose standing in the adjoining room with no one else around. I know we have to do this quickly, so she doesn't get caught. With a big smile on my face, I say "Hi. Here it is," as I quickly drop it into the pocket on the front of her shirt. She smirks, immediately grabs it out of the pocket, and plops it down the front of her shirt into what I can only assume is her bra. I can't see the outline of the phone under there—that's good. She is glowing. And damn—she is beautiful. I so badly want to wrap my arms around her—to hold her close—but I don't.

She says, "thank you *so much*," and then she closes the short distance between us to wrap her arms around me in a tight embrace. I feel her clinging to me. I pull her even closer. I feel like she needs me. I feel myself taking her in. Body to body, with no space between us, we remain. She isn't moving away yet. She is going to have to be the one to step away from this—because I won't. I will let her take what she needs of me. I'll be the one who gets us caught because I can't step away. Finally, she drops her hold on me, takes a short step away, throws me a quick smile and says, "I'll text or call you."

"Okay. I'll talk to you soon."

RUDY

AGE 30
January of 2014

Hello, Girlfriend

*T*hat same day, later in the evening, I text Abby on her new phone. "Does this mean that we're together?"

"Well, that's not usually how you ask someone."

Dang. She's right. I guess I better step up.

"Will you be my girlfriend?"

"Yes."

And just like that, I found myself in another relationship—like I totally promised myself I wouldn't be—just weeks after breaking things off with my girls' mom. I guess my mom was right. We did move fast. We may have barely known each other, but there was just something that drew us together. I couldn't be happier about it. I really like this chick. She's beautiful, kind, sweet, really shy to the point that it's cute, and she seems like a great person who is really family-oriented. Since I am too, I think we're a good match. I want someone who wants to spend time with me, is interested in building a life together, and wants to grow closer each day.

In the following weeks, my communications with Abby pick up big time. Ever since I got her the new phone, she seems to have a lot more freedom to text me. She even calls me during the day now. We talk every morning for several hours, but she always has to be off the phone before 1:00 in the afternoon. She said that's when her dad gets home for lunch. She always cooks him something to eat each day. She then texts me every night at 10 or 11 to tell me *goodnight*. I start and end my days with Abby now.

I'm happy things have worked out the way that they have. I am grateful that I went to visit the little broken-down chapel with the Bishop that day, or I never would have met her. I guess it was fate. The whole healing thing may not have worked out, and I didn't learn anything more about that, because the chapel feels like a bit of a sham—maybe even a scam—but at least I met Abby.

Her dad may be protective over her, but as her boyfriend now, so am I. I'm not sure what his problem is with her dating someone, so long as he's a good man. I know that I am one. I'm hoping this dude warms up to me over time.

As of now, Abby said her parents don't allow her to date, much less have a boyfriend, so I am a secret. As a grown-ass man, I gotta say that it seems crazy and honestly, completely ridiculous that I'm a 30-year-old sneaking around to see my girlfriend.

But here I am,

Abby's best kept secret.

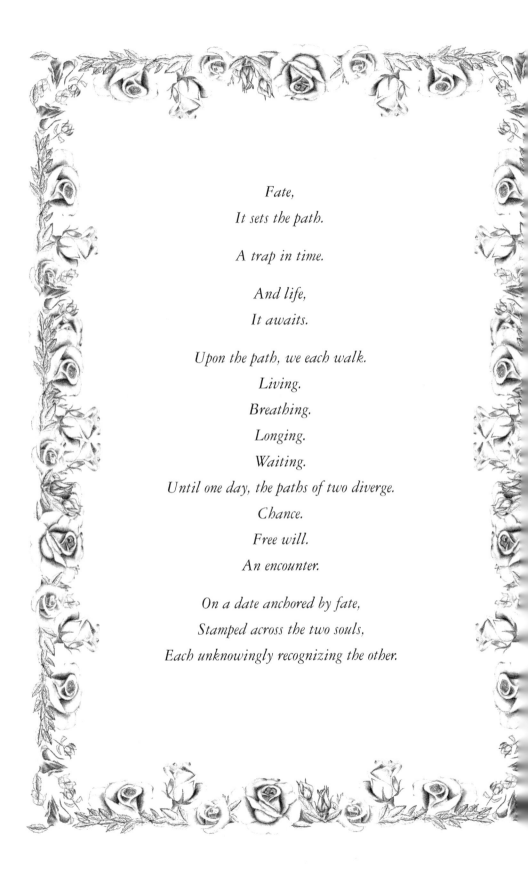

Fate,
It sets the path.

A trap in time.

And life,
It awaits.

Upon the path, we each walk.
Living.
Breathing.
Longing.
Waiting.
Until one day, the paths of two diverge.
Chance.
Free will.
An encounter.

On a date anchored by fate,
Stamped across the two souls,
Each unknowingly recognizing the other.

By light cast upon cheek bones,
Heartbeats skittering on wind,
Whispers of words perched upon beautiful moments,
Caught in time,
Held in reverence,
Respect,
Acknowledgment,
Undeterred by all that surrounds them—
TWO SOULS STAND.

After dancing across the days,
Waiting, longing.

Together. Tethered. Found.
For her and him,
'Twas fate.

—JAMIE COLLINS
(For Abigail & Rudy)

RUDY

AGE 30
February of 2014

The Parking Lot

*A*bby and I text each other and talk every day. It's still in limited blocks of time, but at least I know when I can expect to hear from her now.

Early one morning when we're talking on the phone, I'm surprised when Abby says, "You can come see me today, but park your car at the store down the street from my house. Meet me at 7:45."

"Okay, I'll be there. I can't wait to see you!"

"Okay. See you soon!"

I throw on some clean blue jeans, a light gray tee shirt, and pull on and lace up my Nikes. I hop into my gray Mustang to make the short, ten-minute drive to meet Abby. I pull my car into an empty parking space in front of the corner store to park and to sit and wait on Abby to arrive. Part of me is eager to see her and excited that we're finally gonna have some alone time, together, in person, even if it is in a parking lot. The other part of me is chastising myself because I feel like an idiot to be a 30-year-old-man sitting here sneaking to visit his 24-year-old girlfriend in a store parking lot. Yet here I am. Honestly, there's no place I'd rather be. (I take back what I said about being an idiot.)

The kids' school is right next to the store. Abby, who walked the kids over to school to drop them off, walks up to my car. She opens the passenger door and slides in. I lean over to hug her, breathing her in. We then just sit here and start talking about random stuff. It's awesome to be with her, to be able to see her, like this. In a way, it's thrilling to see this shy girl starting to come out of her shell. It makes me feel special to know that she is allowing me to see the real her.

I like what I see. I like what I'm hearing. She is an amazing person. She is kind, caring, beautiful, and respectable.

After about 10 minutes, Abby's cell phone—not the one I bought her, the regular one—rings. Abby's face flashes with a look of worry. She glances over at me holding her finger up to her lips telling me to stay quiet. Then she pushes the button to accept the call. I can hear a man's muffled voice but can't make out his words. I can only hear what Abby says in response.

"Hi. I'm at home."

(A lie.)

"I just dropped off the girls at school."

(A fact.)

"Now, I'm cleaning."

(A lie.)

"I just started a load of laundry."

(A lie.)

"Okay, I'll see you at lunch."

"Bye."

Abby seems to swallow back some anxiety as she hangs up. It seems like she's nervous all of a sudden, like she's worried that she'll get caught or something. I sense an underlying current of panic.

I casually ask, "Who was that?"

Abby replies, "Oh, that was just my dad."

I intentionally don't say anything more and just sit looking at her, hoping that she'll say something more.

"He's just protective of me. He always calls to check on me and to make sure the girls made it to school okay—to see what I'm doing."

"Oh. Okay."

"He's really strict."

Weird. But again, she has an over-protective Hispanic father who believes in traditional Mexican values. And his belief in those values, puts me, as a 30-year-old man, in a position to have to play along with his stupid rules that require us to sneak around the way we are right now in my car in this stupid store parking lot.

It's a good thing I like Abby so much, or there's no way I'd be able to deal with this shit. This is crazy. It's not like she's 18 or something. She's 24-years-old.

Not long after that, Abby says, "I better go. I have to get the house cleaned and I really do have to start the laundry."

"Okay."

"I wish I could stay here with you longer."

"I wish you could, too. I loved getting to spend time with you today, Abby."

"I know. I did, too. But I'll see you again soon."

"Okay. Call me later, beautiful."

"I will."

She swings the car door open, steps out, and shuts the door behind her. She waves to me, then walks toward her house. I reverse out of the parking lot, looking up to take one last glance back at her.

As Abby leaves, I realize that she is carrying a small piece of my heart with her. (Traditional Mexican values and parking lot idiots be damned.)

ABIGAIL

AGE 24

The Rush

I Am Swooning. I like Rudy so much. Not only is he a really cute guy, but he's so sweet, kind, and caring. He seems to genuinely like me and to want to get to know me better.

I know that I should be afraid of getting caught, but the excitement of seeing him seems to strip away my fear. He makes me feel safe when I am with him, like he will protect me. Although he's nice and mannerly, I don't think he'd take any shit from anybody. I just have to keep him separate from my home life *with them.*

I grab a bowl from the cupboard and pour some cereal and milk into it. Then I shoot Rudy a quick text as I sit down to take my first bite.

"Thanks so much for coming to see me today!"

"Anytime. I'll come see you any time you ask me to."

"Um, how about tomorrow morning?"

"Okay. Same time and place?"

"Yeah. I'll meet you after I drop the girls off at school."

"I'll be there. I'll see you tomorrow, beautiful."

"Okay, I'll text you later."

As long as I pick up my dad's early morning call, I totally think I can pull this off again. It sounds utterly ridiculous—well, perhaps psychotic is actually a better word for it—but my dad has actually timed the amount of time it takes to walk from our house to the school and back home, so he knows precisely when I should be back home. That is why the early morning call always comes at 7:50 a.m. I'll just have to lie to him the same way I did this morning. Thankfully, Rudy didn't seem to find it weird at all, since I already warned him that my dad is over-protective and has a lot of rules.

Rudy is the only person I have in my life outside of this house. My sister and I hardly ever talk. He is the most important person in my life now, aside from my children. My parents would lose it if they knew I had a secret phone, secret boyfriend, and secret morning meet-ups. But I don't care what my parents want. For the first time in a long time, I feel happiness, excitement, and hope. I forgot what it felt like to have something to actually look forward to. Someone that I can talk to for hours and still never get enough of. Everything about my life has been better since Rudy walked into it. Granted, it doesn't change any of the bullshit that goes on inside the walls of this house, but it does give me something to look forward to. It gives me a place to go in my head. A place to go in my heart.

I can't wait to see Rudy tomorrow.

RUDY

AGE 30

The Next Day

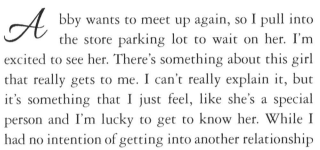

A bby wants to meet up again, so I pull into the store parking lot to wait on her. I'm excited to see her. There's something about this girl that really gets to me. I can't really explain it, but it's something that I just feel, like she's a special person and I'm lucky to get to know her. While I had no intention of getting into another relationship right after my last one, here I am, engaging in covert parking lot meet-ups with my girlfriend—a Catholic rebel—who is forced to sneak around with me. It's just the typical "Mexican family" and overly-strict-and-protective-dad type of shit.

I see Abby walk across the grass lot. She approaches my car, opens the passenger door, slides into the seat, and reaches across the car to hug me.

"Hi, Abby."

"Hi."

We hold one another for a minute before letting go. Then we engage in our normal conversations while sitting in the front seat of my Mustang. We listen to music. That's something that brings us closer. We like a lot of the same songs. About five minutes later, Abby's cell phone rings. She is expecting the call. At this point, I realize this is going to be "a thing" and I'm not shocked at all to hear it ring.

"I have to take this. It's my dad. Be quiet while I'm on the phone, okay?"

"Okay."

"Hello. Yeah, I just got back home. I just threw a load of clothes into the washer and I'm gonna start cleaning the kitchen now. Yeah, I talked to their teachers for a few minutes, so that's why it took me a little longer to get back home today. Okay. Yeah. Okay, I'll see you at lunch."

She ends the call. I decide to ask her about it. "So, your dad calls you every day?"

"Yeah."

"And he always calls you about the same time in the morning to check in on you?"

"Yeah, he does."

"And he calls you every single day—in the morning—at the same time?"

"Yeah. He just wants to make sure I'm doing what I'm supposed to be doing, that I made it home okay. He wouldn't like me being here with you right now, so that's why I have to say that I'm at home."

"So, he doesn't let you go out on dates?"

"Nope."

"Like, ever? With anyone?"

"Nope. I had a boyfriend once and he was allowed to come over. He eventually moved in with us, but that was the only person I've ever been allowed to date. And we didn't go anywhere together, we just stayed home and hung out."

"So, he wouldn't be cool with you having a new boyfriend?"

"Oh no, he definitely wouldn't be cool with that at all. He doesn't want me to do anything with anyone. He and my mom act like I get into trouble. I think they worry that I could get pregnant or something. I'm not sure what they are worried about. It's not like I ever really do anything wrong. They're just over-protective."

"Yeah. I get that. It's kind of crazy that your parents still act like that when you're 24."

They must have really liked her ex for that to actually become a thing.

"Yeah, they've always been like this though."

"I bet you get tired of dealing with it, huh?"

"Yeah, I do, but it's just the way that it is."

"So, you couldn't even go out to dinner or to the movies with me then, huh?"

"No, I can't. I'm sorry."

"Don't be sorry. It's not your fault it's that way, but like I said before, it's not gonna stop me from being with you."

"Okay, good. I don't want it to."

"I wish I could take you out though, on a real date."

"I know. I wish you could, too."

With a big grin plastered across my face, I reply, "I really like you, too, Abby. Your dad isn't going to get in between us. He can't stop us from being together."

Smiling, she replies, "I know. I still have to follow his rules though."

"We're together now, Abby. He doesn't get to control everything you do."

I see a flicker of something cross Abby's face, but it's gone so quickly I can't be sure that I even saw it. *I'm pretty sure Abby is sick of dealing with her dad and his controlling ways. I know I am and I just started dealing with it.*

"I mean it, Abby. Your dad doesn't get to be in control of us choosing to be together."

"I know. That's why I'm here with you right now. I *want* to be with you."

"I want to be with you, too. Do you want me to come and see you tomorrow?"

"Yeah. I want you to come see me every day! I really like hanging out with you."

"Alright. Then I'll be here -- anytime you ask me to be."

"Well, I guess I better go now. I really need to start doing laundry and I have to clean the kitchen, for real."

"Okay. Call me later on, okay?"

"Okay, I will."

ABIGAIL

The Park

O n Saturday, my brother and I decide to take the kids to the park to play for a while. He grabs his basketball to take it along. It's a beautiful day for a walk outside, the sun is shining, the birds are chirping, and the kids are happy to get out for a bit.

We arrive at the park and the kids all run toward the playground equipment to play. I walk over to a wooden picnic table and sit on the top of it, with my feet on the seat part below. My brother is shooting hoops on the basketball court. I ask to borrow my brother's phone, so I can call Rudy. I have his phone number memorized, so I dial it.

"Hi Rudy."

"Hey babe. How are you?"

"Good. My brother and I brought the kids to the park. I'm on his phone right now. I'm just sitting on a picnic table, watching them, while my brother shoots hoops."

"Ah, that's cool. Yeah, it's a perfect day to be outside, babe. I'm glad you're out enjoying it."

Oh my God. All of a sudden, I see my dad's gray Honda drive by, circling the perimeter of the park. Quickly, I chirp out, "Rudy, I gotta go."

"Uh, okay . . ."

"I'll talk to you later." I hit the button to end the call quickly and hand the cell phone to my brother because I don't want my dad to see that I was talking on it. Sensing my trepidation, my brother quips, "Fuck him, Abby. You can still talk on the phone." But that is not a risk I am going to take. *I hope he didn't notice that I was on the phone. Maybe he was too far away to notice.* A minute later, he circles back around again, driving by slowly, so he can leer over at us. *Oh my God. Why can't he just leave me alone? Why is he worried about me being at the park with the kids? Why?*

He makes another loop around the park. *I fucking hate him.*

I ask my brother, "You see Dad driving around the park?"

"Yeah, I see him."

"I'm so sick of him, always checking up on me, watching what I'm doing."

"Yeah. He's just protective, Abby."

We decide to leave the park and walk home. With each step I take, frustration surges within me, followed by anger. *Why is he like this—a psycho? Why can't he just be normal and leave me alone? Why?*

I feel like it's just a matter of time before my dad manages to find out about Rudy. And when he does, it is not going to be good.

ABIGAIL

AGE 24

Later That Night

*A*fter eating dinner, I go to the laundry room. Stooping down onto the large white squares of tile flooring, I run my hand underneath the washer to fish my phone out from beneath it. Glancing at the doorway to make sure no one is watching me, I quickly slide it into the front pocket of my hoodie, then pad my way down the hall to the bathroom. This is the only way I can sneak in a quick text with Rudy during a normal time in the early evening, but I can't text for too long. Seconds are all I have.

"Hi, Rudy."

"Hey, Abby. What're you doing, baby girl?"

"I snuck my phone into the bathroom to text you really quick. I just got done with dinner. Kids are doing homework. What are you doing?"

"Just chillin'. Listening to some music. I'm glad you texted me."

"Yeah, I just wanted to say 'hi,' but I can't talk real long, since I snuck my phone into the bathroom."

"LOL. The bathroom, huh? Whatever works. How are things at home?"

"They're okay, Rudy. I'll meet you tomorrow at the usual spot?"

"Sure. Sounds good."

"Yeah. I'll see you then. I gotta go!"

"Okay. Have a good night! I'll see you tomorrow, beautiful."

Being able to talk to Rudy throughout the day makes living in this hellish house a bit less hellish—just slightly, like it takes the edge off of the insanity that is my actual life. I can't believe how we just clicked as soon as we started talking, and now, we're actually together, like a real couple.

I never thought I'd ever get to have another boyfriend. I don't like having to sidestep the truth all the time, but we just got together and I'm not sure that he could handle the truth. I think he seems like a stronger man than Football Guy. But still, I just don't know that I can tell *anyone* about what goes on here, much less *him*. I like him way too much for him to know those things about me—the things that I've done and the things that have been done to me. All these years of abuse. The rape. The babies. It's all too much for someone to handle. Maybe, in time, I'll be able to tell him a little here or there.

Rudy is protective. I feel safe when I'm with him. He bought me this phone just to help me out and make it to where he can talk to me more often. He comes to meet me every day now, so we can be together.

Fast forward three weeks, dozens more meet-ups, passionate kisses in the front seat of a Mustang, and a lot of talks between us, and this is what I have to say about Rudy:

I. Love. Him.

I love everything about him. Not only is he really good looking, but he's got a good head on his shoulders, he's a sweet and caring person, and a good man who loves his two daughters.

He's exactly the kind of man I want to have in my life, the kind I always hoped to marry. I'm not saying I want to marry him today or anything, but if he asked me to marry him right now, I would. Getting married has always been my ticket out of this house.

But how would I be able to take the kids with me? It's such a screwed-up situation. If anyone finds out who the real father of the kids is, they'll take them away from all of us. I can't let that happen.

At least this way, I still get to be with my kids, take care of them, watch over them, and protect them. Rudy is just going to have to understand that if he wants to be with me, that means secret texts, limited phone calls, and sneaking around. He seems to be okay with it so far. I hope he doesn't give up on everything involved in dealing with me and my situation because I am truly, madly, deeply in love with Rudy Alvarado.

My dad wouldn't like this one bit.

And I don't give a damn.

This is my choice, my happiness, my love, *my* life. And I am going to live it.

ABIGAIL

AGE 25
January of 2014

The House Visit

I walk the girls to school to drop them off for the day. Then I head back home. Emboldened by my strong feelings for Rudy and intoxicated by the safety and protection I always feel anytime I am in his presence, I walk to the laundry room and sweep my hand beneath the front of the washer to grab my secret phone out from its coveted hiding spot, so I can text Rudy.

"Hey—do you want to come over to my house today, instead of meeting up at the store?"

"Alright. To your house? Are you sure?"

"Yeah, my parents will be at work. We'll be the only ones here. It'll be fine. But don't park near my house. You have to park in the alley."

"Okay, as long as you're sure. I'll come over. I'll leave here in a bit."

"Okay! See u soon."

"See you soon, beautiful."

I set my phone on the arm of the couch and walk into the bathroom to glance at myself in the mirror to primp a bit. Using my hands to smooth out my hair, I can't stop thinking about how happy I am that Rudy will be here to see me in a few minutes. I feel like Rudy is the only person who truly "sees" me. He's the only person who actually likes me for who I am as a person—at least the parts of me that I show him.

Rudy walks across the small front stoop and I open the door to let him in. He gives me a side hug as he makes his way past me and kisses me. It feels weird to have Rudy here—in my daily version of a prison disguised as a home—but in a good way. Also, in a forbidden way. My dad would lose his mind if he knew that there is a guy sitting on the couch—his couch—next to me right now.

"Are you sure it's okay for me to be here, Abby?"

"Yeah. As long as they don't come home, it's fine. They won't be home until later."

"Okay. It's just that I know your dad seems to keep close tabs on you."

"Yeah, he does. He already called me to check in this morning though. He won't be home until lunch time in four hours."

"Okay. What would he do if he caught me over here?"

"Um, he'd totally flip out."

"Yeah?"

"Yeah, he would."

"Well, then I hope he doesn't come home, but if he does, oh well. I'll deal with it."

"I don't think you'd want to deal with my dad."

"Your dad can't stop me from being with you, Abby. If you want to be with me, then we are gonna be together, whether he likes it or not."

Rudy and I spend the next few hours talking, watching TV, and eventually kissing on the couch, which quickly leads to his hands pressed against my body and my hands wandering across his. *I love the feel of Rudy's lips on mine. Rudy's hands across my body.* This feels different—because it is my choice.

But when I'm here with Rudy, the whispered words, lightly scattered kisses, and soft caresses of his skin upon mine are something that blaze me to the core. I choose to claim this—this feeling, this love. I choose to own it—these moments spinning in a lust-filled haze. The words spoken in whispers that are born of love. Being physically worshipped with soft eyes, and reverent hands is a beautiful thing. It is a risk worth taking. THIS is the life worth living. The passion between us consumes us, dances between us, body to body, skin to skin, and it's enough to cast a small glimpse at heaven. It may even be enough to burn this horrible home into a heap of smoldering ashes.

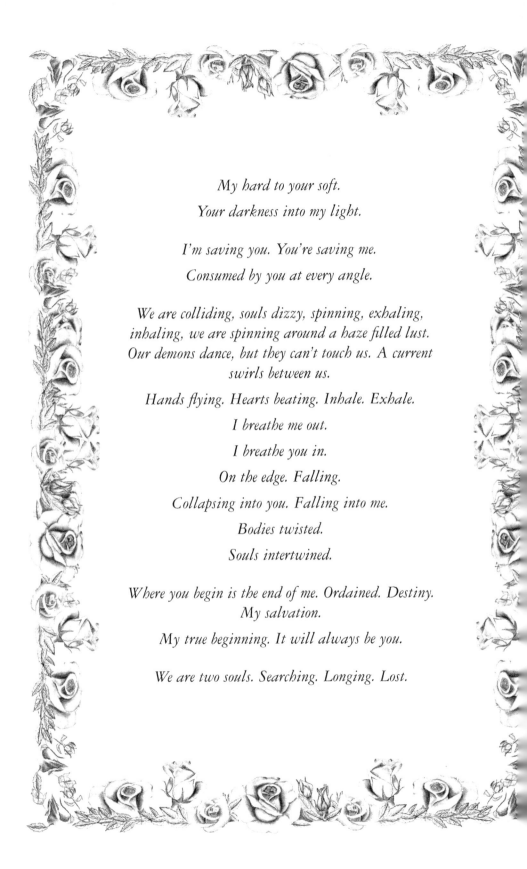

My hard to your soft.

Your darkness into my light.

I'm saving you. You're saving me.

Consumed by you at every angle.

We are colliding, souls dizzy, spinning, exhaling, inhaling, we are spinning around a haze filled lust. Our demons dance, but they can't touch us. A current swirls between us.

Hands flying. Hearts beating. Inhale. Exhale.

I breathe me out.

I breathe you in.

On the edge. Falling.

Collapsing into you. Falling into me.

Bodies twisted.

Souls intertwined.

Where you begin is the end of me. Ordained. Destiny. My salvation.

My true beginning. It will always be you.

We are two souls. Searching. Longing. Lost.

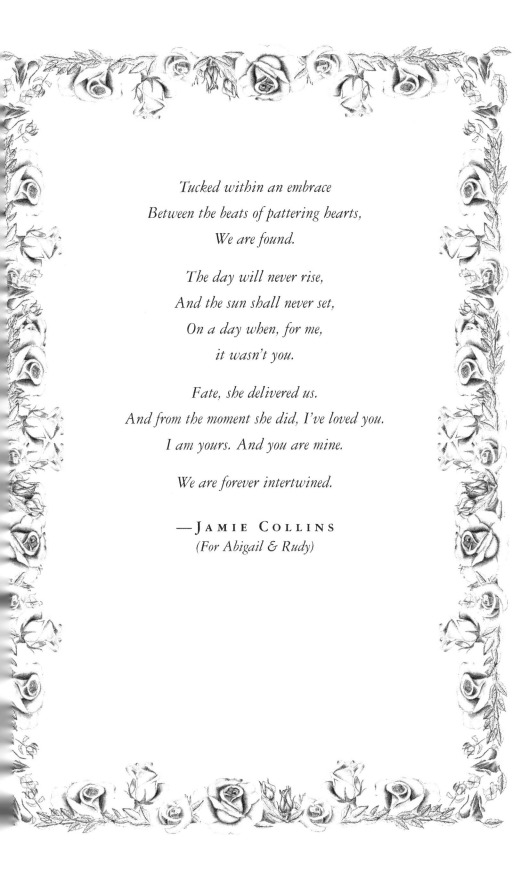

Tucked within an embrace
Between the beats of pattering hearts,
We are found.

The day will never rise,
And the sun shall never set,
On a day when, for me,
it wasn't you.

Fate, she delivered us.
And from the moment she did, I've loved you.
I am yours. And you are mine.

We are forever intertwined.

—JAMIE COLLINS
(For Abigail & Rudy)

RUDY

AGE 30
Early March of 2014

The Date

I'm talking to Abby on the phone. I've been really wanting to take her out on a real date, so I ask, "Abby, Can I take you to see a movie tonight?"

"I can't—because of my parents."

I'm not at all shocked by Abby's response, but it annoys me, nonetheless. I love Abby. She's my girlfriend and I would do anything for her, but all this sneaking around just to talk on the phone, text, or meet up to see one another is getting old fast.

Abby adds, "I have an idea though. Since they already know who you are, me, my brother and my brother's friend and you can all probably go to a movie together. They trust my brother and he'd be there, so they will probably let me go."

"Okay. If that's what we need to do—I'm down."

"Okay. I'll talk to my brother about it and will let you know."

"Alright. I hope it works out. I'd really like to take you on a proper date."

"I know. Me, too."

A few hours later, Abby calls. "Hey, it worked. They said I can go!"

"Alright. Do y'all wanna go see John Wick then?

"Sure!"

"What time should I be there to pick you up, Abby?"

"Um, you can't pick me up. You need to park down the street behind that Mexican restaurant on Old Laredo. My brother's friend will pick us up and we'll drive to meet you."

So, I find myself—a grown-ass-man—sitting in between the white lines of a parking lot space yet again, waiting on my girlfriend to arrive via her "security" detail—her younger brother—who I guess is supposed to make sure nothing crazy goes down.

I'm not sure what the hell they think could possibly happen at a public movie. And we're not young teenagers. Abby is now 25-years-old. I gotta say something. The whole thing seems a bit weird to me, because he is her younger brother. Why is he trusted to watch Abby, when she's a woman who can look out for herself? Why is anybody watching anybody at this point?

Seriously. It makes me wonder. So, while I'm slightly perturbed to be sitting in my Mustang waiting for a date to begin, I'm really excited to see Abby tonight. I've been looking forward to taking her out.

Abby and her security detail pull into the parking lot and park next to my car. Abby holds the passenger door open so her brother and his friend can climb into the backseat. She then sits beside me up front.

The brother's friend says, "Man. We went through all this just so y'all can go to the movies?"

I reply, "Yeah, man. It's crazy. Thanks for helping us out though."

Abby's brother says, "Yeah, man, my parents are assholes. They don't trust us, especially Abby."

Abby jumps in, "Don't forget—I have to be home by 10."

I reply, "Okay, no worries, Abby. We'll make sure y'all are back by then."

We travel the short trip to the local movie theater. Abby and I walk up to the snack kiosk. "Get anything you want, Abby." She opts for a big tub of popcorn, which she shakes the butter-flavored salt on, a large Coke, and a package of Twizzlers.

I pull my wallet out and hand the cashier a handful of bills to cover it, and we make our way into the dark theater. We find two empty seats near the middle of the theater, take a seat, and get settled with our snacks. Abby tosses a few pieces of popcorn into her mouth and looks over at me with a huge smile on her face.

It's become apparent to me that I seem to be the only person with whom she interacts outside of her house. I've definitely noticed that her confidence has grown over the past several weeks. She seems to feel bolder when she's with me, but I still see the glimmers of worry about being caught or getting back home by 10 tonight. We eat handfuls of popcorn and chew on Twizzlers until we've had our fill. I look over at Abby and can't help but think how damn beautiful she is. I grab her hand and hold it for the remainder of the movie. We definitely fail to watch a few parts of the movie because passionate kissing pulls us together.

When the credits finally start to roll, I turn to Abby, "That was a good movie!"

"Yeah, it was!"

"Do you want me to take you home now?"

"Not yet. We still have a little bit of time together."

"Okay. We can all go to my aunt's house to hang out, if you want. She lives close to here."

"Okay. Let's do that! Let's see if they want to go."

Abby's brother and his friend are down to go, so we all pile back into my Mustang to drive over to my aunt's house. I'm excited for Abby to meet my younger sister, who is at my aunt's house tonight. We walk in and I introduce Abby to everyone as "my girlfriend, Abby." We just sit in the living room telling stories, talking, and laughing. At one point I glance at my phone and see that it's 11.

"Abby, it's 11! We have to go! You're late!"

"So."

"I thought you said you need to get home on time tonight. We're already late."

Abby's brother chimes in, "Abby—you KNOW we've got to go," to which Abby curtly replies, "Fuck them."

Abby's grandstanding only lasts about another 20 minutes. Her brother prompts, "For real, Abby. We gotta go. It's time." His words seem to nudge her out of her newfound rebellion, out of my aunt's house, and back into the passenger seat of my Mustang.

I drive us all back across town to the parking lot behind the Mexican restaurant on Old Laredo to drop her brother's friend back off at his car. I pull $10 out of my wallet and hand it to him. "Hey man, here's some money for gas. Thanks for helping us out tonight."

"Ah, thanks. Yeah, no problem, man. It's crazy y'all gotta go through all this just to hang out."

"Yeah, it is."

"Y'all have a good night."

"You, too. Hey, thanks again, man."

We collectively decide that it will be okay for me to drop Abby and her brother off somewhat close to their house, but not near enough to it to be spotted. As a now self-proclaimed expert on running covert ops for dates—consider it done. It's dark out. I drop them off four houses down on the opposite side of the street. With a caress to Abby's cheek and one last passionate kiss, she exits my car into the darkness to walk down the street toward home with her brother.

As I pull away in the darkness to drive home, I can't help but wonder if she's going to get in trouble for being out too late tonight. While I don't regret a second of the time we spent together, I do hate that she's in a position to potentially get in trouble for staying out too long. If she does get in trouble with her parents, I wonder what kind of punishment it will be? Again, she's a grown-ass woman. Why is she getting in trouble at all? Why can't she go to the movies with me without sneaking around? I don't understand it.

An hour later, my phone pings with a text from Abby.

"I'm gonna go to bed. I'm fine. I had fun tonight!"

"I had fun, too. I loved spending time with you. I'll talk to you tmrw."

Still high on the time we spent together—the hand holding, the kisses, her head on my shoulder during the movie, laughing and talking with her at my aunt's house—I find myself wondering why we have to do all this sneaking around. *Why is she so restricted from doing anything? From seeing anyone? Why do they treat her like a young teenager who can't be trusted? Why doesn't she have any friends or anyone she hangs out with besides me?*

Something is off.

I'm not sure what, but I feel deep down that something about the situation isn't right. I just need to figure out what it is.

RUDY

Early March of 2014

Truth Be Told

I arrive at the mail processing facility where I work around 10 in the morning to begin my shift for the day. Standing before two hundred tall plastic filled bins with white, rectangular trays stuffed full of envelopes bearing postage, I glance down at each one to double check that each black barcode of freshly inked postage is properly affixed. While the work is fast paced here, it can feel monotonous at times. That said, it keeps me busy, especially when someone isn't doing their job efficiently, one of the machines breaks down and needs to be repaired, or we are short a crew member. I know my way around the machines pretty well since I've worked here for the past 12 years. I know how to keep things running smoothly, so we can get the 300,000 plus envelopes out the doors each day.

About an hour into my shift, I'm repairing one of the machines, fidgeting with an ink cartridge, when I feel my phone vibrate with an incoming call. I lift it out of my pocket, look down at the screen and see that it's Abby calling.

"Hey, Abby."

"Hi. How's your day going?"

"It's good." I'm glad you called me. There's something on my mind that I need to talk to you about."

After a few seconds of silence, Abby faintly replies, "Oh, okay. What is it?"

"Look, Abby, I love you. I really do. But I can tell something is off. That something just isn't right. And you aren't talking to me about it."

With my heart beating erratically in my chest, I summon the courage to finally initiate a conversation that's been a long time coming about some things that have been gnawing away at me bit by bit since I met her.

"Look, Abby. I *know* something is going on. There is some stuff that's been bothering me, and we need to talk about it. I'm a grown-ass man. You're a grown-ass woman. You should be able to do what you want. You can't do *anything* except see me in the mornings. No movies. No breakfast. No dinner dates. You can't come over to my house. You can't even just hang out with me at any other time. I'm crazy about you—you know that. I've dealt with this the entire time I've known you, but I need to know what's going on. Either you're going to tell me *right now* what's going on, or that's gonna be the end of us. I'll delete you on Facebook. I won't call you anymore. That'll be it, Abby. That'll be it."

The bold words leave my mouth freely and confidently sounding a whole lot like an ultimatum, but I know in my heart that I don't have the balls to actually walk away from her. I feel more like I'm playing a reverse psychology game with Abby in an effort to get her to finally spill her truths. I'm the chump who is too in love with her to walk away. Maybe she'll believe that I could though.

Several heavy seconds of silence greet me on the other end of the phone line. She says nothing. I keep fiddling with the machine I'm working on and allow the silence to linger for as long as it needs to, hoping that Abby will finally tell me the truth about her situation.

But will she?

ABIGAIL

He Knows

O*h my God. Oh my God.* He knows. Rudy knows that something is up. As soon as I hear him say, "we need to talk," I know where things are headed. It wasn't so much in the words he spoke, but in the severity of his tone.

What am I going to do? I can't tell him. I can't. The one and only time I tried to tell someone about this—Football Guy—he walked out on me forever. I never saw him again. I can't lose Rudy that way. I can't. But if I don't tell him, he said I'll lose him anyway. If I do tell him, I'll lose him. No matter what I do, I am going to lose him. What do I say? Do I tell him?

With my pulse pounding in my veins, my heart thudding in my chest, and my voice shaking, I finally break the silence.

"The kids are mine."

"Okay. I already know that."

"Well, *how* do you know that?"

"From the moment I saw the kids and that you had a tiny bump across your belly like a new mom would, I knew. Plus, you have stretch marks, so I knew that I was right about it—that you had kids."

"Well, there's more . . ."

"Well, then, continue then . . ."

Holy crap. He wants me to tell him. He expects me to tell him. But how can I tell him that? The weight of what comes next sits heavy between us. To tell or not to tell. What do I do?

My face soaked in tears, my heart thumping erratically in my chest, voice shaking, I softly whisper, "The kids are *his*."

"Whose?" Rudy asks.

"My dad's."

"Chevo?"

"Yes." I am quietly sobbing, holding my breath with my arm wrapped around my stomach, and fearing what comes next, waiting for him to respond.

In a calm and level voice, Rudy replies, "Okay. I already kind of figured that."

Silence wraps itself around the phone line again.

He figured that? How did he know? Oh my God. He is going to leave me. He is going to leave me. He can't deal with this. There is no way anyone could deal with this. It's too much. Too terrible. Too twisted. No one could possibly want to be with me after this.

There is nothing else I can say to make this sound any better. There isn't a way to dress up the despicable truths I hide and clumsily carry. Maybe that's why I'm sitting in silence. I'm waiting on him to freak out. I'm waiting on him to tell me that he's done with me. That he "can't do this shit." That he can't deal with me. To leave me the same way that Football Guy did.

RUDY

The Reality

*A*s we sit in silence on the phone line, one thought permeates my mind—that I'm going to drive over there tonight and I'm gonna beat Chevo's ass. And if I get arrested? Oh well, I guess that'll be what happens.

What a sick bastard—touching his own adopted daughter like that. I fucking knew it. The signs were there to be seen if somebody was watching. I was—watching. "Traditional Mexican values," my ass. More like an evil sadistic old man with certifiable problems who can't keep his dick in his pants. My next thought? *Fuck. Here we go again. I'm always getting myself mixed up in some kind of craziness.* My mom's words ring in the back of my mind. "Don't put yourself in danger for a girl you don't even really know." But what am I gonna do? I *do* know Abby. And I *love* her.

Man, Rudy, you can never fucking have anything easy. Always the hard route.

I'm just gonna hear her out and go from there. But I'm going to be there for her no matter what—that much, I know deep down.

On a broken whisper, Abby jolts me back to reality. "Are you going to leave me?"

"No. Why would you say that?"

"Because that's what happened before."

"What did?"

"I told somebody else that I really cared about. And he walked out on me."

"Well, I'M NOT HIM," I fire back in a cocky tone.

We sit in another uncomfortable silence, until Abby finally breaks it. "So, what's going to happen with us now?"

"This needed to happen, Abby. We needed to talk for us to be able to continue our relationship."

"What are we gonna do?"

"I'm gonna get you out—like, right now."

"So, you aren't going to leave me?"

"No. Never."

"I can't. I can't leave the house. I can't leave the kids."

"That's what I meant—you and the kids are coming."

"Oh. I thought you meant just me and not the kids."

"No, I mean all of you."

"I'm afraid to leave the kids behind or for them to end up in an orphanage if anyone finds out the truth."

"I want to come get you today—all of you."

"You can't. He's crazy, Rudy. If I leave, he's gonna hurt me, or he's gonna hurt the kids. You don't know him."

"Well, he doesn't know me either, Abby."

Against my own self-protective interests, I ask a question that I don't really want to hear the answer to.

"When was the last time it happened?"

"December."

"Well, how often is he doing it?"

"He hasn't touched me since December."

"Okay. If you feel like you're okay and he's not been bothering you, and the kids are safe, I'll leave it alone for now."

Treading further into the depths of craziness, I ask another question.

"Does your mom know?"

"Yeah. She's in on it."

"What do you mean 'she's in on it'?"

"She participates."

She participates? Laura actually participates? Like, a threesome? I don't dare say the words aloud, but they crash through my mind like a grenade with the pin pulled out. Her mom participates. What the actual fuck. For real.

We sit on the heels of silence, yet again, with neither of us speaking after Abby's latest admission. In all honestly, I'm not sure what to say. What can I say?

Those two old, ugly, disgusting pieces of shit—them motherfuckers are married and apparently, they don't want to fuck each other, so they're using Abby as a sex slave.

Abby finally says, "Ever since we moved to San Antonio—she's been involved with it."

"Like, she is in the room and participates in it?"

"Yeah. She is—she does."

Five more seconds of silence sit heavy with the weight of the truth.

Abby finally says, "Hello? Are you there?"

"Yeah, I'm still here. We're going to deal with this, Abby. And I'm going to get you and the kids out of there. I know you said you aren't ready today, but y'all are gonna get out of there soon."

"Okay."

"Call me later tonight."

"Okay. I will."

Hitting the *end* button on my phone, I stare down at it sitting in my hand, replaying the conversation in my mind. I feel heartbroken for Abby. And admittedly, a bit for myself. It's such a messed-up situation. *No one deserves to live like that—to experience that—to have that happen to them. She said he hasn't touched her since December. Her mom actually takes part in it? What the fuck? I knew there was something off about both Chevo and Laura from the first time I met them at the broken down chapel in September.* They hide from the world wrapped in church clothes, pretending to be good people, and they talk a strong, manipulative game. But I saw them, at least on some level. I felt the bullshit, heard the lies.

One thing I do know with absolute certainty is this:

When I get my revenge on the two of them, I'm bringing hell with me.

ABIGAIL

The Ugly Truth

*A*fter we end the call, I sit on the couch in the living room and allow the reality of what just transpired to roll over me in silent waves. *Disgusting. Dirty. Nasty.* I am all of these.

Rudy knows. Our lies now stand before the one I love for him to consider, to ponder, to judge. *Evil acts. Group sex with my mom. Rape.* I know that he will judge them—that he will judge me. How could he not?

He promised he wouldn't leave me. It sounded like he truly meant it. But is he gonna freak out? Is this gonna be too much for him when he sits and thinks about it? Is he lying when he says that he won't leave me? How are we gonna do this? How am I going to get out?

Attempting to busy my mind and steady my emotions, I begin to clean our entire house. I walk into the kitchen, grab a dishrag, wet it, wring it out a bit, then scrub down the counters. Next, I sweep the floor. I then vacuum the entire house.

Rudy is so clean cut, so kind, so mannerly. He is a good man who has morals. He has no idea who he's dealing with. He thinks he knows, but he can't possibly fathom the intensity of evil that runs through my dad's veins. He is a violent man who drinks to excess, abuses me, and rapes me. I doubt that Rudy has ever even been in a fight in his life, and if he has, it was probably nothing major. Nothing like the threat that my dad will pose. I fear that my dad will kill Rudy or could hurt him badly. I can't allow that to happen. I know what my dad is capable of when that evil sneer contorts his face and his fists come raining down on a body squirming beneath him. I have been that someone—that squirming body, fighting against him—so many times.

Rudy underestimates Chevo. He also underestimates Laura and the lengths that I know they will go to in order to keep the kids—*my* kids. They would do *anything* to keep me from taking them away from them. *We need to be smart about this. We must be calculated. And above all else, we have to be patient and wait for the perfect time.*

Even if I do get out of here, and finally manage to escape, I know that not only will my mom and dad go to jail for this, but I will, too, because I allowed this to happen to me for all these years. I was a part of it, even though I never wanted to be. And for that, I will be judged. For that, I will be punished. My kids will end up in the foster care system. I can't live with that. If I go to jail, I won't be able to care for them and protect them. Besides, if I leave here, they will probably try to kidnap the kids, and flee to Mexico. They have the connections to do it with the help of The Coyote. She'd get them across the border with no problem and I would probably never see my own children again. I can't let that happen. Would Rudy really take in all my kids, too? He says he will, but actually doing it is another thing.

We have to be smart about this. The timing must be right. I have to *know* that we will all be safe once we get out of here. Rudy doesn't understand all of this—any of it, really. He probably just thinks that I'm brainwashed, or stupid, or both. On some level, I probably am, but I know what I am saying is true. They will *never* allow me to leave with the kids. They will stalk me. They will hunt us down. Hurt us. They could kill me. They might even be crazy enough to harm the kids. My dad is a monster. I've seen how evil my mom can be. Together, they are a force. I wouldn't stand a chance against the two of them. I can't leave until I know for sure that I can truly escape and that nothing bad will happen to us.

RUDY
Absorbing the Truth

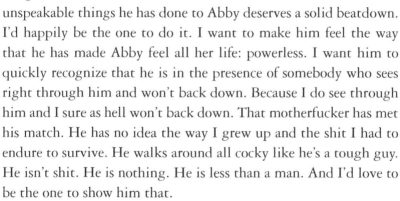

The more I think about Abby's situation, the more infuriated I become. A scorching anger pulsates me to the core. I am eager to step in and seek retribution. Chevo is nothing. He has no idea who he's dealing with. I grew up on the streets of San Antonio. Chevo walks around like he's so hard but, in reality, I'd pound that motherfucker into the ground in ten seconds flat. A man who does the unspeakable things he has done to Abby deserves a solid beatdown. I'd happily be the one to do it. I want to make him feel the way that he has made Abby feel all her life: powerless. I want him to quickly recognize that he is in the presence of somebody who sees right through him and won't back down. Because I do see through him and I sure as hell won't back down. That motherfucker has met his match. He has no idea the way I grew up and the shit I had to endure to survive. He walks around all cocky like he's a tough guy. He isn't shit. He is nothing. He is less than a man. And I'd love to be the one to show him that.

It's killing me that Abby said she isn't ready to leave yet. After she told me everything that has happened to her, I'd think she'd be ready to leave any minute. But they still seem to have a hold over her. I hear what she's saying about them being evil and crazy, but I would protect her and the kids. I wouldn't let Chevo and Laura touch her. They both need to rot in prison for the things they have done to Abby. I don't even have words for two people as depraved as those two are. They are the lowest of the low. Pedophiles. Scum.

I know Abby telling me everything she did had to be hard on her. And who in the hell was this chump who just walked out on her in the past when she told him? What a low life. She's got me mixed up if she thinks I'd do the same thing to her. For better or worse, I'm entrenched in this shit for real now and I'm gonna get her the hell up outta there—her *and* the kids.

While every fiber of my being wants to drive straight over to her house to pack up her and the kids and get them out of there, I sense that Abby isn't in the headspace to do that yet. She seems so scared of them. They have so much control over her. It's like she can't shake the power they seem to have over her. I can't say that I understand it, but she's been abused by them—raped by them—for years.

I know it was huge for her to trust me with the truth the way she did. Nobody would want to own up to that. In the past, she has hopped off Facebook for months at a time and cut off all contact with me. I don't want her to do that again, and for that reason, I'm going to have to try to be patient and play this thing Abby's way, as difficult as that is going to be. It's going to kill me to leave her in that house with those depraved lunatics who abused her, but I can't make her leave until she's truly ready to go. I know that it's not something I can force, even though I really want to. I want her to know that she can trust me, that she can rely on me. I will protect her. I love her and I'm not going to let anybody hurt her anymore.

I'm going to have to bide my time, come up with a plan, and wait for a while to seek vengeance on Chevo and Laura. When it comes to the two of them, I am going to be their worst nightmare. I sure hope they like the shade Inmate White, because that is all they are gonna be wearing in the future—in prison. Believe that.

RUDY
Visit After Learning the News

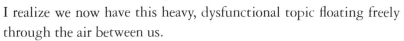

The next morning, as usual, I visit Abby. I park my car in the alley and let myself into the exterior door to her bedroom that she left unlocked for me. After the truth that she was brave enough to finally drop on me yesterday, this visit feels slightly different than the rest. Maybe it's different because I realize we now have this heavy, dysfunctional topic floating freely through the air between us.

"Hey, Abby. How are you today?" I ask, while wrapping my arms around her waist and placing a soft kiss of the side of her forehead.

She hugs me back tightly with no space between us, and replies, "I'm good. I just dropped the girls off at school."

"How are you feeling since we talked?"

"I feel good. I'm glad that you know now. It was hard for me to admit that to you."

"I get that. I'm glad you felt like you could finally tell me what's been going on. You can trust me, Abby. I love you. I'm here to help you. To get you out of here."

"I know. I love you, too. I'm just not ready to go yet, Rudy. We're gonna have to figure things out. I can't just up and leave. They are the kids' grandparents after all—they are family. The kids are used to seeing them every day, being around them, they love them. I can't pull them away completely, not all at once."

"I hear what you're saying, but they're abusers, Abby. That's what they are. This isn't normal—the things they've done to you. The way they make you clean this house, get in trouble if you aren't available to answer their calls at all moments, try to control you and keep you from really doing much of anything."

"I know," she says with a sigh.

"Plus, they are terrible people, Abby. None of this is normal. None of it. It's not okay. None of this should have ever happened to you—it shouldn't ever happen to anyone."

"Yeah. I know. I wish that it hadn't happened. Any of it. But I do love my kids though."

"I know you do. You're a fantastic mom. You do everything for them. You do everything for Chevo and Laura, too. You're the only one doing anything around here. You do all of it. I just want you to know that I'm here for you, and I'm gonna always be here for you, period. I'm gonna get you out of here—you and the kids. All of you. If you are ready to go today, we'll go today."

"I can't go today, Rudy. You just don't understand. There's a lot going on. And Laura has really helped me out over the years. She's done a lot for me. I can't just walk out on her like that."

"Okay, babe. I get that. I know you aren't ready to leave today. Not now. But we can come up with a plan to get y'all out of here. To make sure that everything is taken care of, that you feel okay about it when we do it."

"Okay. I want that, Rudy. I really do. I love you. I want us to be together—to really be together. To one day get married. To have a house. I want all of that—*with you.*"

"I want all that, too, Abby. I just want to make sure that you were telling the truth when you said he hasn't touched you since December, right?

"Yeah. That's the truth," she says sheepishly. I can tell that it is humiliating for her to have to talk about this and to own these truths aloud to me.

"Is there anything else that you didn't tell me?"

"Not really. They just make me do a lot of stuff for them."

"Stuff for them? Like, what kind of stuff? Cleaning?"

"Yeah, cleaning. And they also make me draw their baths each night. After their baths, I have to rub cream all over their bodies. I have to clip their toenails. I give them their medicine. I have to shave my dad's face for him while he's in the bathtub."

"What do you mean you massage them? Like, for how long?"

"For an hour and a half each. My hands cramp up. I hate doing it. It's way too long of a time to give someone a massage. My fingers can't take it. And then once I'm done with one of them, I still have to massage the other. It takes so long. My fingers actually go numb."

"An hour and a half each? That's crazy, Abby. Every single night?"

"Yeah, it's every night to 'help them relax and unwind after work'."

"Do you rub just their backs that whole time?"

"No, it's a full body massage. All over. Their backs, necks, legs, arms, their ugly feet."

"For real? That's crazy, Abby—that they expect you to do that for them at all, much less every night."

"Yeah, I know. But they expect me to do it. I've been doing it for years."

"Do the massages ever lead to other things?"

"They used to, sometimes. But not anymore."

"You should tell them 'no,' Abby—like, 'hell no,' you're not going to rub the cream on them anymore. That's their problem. They're adults. They can rub in their own damn lotion. They can run their own bath. Chevo can shave his own damn face. I shave mine every day. He's a grown-ass man. He doesn't need you to do that for him. It's not right. It's too much. It's not normal. Nothing you are telling me about right now is normal. None of it."

"I know, I know. I want to stop doing it. I really do, but I can't. They expect me to do it."

"Again, Abby, there's nothing normal about that. Normal people don't ask their kids to do that. They go to a place and pay someone to massage them. They're treating you like you're their house slave, Abby. You have no life, aside from the time you sneak with me in the mornings. All you do is cook, and clean, and take care of the kids, then you take care of their ugly asses too—like *they're* your kids. It's too much, Abby. It's way too much. They can clip their own damn nails. They need to take care of themselves."

"I know."

Sensing defeat in Abby's tone, I decide to back off, at least for now. She's already told me more than I expected she would. But this conversation is *far* from over. I'm getting her and the kids the hell up out of this nuthouse. This is insane. Laura and Chevo have lost their damn minds thinking they can treat her like this and have her doing all these things. And I can't even think about Chevo touching her or I'll lose it. I try to tuck that unpalatable tidbit behind a thick wall in my mind.

Abby and I cuddle for a bit while watching random TV shows. When it is time for me to go, I pull her in for a tight hug. "I'm so glad you trusted me with all of this, Abby. That you talked to me about it finally. I'm here for you. For real. We're gonna figure this out."

"I know. I love you, too, Rudy. I really, really want us to figure things out, so we can be together—really be together."

"Text me later to let me know you're okay."

"I will."

Driving to work, I feel the bricks of that tall wall in my mind beginning to erode, crumbling down into the seats of my Mustang one messed-up-thought-brick at a time. Chevo. Abby. Rape. Pregnancies. Three of them. Years of rapes. Years of abuse. Chevo raped her. As a kid. For years. Her entire life. That motherfucker raped her, over and over again. Night after night. He got her pregnant. Three freaking times. He's gonna get what's coming to him. He's gonna pay the price for that. 100%. It's my number one mission to take him—both of them—down.

I just gotta convince Abby to get out of there. I know she's not ready yet. I'm not sure exactly what she means by us "working it out." What is there to work out? They're abusing you. You need to go. It seems pretty straightforward to me.

But I know it doesn't seem to be that way for her. She feels trapped there by guilt, family ties, obligations, or other bullshit. Her reasons sound a whole lot like excuses to me. They aren't real reasons. She should have no guilt whatsoever over walking away from them—from all of it—after the way they've treated her and the things they've done to her. But I don't want to lose Abby. I'm not going to allow that to happen. I have to try not to allow her to push me away. I'm gonna have to try to do things at her pace, even if it kills me. It probably will—kill me. Just to know about all the ways that they have abused her chisels away at me.

I'm going to try to let things play out her way for a bit, but I'm not happy about it. At all. I feel like a fucking dummy. A chump. A love-struck moron. Some idiot who is listening to his girlfriend—who has been raped and abused all her life making a whole bunch of excuses for why she just can't leave—and allowing her to pretend that it's okay for her to stay there, with them, for now.

Am I stupid? I think I probably am. But I'm also in love with a beautiful woman who truly needs me. I'm a fool in love who is willing to wait around a while to see if things will eventually go his way.

But will they?

RUDY
Let Me Count the Ways

*T*he events have been playing through my mind endlessly. It's all I think about. He raped her. For years. She had his babies—three of them. Laura participated in it. What kind of parents are those? Terrible ones. Evil ones. The vilest type of human beings that walk the planet.

Having thought about this for days on end at this point, I can tell you that the fact that I have sex with Abby and know that she has had sex with—been raped by—Chevo isn't what disgusts me. But I am disgusted that this actually happened to her. That as a beautiful little girl, this motherfucker thought it was okay to touch her like that to fulfill his own sick needs. If someone did that to either one of my girls, I'd kill the guy—point blank, game over—he would be dead. Chevo needs to pay for what he's done. No punishment would be severe enough. Death would be too easy. He deserves to rot in hell. Laura deserves to rot right alongside him for being complicit and taking part in it.

I know Abby well enough to know that she's a good person. She's also a great mother who would do anything for her kids. She has strong morals and deep family ties. So, while I do feel stupid on the one hand for sitting back and allowing things to play out the way Abby wants them to, on the flip side, I realize that I can't lose her. I simply can't. I don't want to live without her. She's such an important part of my life now and a big piece of my future.

What eats me alive is knowing that if I don't get her out of there, she's probably not ever going to get out of there. I can't live with knowing that she's stuck there, with them, enduring their bullshit and catering to their wants and needs for the rest of her life, while I go on to live mine. I don't want to be looking back one day, thinking about the girlfriend that I was so in love with and wanted to be with, and to have it sitting heavy on my soul that I allowed her to stay in that dysfunctional life. I simply can't do it.

So, that makes it impossible for me to walk away. And it's for that reason that I'm fighting against my strong desire to tear her from them, and also why I'm here sitting on the sidelines, waiting to see how things play out. I'm just gonna have to convince Abby to get out of there as soon as possible. Being stuck in this crazy bullshit with a rapist and his onlooker pedophile wife isn't anywhere I want to be. But, for Abby, at least for now, that's exactly where I'll be—holding Abby's hand and eagerly awaiting her escape from a household of dysfunction and evil.

ABIGAIL

Hours Later

R udy thinks that I can just pick up and leave here at any time. But he is wrong. Things aren't as simple as he believes them to be. He probably doesn't understand that my biggest reason for staying here—in this hell hole with them—until I can manage to figure things out, is my three beautiful kids.

All at once, my mind goes back to the pungent smell of my dad's body odor as it wafts into my nostrils. His face is mere inches away from mine and twisted into a snarl when in a threatening tone, he utters, "IF you ever get away, Abby—and that's a BIG IF—we would FIND YOU. And when we do, it's NOT gonna be nice." That flash of a memory is followed by a memory of my mom, who walks past me while I'm standing at the kitchen sink rubbing a soap lathered brush across a dinner plate to wash it. She smacks one of my butt cheeks hard, with a loud *thwack*, as she walks past me. She then smirks at my dad who is sitting a few feet away at the table, and haughtily states, "That right there, Abby—that's all that you're good for, that ass—lying on your back."

I want to leave here more than anything in this world. But when it comes to getting out of here, it's complicated. The kids don't even know that I'm their mom. They all believe me to be their big sister, because that's the lie that they have been told since birth. That reality puts me in an odd position when it comes to leaving here and taking them with me. I have to tell them *the truth*. Well, maybe not the *whole* truth. But I certainly need to tell them the essential part—that I'm actually their mom. I'm not sure how they'll take the news.

For the first time in a long time, what I feel is hopeful. Sitting right behind my excitement some major anxiety lurks, but I feel like I'm going to be able to finally get the heck out of here one day! I'll be able to go on and live my own life—a real life—with Rudy. I love him. I trust him. Initially, I wondered if he was going to leave me, like Football Guy did, but now I believe he's in this for the long haul. And I am, too. We just have a lot of things to figure out first. Like, *how* do I tell the kids? *When* do I tell the kids? I think that I'll probably have to tell them right before we leave because I can't risk them slipping up and telling my mom or dad that they know that I am their mom.

I also worry about my dad making good on his promise to come look for me, find me, and harm me. If he kills me, then what will happen to my kids? I can't risk that happening. My kids could end up being raised by *them*. What if my dad starts doing what he did to me to my daughters? The mere thought of it makes my stomach lurch. He can't. He wouldn't. But unfortunately, I know him better than anyone else does. One day, he might. One day, he probably will. My eldest daughter is nine now—the same age that I was when my nightmare started. There isn't much time. Rudy is right, we have to get out of here. But I have to be smart about it. We've gotta be really careful about it and make sure they can't find me and the kids.

I hope to God that Rudy can stick with me until we get a solid plan in place. I know that he may get tired of dealing with all of this—dealing with me, my mom and dad, and all of the dysfunction and drama, and he may end up concluding that he needs to move on.

One thing is for certain, we are leaving. We are getting the heck out of here. It's the *when* and the *how* that I have yet to work out.

RUDY
The Call

One night I'm at home, parked in front of the TV, with my two daughters and my mom. We're all sitting on the couch watching cartoons, when my phone rings. I look down at the screen and see Abby's name flashing on the screen, so I pick it up.

"Hey Abby."

In response, I hear deep breaths and broken words. I can't make out what she's saying.

"Abby—are you there, Abby?"

[More muffled breaths and broken words] ". . . I need you to [labored breath] come get me."

"Okay. I'm leaving now."

Turning to my mom, I say, "I gotta go. It's Abby. Something is wrong. She asked me to come get her." I jump up from the couch, walk over to the door, and pull on my sneakers.

"Right now, Mijo?"

"Yes."

"What's wrong with her?"

"I have no idea. I'm gonna find out though. Please keep an eye on the girls. I'm heading over there now."

"Okay, Mijo. But please be careful."

"I will. Be back soon."

Grabbing my keys, I head out the door, hop into my Mustang and make the ten-minute drive to Abby's house.

I've got the music cranked and I feel amped up. At one point, a few minutes into my drive, I realize that Abby called me again and I missed it. I immediately pick up my phone and dial her number.

"Hello. Abby?"

"Hey, I'm fine. Me and my dad are picking up McDonald's for the kids now and then we're gonna go back home to eat."

"What? You were so upset earlier. What do you mean everything is fine? What happened? Where are you?"

"I'm riding in the truck, with my dad, to go pick up food."

"Abby, I don't know what's going on right now, but I know it's something. Whatever it is, we need to face this. I'm on my way. I'm still gonna come over. Something's not right."

"Okay. Um, wait like 15 minutes and then come. That way, we'll be back home from getting the food."

"Alright. I'll see you then."

What. In. The. Fuck. I have no idea what is going on, but I know it can't be good. Abby has never called me like that before. She was so upset earlier she could barely speak. I couldn't even make out her words. It sounded like she was winded from running or something. I need to figure out what in the hell is going on. Something went down tonight. Whatever it is, we're gonna deal with it—and we're gonna do it tonight.

I bet that motherfucker touched her again. She said that hasn't been happening anymore since we got together, but that could explain the call to me. Her being panicked and out of breath. I bet he tried to get with her again and she freaked out. Chevo is a fucking low-life. Scum. He is not a man. He is nothing to me. He better hope he didn't touch her.

Pulling up in front of Abby's house, it is now pitch-black out. I have no idea what to expect. Walking up the long driveway, I'm prepared for anything. Things could pop off. This could be an ambush. That motherfucker may try to pull a knife or gun on me. All I am armed with is my fists and the undercurrent of rage seething in my gut for the shit that has happened to Abby—whatever that may be today.

I walk up to where Chevo's pick-up truck is parked in the driveway and I stop, cautiously standing beside it. Like I said, it's pitch-black out, so I can't really see much of anything, which places me in a state of high alert. There are lights on inside the chapel that stands at the end of the driveway. Through the doorway, I see Chevo and Laura sitting on folding chairs inside it.

I guess I'm just gonna stand right here by this truck until I figure out what's going on. Walking into the closed space of that chapel would make me an easier target. I have no idea what's waiting on me in there. Chevo may be looking to fight. If so, I'm down. Out here, I'm not boxed in, which gives me the advantage. About five minutes after taking my standing position by the truck, my phone rings. I look down at the screen and see that it's my mom calling.

"Mijo, where are you?"

"I'm here now."

"Well, then I'm gonna head over . . ."

"No. Don't. I don't want you in danger."

"Well, I don't want you in danger either, Mijo."

"Mom—stay there. I just want to make sure Abby's okay and then I'll come back home. Plus, you're watching my girls. I promise I'll call you as soon as I leave."

"Okay. But please be careful, Mijo. Please."

"I will, Mom. I'll see you soon."

I end the call and re-engage in my waiting game, standing beside Chevo's pick-up truck in the darkness. Waiting. Wondering what is going on. Wondering what happened to Abby to make her call me in a panic. Wondering what's going to happen here tonight.

About five minutes later, Abby finally exits the chapel doorway and walks down the driveway to where I'm standing beside her dad's truck.

She softly says, "Hey."

"Hey, Abby. Are you okay?"

"Yeah." She looks at me, but is looking all around, like she's afraid they might come out of the chapel any minute.

"What's going on? You called me over here and then y'all were just sitting in that chapel for like 15 minutes, while I was standing out here."

I notice that Abby is wearing a black hoodie jacket, which she has zipped all the way up to her neck. *In Texas. In April. It's hot as hell out.*

Why is she wearing a black hooded jacket? I decide to hold those thoughts and tread cautiously because I have no idea what went down earlier, but I know it must have been really bad for her to call me to intervene.

"Abby. Really. What's going on? What happened?"

She is looking down at the ground, so I lift my right hand to her chin to gently tilt her head in my direction, so I can look her in the eyes and get a better read on her and the situation.

"We were just talking. Me and Laura got into it."

"Like, an argument?"

"Yeah."

"Okay, but y'all just got back home. This just happened. What sparked y'all's argument?"

"My dad found out about us. He saw me on my main phone—the one they bought me. He knows I was talking to you."

It's so dark out that I can barely make out Abby's features and all I can see of her is her face. Everything else is covered by the black hoodie.

"Abby. Really. Are you okay? I feel like there is more to this than you are telling me right now." Lifting my hand to her face again, I gently rub the side of her cheek. I notice a fairly large bump on her forehead. Looking at it and rubbing my finger near it, I say, "What happened?"

"Oh, when I ran outside to call you earlier, I ended up tripping on my way down the steps and fell. I hit my head."

"Are you okay?"

"Yeah, I'm fine.

What she's saying makes sense. If she left the house angry, maybe she did miss a step. I see how that could happen.

"So, you're fine?"

"Yeah. But they want to talk to you."

Again, I find myself wondering why in the hell she's wearing this damn hoodie, but I'm treading lightly and just happy that she appears to be okay.

"Where are the kids?"

"They're inside with Tio." ("Uncle" in Spanish).

"Well, lead the way . . ."

I have no clue what I'm walking into right now, but trailing behind Abby, we make our way into the chapel. All the folding chairs are stacked and put away, but there are four chairs pulled out. Laura and Chevo are sitting in two of them. Chevo is sitting facing the doorway to the chapel. Laura is sitting on the right side of the room. Abby takes a seat in the chair beside Chevo and I take the only empty seat remaining, the one beside Laura.

Upon entering the room, I don't notice anything threatening. I am definitely on high alert and cautious, unsure whether something is going to pop off. I have no idea what this is about, why we're all sitting in here right now, or what happened earlier tonight.

Laura is the first to break the silence.

"Hi, Rudy. We brought you in to talk. We just found out that y'all have been talking. Well, actually, that you've been coming to our house without our permission."

"Uh-huh," I utter in a defiant, smart-ass way.

"And Abby isn't allowed to have a boyfriend and isn't allowed to see anybody."

"Uh-huh." (Yep, still uttered like a smart-ass. Not sure where this is heading.)

I look over at Abby and notice she's staring down at her knees, never looking up. *She looks ridiculous with that hoodie pulled up tight and cinched closed around her face.* She has to be sweating in that thing. I can't help but notice that she looks like a scared puppy—cowering. Why? I have no idea.

Laura continues, "She's not allowed to do this—see anybody. So, I'm not sure how she got to sneaking around."

"Uh-huh." (Yep, still being a pompous jackass and proud of it.)

I look over at Abby—who is still staring downward—and ask, "Abby, how old are you?"

Never glancing up, she softly replies, "25."

Laura jumps in, "Okay. This conversation will stop right now."

I let out a guffaw. Laura looks offended and agitated. I don't give a damn.

She continues, "I'm dead serious. If you don't stop with the fucking attitude, this conversation will fucking stop right here."

I follow her statement up with another guffaw. *I give zero fucks about what this lady has to say. I'm fucking grown.*

Right then, Abby reaches over to touch my left hand and says, "Babe. Stop."

I think to myself, O*kay, let me see what these dumbasses have to say and then we'll see which way this is gonna go.*

I glance over at Chevo, who is blankly staring at Abby with a look of disbelief.

Laura then prompts, "Do we have an agreement? To stop with the attitude?"

"Yeah."

"And with the smart-ass laughing?"

"Okay."

She continues, "We don't appreciate that you've been coming around. This is causing friction in our family. We had no idea y'all were seeing one another. How long have you been coming over?"

I allow her words to pass over me without guffawing. (Self-control mode is engaged.)

"About two to three weeks."

My response is also a lie, but one that flows easily from my lips to protect Abby. In reality, we've been together for about eight months. Not really their business.

Chevo finally chimes in, "Well, where have you been parking?"

"In front of the house." (Another lie, but I want to rile him up a bit.)

"Well, that's weird because I swing by sometimes and I've never seen your car here."

He left out the part where he used to come home at lunchtime to rape Abby before December. In the mood to mess with him a bit, I throw both my shoulders up in response and say, "Okay," with a confident smirk plastered on my face.

"Well, you're lucky I never caught you."

I look him dead in the eyes and tilt both of my hands up in the air in a pose that says, *whatever* and infers *I'm standing here right now if you want to do something about it.* (Actually, my body language makes it less of an inference and more of an open invitation.)

Laura responds, "There needs to be ground rules if this is gonna continue."

Surprisingly, Chevo shows no reaction. It almost looks like he's in a state of shock sitting in this chapel with us. I expected something more from him: anger, rage, frustration, a desire to fight—something, anything more than this.

In that moment, I decide to let him know who he's dealing with. I shift my body toward him and look him straight in the eyes with no intention of looking away—a non-verbal taunt—to see what he'll do. He looks back at me for a few seconds and meets my gaze, then diverts his eyes away. *That's right, motherfucker. You are nothing to me. You are no one.* Those are the unspoken words I sent his way with that glance. It wasn't just a taunt. It was a warning. I wanted him to know he was nothing to me.

Laura starts back in with, "Okay. You aren't allowed to come to the chapel anymore."

"Okay." *I haven't been back to the broke-down chapel since December, lady. I have no desire to be there, except to see Abby.*

"And y'all can't go nowhere, so if you do come over, it's gonna be on the weekends, mainly on Saturdays and with all of us."

"Well, that's weird."

"Well, we don't really trust Abby."

"With what?"

"Well, she's very immature for her age."

"Okay?"

"She's, um, in special-ed."

"What does that mean?"

"She was in special ed through all her school years, so she needs special attention. She's slow. She doesn't know how to do stuff for herself."

All I can think to myself is what a bunch of bullshit this is. This lady is full of it. Abby is the one doing *everything* in that house. But I somehow manage to hold my tongue and keep my composure to get through the rest of this conversation for Abby's sake.

"She's been very rebellious toward us and I see why now."

"So, you're blaming me for, like, talking to her?"

Interesting, since I know that they abuse her. That he rapes her.

"Yes, because she doesn't go to school. She doesn't work. She doesn't do nothing. So, she gets to be home, but she's supposed to be cleaning, washing, putting away clothes, cooking meals, and taking care of the kids."

"Well, that's a lot of work in itself right there. So, she does that every day?"

I already know the answer but feel the need to force her to answer my question anyway.

"Yes."

At this point, I'm just playing along and letting them say whatever they want to say to let this lady think she's gonna play this mind game on me. (She's not. Also, this is a bunch of bullshit. They are terrible people who only pretend to care about Abby.) I'm still somewhat on edge because I realize that at any time Chevo could stand up and try to fight me. If he does, I'm ready to throw hands.

"So, what you're saying is that we can only be together on Saturdays?"

"Yes, that's right."

"Well, when I get off work, I'd like to come see Abby."

"Well, what time do you get off work?"

"Around 7 or 8 o'clock." (A lie. At this point, we're all trading lies. It's an even exchange. Their bullshit lies for my well-crafted ones. I want them to think it's not possible for me to visit Abby during the day. In reality, I go in to work at 1 o'clock and work until 10 or 11 at night. But they don't really need to know that.)

"Well, no. That's not possible because at that time, we're closing down the chapel and putting the kids to bed."

She then continues, "So, y'all talk in the mornings?"

"No. We don't talk all that much. I go to work at 8 in the morning and get off work at 8 at night." (Another lie. We talk all the time. I don't want them knowing how much Abby and I talk, much less when.)

"Let's keep it slow. We'll let you come see her on a Saturday. But it'll be with all of us. And y'all can't be alone."

"Okay, that's fine." (Another lie. It's not fine, but I'm just playing along for Abby's sake.)

Laura then says, "Is there anything else?"

"No, not really."

She then looks at Abby, "Abby—do you have anything to say?"

I sit there waiting to see how Abby replies. She always talks a big game to me about how she's ready to stand up to them. Let's see if she backs it up.

Abby softly replies, "No."

I ask Laura, "Is it okay if I speak with Abby alone for a minute?"

Laura glances over at Chevo, whose face is twisted in a scowl. (*Not that I give a damn.*)

"Yes, but only for a few minutes."

Abby stands and walks across the chapel toward the exit with me trailing behind her. We walk in silence down the driveway and out to the street where I parked my car. I want to hold Abby's hand. I want to kiss her, but I know that they are probably watching, so I do none of these things. Standing beside my car, in a light-hearted, but sarcastic tone, I say, "Well, that was a lot of fun."

Abby smirks in response, "You're fucking necio." (Spanish for "foolish").

"Really, you shouldn't have stopped me. I seriously could just go back in there and fuck both of them up."

"No. No. You never know what could happen."

"I'll go in there and kick Laura in the stomach—and then give me about ten seconds with Chevo—and you can call the cops if you want, whether you like what you see, or you don't."

"No. Behave."

"Are you sure you're gonna be fine?"

"Yes. They're not gonna do nothing."

I put my hand beneath her chin, look her in the eyes, and say, "If you don't text me before you go to bed, I'm coming back."

Closing the evening's events with a simple hug, I get into my Mustang and head back home.

A few hours later, I receive a text from Abby.

"Just wanted to tell you goodnight. Thanks for coming and talking to them. I really want it to work."

"Did they bother you after I left?"

"No. We ate dinner, I gave the kids their baths, and then put them to bed. I'm really drained. I just want to go to sleep. I love you. I'll text you in the morning. Like always."

"Okay. I love you. I'll see you tomorrow, babe."

As I set my phone down on the nightstand beside my bed, I realize that it feels like I'm walking through a nightmare with someone who refuses to wake up. That's all she has to do is wake up and willfully take the power over her own life back. Be her own person. Live her own life. Why can't she see that she doesn't have to play along with their stupid rules anymore? She's a 25-year-old woman who cowers to them like she is a scared little girl.

Why can't she see that there is a way out? Why doesn't she just wake up and walk out of the nightmare? I'd hold her hand the whole damn way.

She's going to have to make a choice at some point. But will she actually walk out? And if she does, will she be walking away from them, or walking away from me? A terrifying question. No clear answer.

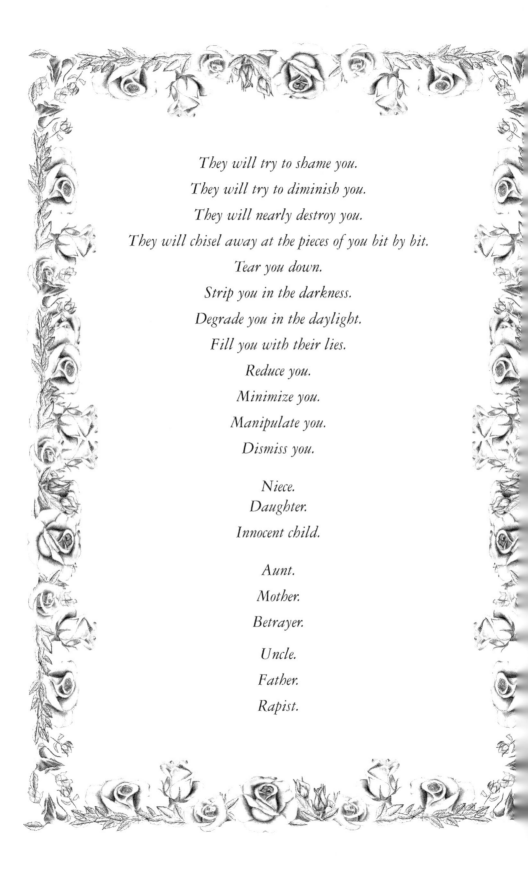

They will try to shame you.

They will try to diminish you.

They will nearly destroy you.

They will chisel away at the pieces of you bit by bit.

Tear you down.

Strip you in the darkness.

Degrade you in the daylight.

Fill you with their lies.

Reduce you.

Minimize you.

Manipulate you.

Dismiss you.

Niece.
Daughter.

Innocent child.

Aunt.

Mother.

Betrayer.

Uncle.

Father.

Rapist.

Lies.

Truth.

Blurred edges.

*The unbecoming of a twisted-up girl, who lurks within
the cloak of an evil shadow, seeing no way out.*

Desperate.

Burdened.

Broken.

Undone.

Girl.

Woman.

Victim.

SURVIVOR.

—JAMIE COLLINS
(For Abigail)

ABIGAIL

AGE 24

Sunday—Earlier That Evening

The Beat Down

*M*y parents and I drive four and a half hours to visit the Bishop in Dallas. We then climb back into the van to travel the four and a half hours back home. When we walk into the house, I am completely exhausted. All I want to do is lie down on my bed and relax, but my mom has other things in mind. "Abby, you need to start cooking dinner, you need to give the kids their baths, and you also need to throw a load of clothes into the washer."

Oh. My. God. No way. I am exhausted.

Why is it my mom and dad get to sit on the couch after our long day today, but I am the one expected to do *everything* in this house that needs to be done? I'm totally over it. Depleted of energy and unwilling to appease them, I remain seated on the couch. My mom's voice chimes in again, "I'm serious, Abby. Everybody is hungry. You need to get up *right now* and go cook us all something to eat." In no way attempting to move from my comfortable spot on the end of the couch, I look my mom straight in the eyes, and for the first time in my entire life—defiant words flow freely. "No. I'm not doing that. I'm not cooking. I'm tired. We've been traveling *all day long* and we *just* got home. I'm not doing that."

"Oh YES YOU ARE, Abby. And you're going to do it RIGHT NOW."

Who does she think she is? Trying to act like she's the one in charge of everything? Like I have no right to be tired, when we all are. I'm over it. Still not moving, I reply, "No, I'm not."

"YES, you are. And you're going to get up RIGHT NOW to go do it."

My next words are raw and unfiltered as they pass from my mind and my mouth, a rebellious combination of stupidity and rage. "You know what? Maybe we need to tell everybody who the kids' REAL mom is." A heavy silence fills the room. The type of silence that can be felt by everyone in it, especially me.

My hands are shaking I'm so emotionally charged right now. I've never openly defied my mom like this, much less refused to do what she asked. But I'm completely fed up with this entire situation. I am their house slave. They are my keepers. My commanders. My abusers. My rapists. My tormenters. The thieves of my children, my life, and my future. So, hell-to-the-no, I'm not getting up. Not this time. Fuck that. Fuck dinner. Fuck running bubble baths for anybody. And FUCK THEM. (This time, figuratively—for once.)

All of a sudden, my mom is standing in front of me and looming over me with her face twisted in an angry sneer. "WHAT did you just say to me?" But it wasn't really a question at all. It was more of a snarky statement that awaited no response.

Then . . . impact.

Her closed fists pummel me in the face over and over again. She is furious and I feel every bit of it as she pounds her knuckles into my eyes, cheeks, and jaw. She is standing over the top of me as I'm pinned in a seated position on the couch, and—THUMP—another punch lands on my cheek and slides off. THUMP. Another fist strikes me in the side of my forehead. With my arms up, I am attempting to fend off her punches the best I can while trying to get up from the couch at the same time.

My mom is not a small woman, which gives her a major size advantage over my small shifting frame—especially the way she's towering over me right now—so it is difficult for me to pull myself up to a standing position with her punches raining down on me left and right from above. She lands a few hard blows to my face, more jabs to my ribs, and I somehow manage to twist to the right and to lift my body upward to stand. Once I am finally up on my feet, I immediately take off running down the hallway to the bathroom, so I can hopefully lock the door to get away from her.

I make it to the bathroom. I step across the threshold, but as I go to push the door shut behind me, my mom runs up to the doorway and is now pushing the door against me to try to gain entry to the bathroom. She's so big and pushing it so forcefully that my feet are sliding backward on the white tile. All at once, she shoves the door forward and I fall backward and slide down the wall in front of the washer and dryer. In two long strides, my mom lunges for me. I end up lying on my back on the porcelain tile bathroom floor with my mom straddling over the top of me.

She is punching me as hard as she can—everywhere that she can land a punch. THUMP. THUMP. I am turning my head to avoid getting hit. THUMP. I am trying to lift my arms up to cover my face, but my arms are pinned beneath her weight. THUMP— another punch to the center of my forehead. *Oh my God. She isn't going to stop.* THUMP—a punch near my left eye. THUMP, THUMP, THWACK—punches to my left temple and the side of my face. I struggle to get her off me, but I cannot move. I am pinned by her weight and assaulted by her fury.

"Please stop. *Please* stop." THUMP, THUMP, THUMP. Three more hard punches land on my chin and neck. *She isn't going to stop. She isn't going to stop hitting me. She is going to kill me.* THUMP, THWACK. She lands another two blows to my chest. My body is collapsing beneath her weight. She still has me pinned beneath her, but she isn't hitting me anymore. I can tell that she has worn herself out.

The fury in her face is replaced by a flicker of exhaustion. All at once, I buck my hips upward and twist at the same time and manage to wiggle out from underneath her. My mom does not resist my maneuver to get up—because she could have, if she tried—and I am finally back up on my feet. I am shaking so bad. Tears are flowing down my face and I am breathing fast. I run to my bedroom, grab my regular cell phone, and run out of the house. With tears and snot streaming down my face, I take off running up the road.

I hear my mom call out to my dad, "Go get her. She is going to tell people."

Oh my God—they are going to chase me.

Running at a clipped pace, I turn to look back. I see my dad driving his truck toward me at a steady pace—he is going to catch up to me. He is almost to me. All at once, I feel a stream of wetness trickle down my legs. The realization sets in—I just peed my pants. *I can't let him catch me. I can't let him catch me. I can't let him catch me.*

I want to get away. I need to get away. I cannot go back there. I have no idea what's gonna happen if I go back there. She might kill me.

But my kids are there. I cannot leave them. I have to go back for them. What will happen to them if I don't go back?

And so begins the vicious circular pattern of thoughts looping in my mind. To leave? Or to stay?

Leave. Stay.

Leave. Stay.

Leave. Stay.

Should I leave or should I stay?

Leave.

I'm totally leaving. I can't do this anymore. She might kill me. I'm out.

My kids—I have to stay.

I don't have a choice. I can't leave them behind. What would happen to them if I leave?

Fear,
Whether real,
Proven,
Perceived,
Or pondered,
Is a powerful trap.

Ensnared,
Jagged edges,
Digging into flesh,
Gripped in place,
Alone.
Waiting.
Struggling.
Stuck.

Inside an inescapable psychological cage,
She is perched.

Waiting for someone,
Or perhaps,
Herself,

To unlock it.

But fear, it is an invisible shackle.
It blinds one to possibilities.
Robs one of hope.
Denies one's potential.

From inside the shiny cage.
Perched.
Behind the bars.

It appears that there is no possibility of escape.

—JAMIE COLLINS
(For Abigail)

RUDY

Tuesday

Two Days Later

*A*bby stayed.

She climbed into her dad's pick-up truck. Her dad was talking calmly (calculatingly). He managed to talk her into going with him to pick up McDonald's for the kids that night, before I met up with Abby and her evil ass parents in the chapel for that bullshit meeting.

I know that her staying is a difficult thing to fathom, but at this point, she has her reasons for not leaving, namely, her children. I told her they can all leave—that I'll help them all to get out of there, but she doesn't seem ready to do that yet. It's a frustrating situation to find myself in. I just want to get her out of there right now. But I also know she's been through a lot, so I try to respect her boundaries. It's a delicate dance. I don't want to scare Abby off, but I also can't believe the stuff that is going on in that house with her "parents."

I'm still not entirely sure what all happened a few nights ago, but I know that it must've been major for her to call me and ask me to come over there "right now" the way that she did. I'm curious to learn more about what happened. I'm also afraid to. I know how evil Laura and Chevo are and how defenseless Abby is against them.

But the defender of Abby is definitely a role I'm willing to step in to play. I'll beat Chevo's sick, twisted, evil ass if he ever touches her again. And Laura isn't much better. She's an enabler. A participator. A master manipulator with a quick mind and a fast mouth who seems to always help Chevo to tie pretty ribbons around the disgusting lies they tell and the horrific secrets that they keep—from everyone. I see through their bullshit. Their compounded lies. Their stories about Abby. Their fake portrayal of themselves as caring, over-protective parents when, in reality, they are pathological liars and masterful abusers. Laura mentioned Abby being in Special Ed, but after switching schools so many damn times over the years, how could she *not* struggle in school? I fear neither of them. I only fear what may happen to me if I ever end up seeking retribution against them for the terrible things they've done to my girlfriend because I may not be able to stop.

At 9:00 a.m., I pull my Mustang into the alley to park it. As usual, Abby leaves the door open for me. I step through the open doorway into her bedroom. Abby walks up to me and hugs me. She lingers there for a minute, just holding me, not letting go. When she finally takes a step back, the first thing I notice is a huge goose-egg in the middle of Abby's forehead. *What the fuck.*

"Oh my God, Abby. What happened? What did they do to you? This is why you had that hoodie on the other night, isn't it?"

"It's okay. I'm okay." Abby then proceeds to tell me what happened on Sunday night before I got there for that bullshit talk with her parents at the chapel.

"This isn't right Abby. That she did this to you. Why don't you just leave? I'll help you leave. ALL of you."

"I know. I know you will. I'm just not ready to go yet. I have to figure things out—with the kids. They go to school here. The kids think they're their mom and dad. I have to sort out what I will tell them."

"Okay. But this is killing me, Abby. This isn't okay. Any of it. The things they do. That bitch has no right to put her hands on you."

"I know. I was afraid she wasn't going to stop."

"That's exactly what I'm saying, Abby. You don't deserve that. You're not safe here."

"I hate them. But things have calmed down a bit. Just give me some time to get things figured out."

"Did he bother you again? Is that what started this?"

"No, he didn't. I promise."

"Okay. But if he did, you could tell me, Abby. You could tell me."

"I know I could, but he didn't."

"This isn't right—the stuff they do to you. The way they treat you. All the stuff they make you do. It's crazy."

"I know. I'm sick of it. I know that it's not right."

"I love you, Abby. You could tell me anything. I'm gonna be here for you."

"I love you, too. I really want this to work out between us. I want us to stay together."

Glancing over at Abby sitting on the bed cuddled up beside me, I see that she has bruises in other places. I'm filled with three distinct emotions: empathy, rage, and an overwhelming desire to extricate Abby from living here with these lowlifes.

Instead, I kiss the side of Abby's head, being careful not to touch the bump on her forehead, and I begin to softly run my fingers up Abby's bruised arms and battered legs, then back down them again, in an effort to quell my anger. Considering that Abby is beautiful and I love her, it works, and my mind wanders to another place for a period of time. But I realize it won't be long before my thoughts return to that newly found baseline of empathy, rage, and a deep-seated conviction to help her escape.

RUDY

Saturday

Four Days Later

$\mathcal{A}$ bby told me that I'm invited over to her house for a barbeque today with the family, including her crazy-ass parents. It is going to be *interesting*, to say the least. Her parents have no clue that I know all about them and the despicable shit that they do to her. I'm sure they assume Abby is either too ashamed or embarrassed to confide in me. While I'm sure she felt both, she did finally admit to me the vile, unimaginable truth of her reality. Sick bastards. I'm sure they'll be on their best behavior today. No way are they gonna mistreat Abby with me standing around to bear witness to it.

Admittedly, I'm a bit nervous to take my two daughters along to the barbeque with me, but I'll be there to watch over them closely. I want my girls to finally meet Abby, since she's an important part of my life. I buckle the two girls into their car seats and drive us over to Abby's house.

When we pull up, I see that all the kids are running around playing outside. My girls are gonna love it. Abby walks up, "Hi Rudy. Hi girls. I'm so glad you were able to come over today to hang out with us."

"Hiii," my eldest daughter responds. My youngest, pointing in the direction of the kids running around, says, "Can we go play with themmm?"

"Sure. I'll be over here talking to Abby. Let me know if y'all need anything."

"Okay. Byyyye." And off they both sprint straight toward the trampoline. For them, this place is a mini fun park with playmates. For me, it's an opportunity to try to pretend I'm adhering to Abby's parents' bullshit rules in an effort to spend more time with her. They don't realize I still talk with, text, and see Abby every day while they're at work.

Laura steps out of the house and comes over to greet me. In reality, I'm pretty sure it was more of an assertion of her ever-shadowing presence than her desire to be friendly. I don't think she likes me any more than I like her, which is *not at all*. Laura then says, "Hi Rudy. Looks like the kids are having a good time. Well, I'm gonna head back in to finish preparing the food." Right behind her departing words, Chevo calls out, "Rudy, can you come up front to help work on the yard?"

I reply, "Sure." I'm willing to play along. That said, I'm here to see and talk to Abby, not to beautify their lawn, but whatever. Chevo shuffles off to the garage to grab some tools and we work to clean out the fire pit. I'm working alongside Chevo and I can't stand him. I know who he is—WHAT he is. A deplorable man who gets off sexually abusing his adopted daughter. Fury fills my veins when I think about it.

Abby heads back into the house to help Laura. At this point, I'm wondering why I'm over here at all. I'm not even getting to be around Abby, much less talk to her. I'm apparently here to provide manual labor for the last two people on earth I'd actually want to help out. Yet here I stand, with a fake smile on my face, shoveling away heaps of ashes. Chevo walks over to the porch where an old radio is sitting. I hear him messing with the stations until he finally lands on one that is playing classic rock. It figures that this guy doesn't listen to any music I like, or even Tejano music, which is what I expected him to listen to. Songs by Ozzy Osborne and Led Zeppelin blare through the speakers as I keep shoveling out the fire pit.

At one point, Chevo turns to me and says, "Who is this one?" asking me about the current song playing. *No clue. I don't listen to this.* "I'm not sure who it is." He asks me again a few more times when songs he must deem to be "classics" play, to which I either say "I don't know" or proffer a wrong guess. Chevo chuckles. *I'd like to wipe that smirk right off his face.*

I glance over when I hear my girls giggling and see them jumping as high as they can on the trampoline. *I'm glad somebody is having a good time. I'm definitely not.* It makes me happy to see my girls having fun playing with Abby's kids. After finally scooping out the last of the ashes, Chevo leads me over to a flowerbed beside the house to dig up dirt and plant flowers. Driving over here today, I had no idea that I was going to be stepping in as Chevo's assistant landscaper, but here I stand, digging and planting away, all the while hoping to see Abby.

Laura comes outside, "Hey Rudy, would you mind running to the store to grab a few things?"

"Sure." As the word drops from my mouth, I find myself internally questioning whether it's okay to leave my daughters here with *them*. But then I realize that Abby is here, I trust her, and I know she'll make sure everything is okay while I'm gone. I don't trust Laura and Chevo at all. I do trust Abby.

When I return from the store and walk back up the driveway, I don't see Chevo and Abby. My girls and the other kids are still jumping up and down on the trampoline. Laura walks up to grab the newly purchased grocery items from my hands and heads back inside. I decide to stay outside where I can keep an eye on my girls.

Where are Chevo and Abby? I walk around back and see that Chevo is standing beside the garden over a hot grill, where he is cooking meat. As I approach him, he says, "I love to grill. I always get lots of compliments." I nod my head in response as I check out the chicken legs, strips of marinated chicken cut into strips for fajitas, and large sausages. At this point, I'm definitely looking forward to eating some chicken. My stomach is growling. I know my girls must be starving. As I stand beside the grill to sweat my ass off for another thirty minutes, I rarely catch a glimpse of Abby, who remains in the house most of the time. *This is bullshit. Why did I even come over here today? I haven't really even seen Abby at all.*

Another thirty minutes pass and it's starting to get dark out. Finally, Abby and Laura step out of the house holding dishes filled with beans, rice, and jalapeno poppers, as well as all the fixings for fajitas. Chevo starts to pull the grilled chicken legs and chicken strips off the grill and place them into a large bowl that Laura hands to him. We all head into the chapel to eat. By this time, it's about 9:00 at night. No joke. It's honestly ridiculous.

This whole day has been weird. Who eats dinner at nine at night? My girls are starting to get cranky and whiney because they've waited so long to eat, especially my youngest. We each take a seat on a folding chair and pull ourselves up to the folding table in the broken-down chapel to shovel forkfuls of rice and beans into our hungry mouths. No one recites a prayer before we dig into the food. That seems a bit weird since we're sitting inside a chapel and eating—clearly, a place where most people would feel inclined to pray—but we're all starving, so I don't really miss it.

I pick up a chicken leg from my plate, take a bite, and notice that it isn't quite cooked all the way. *Disgusting. Figures that Chevo can't even grill a piece of meat right after all that bragging he was doing earlier.* I stifle my strong desire to immediately spit it back out and silently choke down the bite. No way am I going to give my girls any of this chicken. I let them continue eating just the side dishes. Laura asks, "Do the girls want some chicken?" to which I reply, "No, they're kind of picky eaters. They'll be good with just the sides."

"Oh, okay," she replies with a glance of judgment.

Who is she to judge anyone? Seriously.

I find myself seated with the woman I love, my little girls whom I adore, *Abby's three beautiful children*, her rapist, and a lady pretending to be the doting mother to Abby's three beautiful children who aren't actually hers—the last two diners also being pathological liars and some of the worst humans on the planet.

The company definitely makes for an awkward dining experience, even without taking the salmonella into account. Laura and Chevo don't really like me. And I don't give a damn that they don't. The room is cloaked in silence because we are all too famished to stop eating long enough to speak. Forks are scraping across plates, the kids occasionally chit-chat with one another, and there is the occasional passing of side dishes to people who can't reach them.

I've spent the past few minutes picking at my plate, eating rice and beans in an effort to avoid food poisoning, while sitting in uncomfortable silence. Chevo glances right at me then quickly diverts his eyes to Laura before saying, "It's getting late." He detonates the words into the air to put us—mainly me and Abby—on notice that it's getting close to time for me to go. At this point, I've spent about a total of five minutes with Abby today—tops. I did a hell of a lot of yardwork. I cleaned out the fire pit. I planted a bunch of plants and flowers. I watched Chevo man the grill to (under) cook his chicken even though I can't stand being around the guy.

Time with Abby? Pretty much non-existent.

This could've been a great day. It wasn't one.

I hope Abby doesn't think I'm gonna come over to do this shit every weekend. No freaking way.

Laura says, "Well, it's been a good day today! It was nice to see everyone playing outside. I'm going to head into the house and y'all can say your goodbyes."

Feeling half-drained and fully disheartened, I get up from the table, do my best to clean up the tabletop where my girls ate, and walk down the driveway with Abby and the girls. I turn to Abby and say, "Is it going to be like this all the time? I barely saw you today. I didn't even get to talk to you."

"I know."

"Seriously. Because if this is how it's gonna be, Abby, then you are crazy to think that this is gonna work out."

"Please don't say that. It has to work out. I really want it to. I want to be with you."

"I really want it to work out, too, but I'm not sure I can deal with this part—with your parents."

Heavy in the back of my mind sits the disturbing reality that my kids and I spent the entire day with a damn rapist and a lunatic lady who treats Abby like garbage, like she's nothing more than their servant. The thought of it makes me feel ill and angry.

I love Abby. I want us to work out. I really do. But I'm not sure that I can do what she needs me to do to appease her parents in order to make our relationship work. Some boundaries are drawn too deep to trespass across. Hanging out with her parents is one of those boundary lines. It's too much. Too twisted. Too dysfunctional. Too emotionally exhausting. As much as I want to be with Abby, I want nothing to do with Laura and Chevo. I want to get Abby and the kids out of here. Whether I'll be able to stick it out long enough for that to actually happen remains to be determined. One thing of which I am certain is that my days spent with a rapist and a lunatic are definitely limited.

ABIGAIL

Channeling Fidencio

*I*n the days that followed the barbeque, my mom began to tell me that she was "channeling" Fidencio—that is, that she was receiving messages from him via some invisible spiritual tether, about me and Rudy. I am standing in the kitchen making dinner, when my dad comes into the house from the chapel and says, "Your mom needs to talk to you. She's in the chapel. Go talk to her. It's Nino! She has a message from him." (Referring to Saint Nino Fidencio, Rudy's namesake, and the saint that he prays to).

Wiping my hands on a nearby dishtowel, I sit it back down onto the counter and make my way out to the chapel beside our house. I walk in to find my mom sitting on a chair with her head down. In a slightly different voice, my mom says, "Sit down, Abby. I am here to tell you something. Come sit close to me." In a clueless state, I take a seat beside my mom, who still has her head bowed. "Abby, I see everything, and I know what is going on. You are not listening to your parents, and you are being a rebel. You need to obey them. And Rudy isn't the one for you. He isn't good enough for you and he isn't the one. Someone is going to come into your life, and he will be the one. You will marry him and have a beautiful life together."

Her words are met by my silence which is quickly consumed by a thick cloud of confusion. I have nothing to say to her on this topic and I know that there is no point in attempting to argue. *Is she really channeling Nino? Is she just pretending to? I'm not sure.* But what I do know is ever since she found out about Rudy, she hasn't seemed happy at all about me being with him. Now that everybody is on the same page with Rudy and me dating, it's like she's doing what she can to derail my future with him. *I wonder if she's for real about this?*

A moment later, my mom drops the channeling and seemingly "returns" to the room we are sitting in together. I am so confused about what just happened. *Is she trying to mess with me? Was this truly a message from Nino to me? Where would I possibly meet someone? I don't even think I'd want to meet someone else. I love Rudy.*

I realize that many people who aren't Mexican Catholic may have a hard time grasping, much less understanding, all of this saints and channeling stuff, but in a traditional Mexican Catholic household, like the one I was raised in, I was taught to believe in the ability of certain special people to spiritually connect to particular saints, for them to sometimes have the ability to channel those saints, and at times, to even to possess the ability to actually heal people of their ailments or afflictions using their spiritual gifts. It is part of the church teachings and at the core of our religious beliefs, as Mexican Catholics. We are raised up immersed into the religion and everything that comes along with it, including the creation of beautiful shrines at which we pray before pictures and candles depicting the faces of various saints. So, while channeling isn't mainstream for some, it is a common belief of those in our religion. And as such, it is plausible to me. I walk back into the house as confused as I have ever been, my mind swirling with thoughts, riddled with uncertainties, and plagued by a strong undercurrent of doubt. I love Rudy, but what if he really isn't who I am supposed to be with? What if he really isn't "the one" that I am supposed to end up with in life? Am I betraying my family by being with Rudy and planning to one day leave my parents' house, to get us all out of here? Is what I am doing wrong?

Laura has never channeled anyone before. Well, if she has, I've never seen her do it or heard anything about it, so the whole thing seems like a puzzle for me to sort out. Is this her play at getting me to back away from Rudy? Is this truly a message from Nino to me about my future?

The next morning, I call Rudy, "Hi babe. Some crazy stuff happened yesterday."

"Some crazy stuff?"

"Yeah. Just some stuff my mom said."

"What do you mean? What did she say?"

"Well, I was cooking, and my dad came into the house and told me my mom wanted to talk to me out in the chapel—that it was Nino."

"Nino?"

"Yeah, that it was Nino—that she was channeling him."

"Pfft. Okay, and?"

"She looked like she was channeling and then she basically told me that I'm not supposed to be with you, that I've been being a rebel, and that there is another guy who is actually the one that I'm supposed to be with, who I am supposed to marry. That he is who is going to make me happy."

"So, your mom said she was channeling Nino?"

"Yeah."

"And you believed her?"

"Yeah, I mean, it seemed like she was."

"Well, I guess if that's what you want to believe, Abby. It's all bullshit, but if that's what you want to believe."

"I didn't say I *want* to believe it. I am just telling you what she told me."

"Well, I can't wait to see when this 'dream guy' comes around."

"Whatever."

"You are the one who is going with it—believing her, Abby."

"I didn't say I believe her, but I just wanted to tell you about what happened—about what she told me."

"What do you think, Abby?"

"I don't know. I'm confused. I don't really know what to think."

"Well, next time, you need to ask some questions when Laura pretends to do this bullshit, Abby."

"I didn't say I believe her. But I'm not sure whether I shouldn't, either. I'm just confused, Rudy."

"I gotta go. Let's talk more later. I got stuff to do before work today."

"Okay."

"I'll talk to you later.

"Alright. Bye."

"Bye."

There was no "I love you" to end our call today, just a cloud of confusion and regret for telling Rudy what happened because he doesn't believe a bit of it. I also feel a glimmer of wonder about what my future may actually hold. Is he really not the one for me? My mom also said Rudy isn't a good guy, but I know that's not true. He is definitely a good guy. But maybe he isn't the guy I'm meant to be with? She said I'll be meeting someone else soon. Is that a lie to get me to stop talking to Rudy? I'm not sure about any of it anymore.

Rudy and I talk throughout the week, but less than usual. I'm spending time sitting with my own thoughts and trying to figure out what my life is supposed to be. At this point, I really don't know.

ABIGAIL

The Gasoline

My dad's anger has intensified over the past week, since the day of the barbeque when Rudy came over to our house. I know it is because he doesn't like the fact that Rudy and I are together. Rudy has ruined my dad's sick plan to keep me all to himself, the way he always has.

While I still don't know what to think about my mom "channeling" Nino and insisting Rudy isn't the one for me, the one thing that I am crystal clear about is my dad's intense hatred for Rudy and all that he represents in my life: love, hope, and a future. My dad doesn't want me to have a life unless it's with him, which is twisted and unfathomable.

I am particularly on edge tonight because my dad has been outside drinking all day today. In fact, he called in to work, to apparently sit outside and drink beer like it's his personal mission to get wasted. The more beer he guzzles, the meaner he tends to get. Any time he is drunk, I try my best to avoid him. This has become one of those days of avoidance. I haven't even been able to talk to Rudy today because my dad has been here all day.

Around 10:00 in the evening, I sneak to the laundry room, pull out my secret lime green phone, and dial Rudy's number. I don't have long to talk, so it has to be quick.

"Hey, Rudy."

"Hi, babe. How are you?"

"I can't talk long at all. My dad has been home all day. He's outside drinking. But I just wanted to sneak to call you real quick to tell you goodnight."

"What? He's been home all day? Is he drunk?"

"Yeah, but it's okay, babe. Everything is fine."

"If he's been drinking, you aren't worried that he's going to try to bother you? That something could happen?"

"No. I'm not worried about that. I'll be fine. Don't worry. Okay, I gotta go, Rudy."

"Okay, as long as you're sure. Goodnight, babe. I love you."

"I love you, too, babe." I then quickly hit the button to end the call, scurry back to the laundry room to place my phone back into its ever-present hiding spot, and walk back into the living room, like I didn't just make a secret phone call to Rudy. I sit down on the couch and watch whatever show happens to be on while scrolling Facebook on my other phone that my parents know I have.

About an hour later, my mom walks in from outside. "Abby, it's your dad. He's gone crazy! I can't calm him down, Abby. I've been trying to get him to stop and just come inside and it's not working. He keeps saying that he is going to set the whole house on fire. You have to try to see if you can stop him, Abby. See if you can calm him down. I can't seem to get through to him right now. He's gone crazy!"

Upon hearing her words, fueled by self-preservation and adrenaline, I storm outside to find my dad standing there leering and mumbling under his breath. I am taken aback by the devilish and appalling sight of him holding a gas can and aggressively pouring long wet lines of gasoline all around the back side of our house, along the perimeter of its foundation. Without even thinking, I engage him:

"Dad. What are you doing? What's going on? Why are you doing this?"

With a wild sneer on his face, he quips, "What does it look like I'm doing? I'm going to burn the fucking house down."

"What? Why would you want to burn the house down, Dad? Why would you want to do that?"

"Because of you, Abby. Because *of you*. Because of everything. Fuck everybody. I'm going to fucking set this house on fire and kill everybody in it."

"Dad, please don't do this. Dad, please stop. Look at me, Dad. Please just stop. Don't do this."

"WATCH me," he hisses, as he frantically continues to pour more gasoline around the perimeter of our house.

With my voice turning soft into the form of a plea, I tell him, "Dad—look at me. It's me, Dad. I'm right here with you. I love you. You love me. You love the kids. You love Mom. You don't want to do this. You're just angry right now."

He sears me with a look of hatred. "You're damn right I'm angry—YOU FUCKING WHORE. You're nothing but a stupid slut. A good for fucking nothing whore." He pours the gasoline more aggressively, saturating large areas of grass. My nostrils are hit by the overpowering odor, to the point that it gags me.

Sucking in a ragged breath, I turn my head the opposite way, but still plead to him, "Dad, look—I know you're angry—I know that, but I want to work this out. We can figure things out. Please just stop pouring the gas, Dad. Let's sit down and talk—just me and you. We can talk about whatever you want to. Anything. Please. Please, Dad! Just. Stop."

"I'm going to BURN THIS FUCKING HOUSE TO THE GROUND. I am going to kill the kids in the fire and BURN EVERYTHING THAT YOU HAVE, ABBY—all of it. ALL. OF. IT."

My dad briefly pauses his pouring to listen to me speaking, but he has not fully stopped. *I just need him to stop. I'll say whatever I have to. I just need to get him to stop.*

"Dad, look at me. I love you—I love you so much. You are so important to me, Dad. Look at me."

As I speak, his sneer falters slightly before he gazes at me with drunken, wild eyes bearing a flicker of hurt behind them. What I see as he looks at me is the jealous, hate-filled gaze of a scorned lover. But he isn't a scorned lover—he is my freaking dad. I guess in a way, he is both, which is fucking sick, but here we are. The look he gives me makes me want to puke, but if I can get him to stop pouring the gasoline, I'll deal with whatever I have to. I'll say and do *anything* to make him stop.

"YOU don't fucking love me, Abby. You are fucking HIM now. You are WITH him. Just like the fucking WHORE THAT YOU ARE, Abby."

"Yes, I do love you, Dad. I do. Don't worry about Rudy, Dad. If I need to stop talking to Rudy so things will be okay, then I will. I'll stop seeing him. Please just stop. Put the gasoline down." He pauses in his pouring efforts, as my mom gingerly walks up to him, seemingly sensing that his rage was quelled by my words and his anger was by my probably-fake-promises. She gently puts her hand around his right arm and manages to usher him back into the house.

I am left standing outside in the darkness with the overpowering scent of gasoline consuming the air that I breathe, just as his recently uttered words and lover-esque looks consume my soul, eating away at it bit by bit. I feel repulsed by him in every way. I hate him. Behind those feelings, there is also a twinge of relief that he has stopped pouring the gasoline and trying to burn down our house.

My mom walks back outside, interrupting my thoughts. "I got him into bed, Abby. He's going to pass out. Everything is going to be okay now." She then grabs the hose and douses water all over the areas of our house and yard where he had poured the gasoline. Then we both head back inside to our still-standing-house-that-hasn't-been-burned-to-the-ground-at-my-dad's-hands. My mom returns to her bedroom, where she will sleep beside her psychotic husband. I head to my room, still entirely disturbed by what just happened, and I lie down in my bed, where sleep will undoubtedly evade me.

He was going to kill us—all of us. Me and the kids. He was going to burn the whole house down. We aren't safe here. We never have been. He is completely crazy.

I realize that this isn't the first time that I have seen him pour gasoline all around us and threaten to set himself on fire—and us, right along with him. My thoughts go back to the time when I was a kid, when he apparently tried to have sex with the immigrant lady in a car at The Coyote's house. The time when he freaked out to calm Laura down and poured gasoline all over the house and his body and tried to flick a lighter, but it wouldn't freaking strike. (The time when I prayed to God from the core of my being to set him on fire and let him burn. The time when he didn't.) Then this time.

He is a sadistic, evil person.

And he is going to kill us, if we don't get out of here.

We have to get out of here.

RUDY

The Following Saturday

Talking to Abby's Brother

*T*hinking about Abby's situation, I can't help but wonder whether the rest of her family is aware of the years of rape and abuse? I have her brother's number. He and I text back and forth on occasion. Since he's Abby's little brother, I try to be cool with him. There have been times when I've given him a ride when he needed one. There have also been times when I've given him a little money here or there to help him out.

I grab my phone and send him a quick text to ask if he wants to meet up for tacos tomorrow, my treat. My phone chimes a moment later with an incoming text. He's down to have lunch.

I need to know whether he knows about the abuse, if so, how much, and why Abby is still in this situation. Her brother's support could be helpful for me and Abby, especially if things go sideways when I go to move her out of that house. It would be great to know that I have someone on my side if Chevo makes the mistake of stepping up on me, swinging at me, or worse. While my mom knows about Abby's situation and the past abuse, and constantly offers to head over there with me to get her out of there, I really don't want to put my mom in harm's way. It's not her place to deal with this, it is mine. And my way of trying to take control over the situation involves determining whether or not her brother is on Abby's side and willing to back us up.

The next morning, I wake up, jump into the shower, pull on a clean white tee shirt, grab a pair of faded jeans, pull on and lace up my sneakers, and drive over to Abby's house to pick up her brother.

He steps out of the house, walks down the driveway, pulls open the passenger door, and slides into the seat.

"What's up, man?"

"Hey, Rudy. Not much, man. What's up?"

"Ah, just chillin'. I figured we'd drive around for a bit and then go eat at that place with the good tacos."

"Alright. Yeah, sounds good, man."

I have one reason for having Abby's brother in my car right now. And it's not for small-talk and tacos, but I don't want to drop it on him right away, so we drive around San Antonio for a while. Windows rolled down, radio on, we just cruise down the city streets. We then head to the taco joint across town. I still haven't brought it up yet. I guess I'm waiting for what seems to be the right time. But I'm not sure there is a "right time" to talk about someone's girlfriend—or someone's sister—being raped by her adoptive dad. I can't even think about it without cringing with disgust and anger.

We grab a seat in the back of the restaurant. I slide into the booth that allows me to watch the door out of habit. He and I both order tacos, which we scarf down the moment the waitress brings the plates of toasted corn shells heaped with toppings. I'm still plotting the best way to enter this topic of discussion and the best time to do it.

Once we're done eating, we pay the bill, exit the restaurant, and climb back into my Mustang to drive around some more. It is finally time to broach the topic with him.

"Dude, I got something to tell you."

"What's up?"

"Your sister told me some shit about your parents—about the way they are."

"Yeah, they're strict, man. Over-protective."

"Well, *why* do you think *that* is?"

"Well, Abby got around when she was young."

"Yeah?"

"Yeah. They've been strict with her even when she was little."

"Well, what's the reason?"

"Well, she got pregnant."

"Okay, and?"

"And she's just not all *there*, man. She was in special-ed. She can't really do much. She just stays at home."

"Well, there's *probably a reason* why it's like that. It's not for *no reason*."

"I don't know."

"Look, man, Abby told me some shit the other day. That Chevo has been molesting your sister since y'all got adopted."

His face basked in pure shock, he cocks his head sideways, looking at me all clueless like a cocker spaniel being asked a question. *I really don't think that he knew about it.*

He replies, "What? No."

What a dumbass. How could he not see it? All those years? How?

Trying to keep my tone of voice steady and calm, I reply, "Chevo *not only* molested your sister. He's been *raping* your sister. And—the three kids are HIS."

"Where's the proof? I'm gonna need Abby to tell me this."

"What do you mean?"

"I'm gonna need Abby to tell me everything. The details."

"What? She's not gonna be able to tell *you* THAT. She can't even tell *me* that yet."

"Well, I need her to tell me exactly what happened."

"Dude, there's no fucking way she's gonna tell you. The only reason I'm telling you is because I'm hoping you'll help us, when I go to get her outta there."

"Well, if she doesn't tell me everything, I'm not gonna help y'all."

Resisting the strong urge to punch him in the face, I say, "Dude, THE PROOF IS THERE! Look at the kids! Look at Abby's son. He LOOKS LIKE CHEVO!"

My statement is greeted by silence. We are sitting in my car one street over from Abby's house, engaged in what quickly seems to be evolving into a discussion that is getting me—us—nowhere.

Abby's brother sits in the passenger seat facing me and animatedly gesturing with his right hand when he speaks, "I haven't seen Chevo do anything to her since I've been there."

With anger trickling through my veins and venom in my voice, I reply, "YOU'RE AN IDIOT. Do you think he DOES THOSE THINGS when YOU'RE AROUND?"

"Dude, you're getting loud with me and calling me names."

"WELL, YOU'RE PISSING ME OFF."

"If Abby isn't gonna talk to me, I'm not gonna help you."

"But if Abby leaves, something is going to pop off."

"Well, if it happens, it happens," he replies.

"Well, dude, I guess there's nothing left to talk about then."

Swallowing down my fury, I glance over at him and nod my head toward the passenger door in a gesture that tells him that he can get out of my car. Even though we're sitting a street over from Abby's house, I couldn't care less about personally delivering this dude to his front door. At this point, he can fuckin' walk.

As I pull away from the curb, two distinct thoughts consume me:

One: If he really didn't know, he's a moron.

Two: Talking to him was a major mistake on my part.

Abby is going to be so pissed when she finds out. Man, I messed up. This dude might run straight to Chevo and Laura to warn them that I'm planning to get Abby out of there. *Damn it! I shouldn't have freaking talked to him. I never should have trusted him. He's going to back them. Of course, he is.* I just watched his metamorphosis from a clueless brother to resistant listener to a passive person who would rather back his rapist, adoptive father over his abused, raped sister. He now poses a potential threat to our future plans and it's my fault.

How am I even going to try to explain this to her? "Uh, I'm sorry, babe, but I messed up today and I told your brother about your plan to escape. I told him that you were raped for all those years, that the kids are Chevo's, and he wants you to tell him all the details about it, or he's not going to help us." Yeah, that's really going to go over well. Chevo may not need to kill me—because Abby will.

One thing is for certain. With or without his help or anybody else's, I *am* going to help her escape.

RUDY

Monday—Two Days Later

Telling Abby

I roll up to Abby's at 8:30 in the morning, like usual. As I walk through the doorway to Abby's bedroom, she walks up and wraps her arms around my waist. We linger in a tight embrace for a few moments before I bend down to plant a light kiss on her forehead.

"Good morning, babe." She looks up at me and smiles.

"Good morning. I'm happy to see you."

"I'm glad to see you, too. I've got something to tell you."

"I know that you and my brother hung out the other day."

"Yeah."

"What all did y'all do?"

"We went out to eat and talked."

"Well, what did y'all talk about?"

"Well, I kind of talked to him about if he was down to help me if anything went down with the parents."

In a calm tone, Abby asks, "Rudy, what did you tell him?"

Looking her straight in the eyes, I reply, "I told him we were hanging out and I told her that Chevo was the dad of the kids—that the kids were his."

Still displaying no emotion, Abby calmly responds, "Okay . . . what did he say?"

"That he wanted proof."

"What do you mean *'proof'*?"

"He said that he wanted to know everything."

"What? What does that mean?"

"Basically, he wants the details—to know what went down. Blow-by-blow."

Abby's calm demeanor slips into a look of shock that quickly morphs to anger. Her tone drops, "He's fucking stupid, if he thinks I'm gonna just tell him everything. *Who* would ask someone to describe their rapes openly? That's why we don't talk and aren't close."

"I know. That's exactly what I told him. I ended up getting pissed off. And I wanted to hit him."

"*Why* did you tell him?"

"I told him just in case anything goes down when we get you out of here. Your brother walks around like he's all tough, and you're his sister, so I didn't see why he couldn't help."

"Well, this has been going on *for years* and he hasn't helped with shit."

"My bad, Abby. I'm just trying to do the right thing."

Abby's eyes are diverted down at one of her hands. She is picking at one of her nails. A look of concern comes across her face. Her voice is saturated with worry. "Now, *I'm* screwed. *We're* screwed. Because he might tell them."

"Abby, I was just hoping that your brother would help."

"He's a freaking coward. You better hope that they don't find out. This might mess everything up. We might not be able to see each other anymore."

"Well, you can't just *say that*. You don't know."

"Rudy, every time something good happens to me, something bad always follows and I'm stuck—again. Every time."

"Well, that's not gonna happen this time, Abby. I fucked up. Just let it run its course. That's why you should get out of this fucking house then—and *not* be stuck."

"Well, we're getting there."

"*Okay*—we're *getting there*. We shouldn't be worried too much. If your brother gets in the way, then I'll just have to handle him, too."

Abby looks emotionally shaken. We lie down on the bed, and I hold her tightly alongside me to comfort her. Because our early morning visits cut into my sleep time, I doze off. I awaken to Abby's fingers gently running through my hair. With a smile on my face, I open my eyes and glance over at her. I am met by big brown eyes and a smile. She spends the next few minutes kneading the muscles in my right hand. She knows I do a lot of repetitive movement with my hand and wrist at work to feed mailing envelopes through the machine, so my hands hurt all the time.

I know Abby is still quietly feeling the sting of our recent topic of conversation, but it seems like she is happier now. These stolen, quiet moments are the ones that I seek most. The ones I revel in and can never get enough of. Her rubbing my hands. Her running her fingers softly through my hair. Her kissing my greedy lips. Her whispering "I love you" into the space between us. The moments where just breathing the same air and slow strokes across skin set us both on fire. I live for these moments. Not just sex. But love. And I do love Abby.

ABIGAIL

Four Days Later

The Party

*T*oday is Friday. I am standing over a hot skillet frying eggs when my mom walks into the kitchen and sits down at the table. "We're going to have a party tonight, Abby—here at the house. Just a few people over." She and my dad then head out to the grocery store to buy food for the party. They return with not only a ton of food, but a piñata for the kids. They've invited my dad's brother, his wife and their two kids, the aunt of the lady who owns our house, and some people who regularly attend mass at the chapel—mostly older couples.

For everyone else, this will be a fun night.

For me, it will be an awkward one.

My contact with outside people is so limited that I always have to watch what I say to people and what I do. I have so little contact with those around me that I feel like no one really knows me. They definitely know nothing about my situation.

My parents stand guard over me—they always watch every attempted interaction, often step in to intercept, steer the conversation away from me and back to themselves, or pull me away to go perform a task that will remove me from socializing entirely.

The last one is most common. I am constantly told to "go check on the kids," "go get this or find that," or "you can cook the rice and beans." They fear the things that I may one day say—as they should.

The secrets tightly tucked within these walls would upend everything. But we don't talk about that—any of it. I do the random, requested chores. I do what I'm told. I try to avoid talking to people. I try to stay on their good side. It's all a part of the role that I've played all my life. The one that I now play in addition to being their house slave, sex slave, and the bearer of stolen children born to thieves who do not deserve them. It makes my days easier when I just go along with everything. Do I resent them? Yes. Would I ever tell one of their "friends" about what goes on here? No. If I did—we would all go to jail.

So, I remain quiet Abby. Shy Abby. Abby who doesn't talk to anyone. Abby who does what she is told. Abby who is here, physically— barely—but never really allowed to own her own presence in a room. Trapped Abby. That's who I am most of all. And the person I have been all my life. Trapped within these walls. Trapped within their mentally unhinged ways.

I watch my dad, who stands over the hot grill wearing his usual outfit: a pair of dirty jeans and a never-quite-white tank top, while occasionally turning pieces of half-cooked chicken, long smoked sausages, and the sliced onions and peppers for fajitas. He smiles and laughs in conversation with an older Hispanic man who is a church member.

When the meat is finally cooked, we sit at the tables and folding chairs that my mom and I set up in the back yard. Music blares through an old radio—everything from Tejano music to country songs and rock anthems. The kids eat their food, then pile cake and ice cream onto paper plates. Each of them excitedly takes a turn thwacking the piñata until it finally busts and the candy spills onto the ground for the children to scoop into their eager hands.

It's getting dark and everyone has eaten their fill, so things are winding down. Once everybody leaves, my mom and I clean everything up. What I hate most about these impromptu gatherings, aside from the awkward social interactions, is the clean-up for parties I didn't even want to have.

We fold up all the chairs and carry the tables back into the chapel. The yard is littered with pieces of forgotten candy, which I stoop down to pick up one by one. We then head inside to wash dishes, clean up the kitchen, then I bathe the kids—my kids—and put them to bed. It was fun seeing them play outside today and striking the piñata to get to the candy. I did enjoy that part of the day.

I am in my room pulling my nightgown over my head and down my body, when my mom and dad walk in. My mom says, "We need to talk, Abby."

"Okay. About what?"

"Our little boy is gonna need a brother or a sister, so we are gonna need to start trying for one."

"No. I'm not—I don't want to."

With a glare, she replies, "Well, YOU DON'T HAVE NO CHOICE, Abby."

Looking satisfied with the conversation—as I sit fully eviscerated by it—they exit my bedroom.

No way. No freaking way. No way am I going to have another baby. I'm not doing it. It's not happening. They are crazy. Why can't they just be happy with what they have? Nothing is ever enough.

Tears stain my cheeks as I plot my demise. The only way out is to kill myself. That's the only way I will ever truly break free of this—break free from them. But I do have Rudy now. Rudy said he will help get me out of here. How am I going to tell Rudy about this though? This is too much. No way is he going to want to deal with this craziness.

I spend every waking moment, and every attempted sleeping one, looking over my shoulder. Watching. Waiting. Wondering and worrying when they will try to force their sick plan upon me. I don't have to wait long . . .

ABIGAIL

Saturday

The Next Day

O n Saturday night, once the kids are put to bed, my mom says, "It's time for our baths, Abby." My stomach lurches, my breath hitches, and suddenly, I feel sick. I know where this is headed. It's been a long time, but I know the predicable routine.

The baths lead to massages. And the massages lead to other things—despicable things—in their bedroom. Things that I don't want to do ever again. Things my mom believes only happen whenever she is around. Things that have happened in her presence, as well as in her absence, ever since I was a little girl. Things in the SpongeBob bedroom. Things at the kitchen sink. Things that turned me inside out. Things that undid me. Things that she didn't want to know about. Things she pretended to never believe. Things she used to deny happened. Things that *she now does*. The fondling, the touching, the licking, the pressing into me, the large brown eyes filled with evil and marred by lust.

After the baths, the full-body massages, and the foot rubs, the sex begins. In these vile, disgusting moments of skin touching skin, and parts touching other parts, I go numb. I go anywhere other than this room, with them. I am on the beach in Florida. It's a sunny, beautiful day. Sitting on my beach towel, I squish the sand between my toes. Rudy is sitting next to me. He leans over and kisses me passionately.

I am with Rudy.

I am not with them.

Please let this be over soon. Please just let's get this over with. These thoughts remind me that I'm not with Rudy. I am being raped by my dad while my mom looks on, with her hand between her legs, pleasuring herself while cupping my right breast with a guttural groan before her body begins to tremble.

Please just let this be over. Please just hurry up. Chevo thrusts into me over and over again. *Please get this over with. Please hurry up and be done. Just let it be over.* It is not Rudy's body slamming into me. It is Chevo's. *Please hurry. Please finish. Please be done.*

With a few hard thrusts of his hips, his sweaty body finally collapses on top of me as he groans while planting his seed deep inside my body. MY BODY. The whiff of stale beer breath assaults my nostrils. My entire body cringes in revolt. He rolls his sweaty body off of me and I am finally able to stand up, pull my nightgown back on, and flee what just happened to me. I head straight to the bathroom, put the shower on and wait for the water to get hot, then abrasively rub my skin with a washrag in an attempt to scrub him out—both literally and figuratively.

I do not want to have his baby. I will not have his baby. I do not want him to touch me ever again. I am going to get the hell out of here. There will be no more of this.

I am smeared in truth, and shame, and all the things currently left unsaid between me and Rudy. I have no idea how I am going to tell Rudy that I betrayed him—with them. This is betrayal. I cheated on him, even though I didn't want to. How am I going to explain that this happened? He obviously knows the kids are my dad's and that this used to happen to me all the time, but he didn't think it was going to happen again.

Rudy is going to flip out. I just hope that he doesn't leave me. I hope that he understands that I didn't want this to happen. I have *never* wanted this to happen. I love him. I just hope that he makes good on his promise to help me escape with the kids and that he still wants to be with me.

I am done. This is my body—my life—my kids. And it is time for me to take back what is rightfully mine. My body. My kids. My life.

They. Are. Mine.

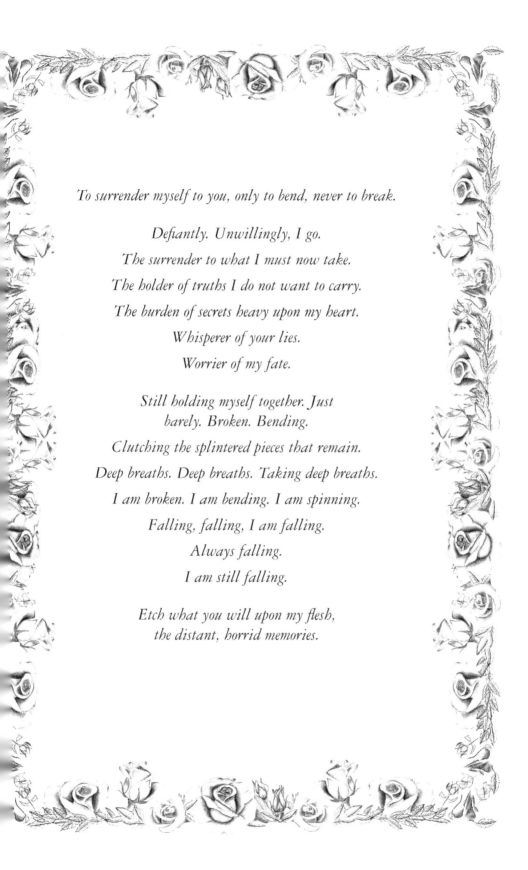

To surrender myself to you, only to bend, never to break.

Defiantly. Unwillingly, I go.
The surrender to what I must now take.
The holder of truths I do not want to carry.
The burden of secrets heavy upon my heart.
Whisperer of your lies.
Worrier of my fate.

Still holding myself together. Just
barely. Broken. Bending.
Clutching the splintered pieces that remain.
Deep breaths. Deep breaths. Taking deep breaths.
I am broken. I am bending. I am spinning.
Falling, falling, I am falling.
Always falling.
I am still falling.

Etch what you will upon my flesh,
the distant, horrid memories.

*Mar it into my bones, your stamp
of horrors inked across me.*

Pain. Sorrow. Trapped. I am trapped.

*I will blink. Expelling breaths of broken
sorrow, innocence stripped bare,*

and pulled away from me. Pulled away.

*Limbs shaking. Heart flailing. As I spiral
down, down, down. Into the darkness, I go.*

*Choking back sorrow. Swallowing my own tears.
The pieces of my soul, forever rearranged.*

I will bend. I will break.

You will twist me.

My heart, mind, body, soul.

*My innocent spirit will shift into the
darkness you deliver to me.*

But—you will never define me.

—JAMIE COLLINS
(For Abigail)

ABIGAIL

Number Four

ast forward a few weeks, and I wake up still feeling exhausted even though I slept, with sore breasts, and a wave of nausea overwhelming me. I know that I am pregnant. Again. Only this time, I don't know whether the baby is Rudy's or my dad's. *Oh My God.* While I haven't told Rudy that my dad got to me again—that he raped me—he did, and it is possible that this baby is *his.*

My mom walks into my bedroom to see why I'm not up yet to prepare breakfast for the kids. I tell her my suspicion and she replies, "Well, let's get you into the doctor today then, for a pregnancy test." I can't argue about that. I need to know. Unfortunately, the information that I *really* need to know isn't going to be revealed to me with a pregnancy test—I need a DNA test.

I climb out of bed, pull on shorts and a pale pink tee shirt, and head to the kitchen to make sure the kids get something to eat, even if it is just cereal and toast. My mom and I then hop into the car and she drives us to the doctor's office. I feel more nervous this time than I have all the other times in the past, probably because Rudy is involved now. I am going to have to tell him about this. I wonder if he will be happy or freaked out? I am freaked out to realize that this baby may not be his. I have no idea how I am going to tell him that.

I walk into the doctor's office. I put on the crinkly gown and lay the thin sheet of paper across my lap to shield myself. At this point, I have already peed in a cup and handed it to the medical assistant, as prompted. *I am going to have to tell Rudy that this could be my dad's baby. He needs to know that.*

The doctor interrupts my thoughts, "Well, we ran a pregnancy test, and it was positive. You are pregnant!" My heart lunges in my chest. For once, my mom doesn't appear excited or happy to hear this news. She replies, "Okay. Abby, you go ahead and get dressed and I'll go outside to talk to the doctor for a minute." Basked in numbness, I softly reply, "Okay."

I spend the rest of the day consumed by thoughts of a pregnancy that I have no idea how to explain to Rudy. Why did this have to happen right now? We should have been more careful. But I guess even if we had been, I still could have gotten pregnant by my dad, so I guess that wouldn't have mattered.

Later in the evening, I'm in my room lying on my bed, when my mom walks up to me and, holding out her hand, says to me, "Here are some vitamins that the doctor gave me earlier to give to you, Abby. Take them." Holding the white pills in my hand, I pop them into my mouth, pick up my glass of water sitting nearby and swallow them down.

The next morning, I wake up with damp panties, go to the bathroom, and realize that I am bleeding, down there. I must be having a miscarriage. Consumed by a mix of emotions, I comfort myself with the thought that God didn't feel it was time for this baby to come into the world. Not the right time or place, and under such completely messed up circumstances.

My mom does not appear shocked when she learns that I lost the baby. Why? I do not know. She has never acted like this before. She has always been excited at the thought of another baby. After all, she wanted another baby.

I wonder what those pills that she had me take were? I thought it was medicine from the doctor to help me, but now, I'm not so sure.

I do end up telling Rudy about the pregnancy. I also tell him about the doctor's appointment, how my mom gave me some pills to take, and that I lost the baby.

What I do not tell Rudy is that the baby could have been my dad's. I just can't own that yet.

RUDY

Tuesday
Three Days Later

I didn't get to see Abby at all last week. We exchanged the occasional good morning or good night text, but that's about it aside from one call, where we didn't really talk about much of anything. How am I? How is she? What did we each do that day? We love each other. We miss each other. We'll talk later. That was about it.

Her parents seem to be keeping her occupied doing family things to prevent her from seeing me on the weekends. They still don't know anything about the frequency and duration of my private house visits—and they don't need to.

I hop into my Mustang to drive the 12-mile stretch of road to Abby's house. When I pull the door open and walk into her bedroom, she's lying on the bed, which isn't typical. Normally, she gets up to greet me with a hug and a kiss. *Something is off.*

I bend down to place a soft kiss on her left cheek. "Hi babe."

"Hey, Rudy."

"How are you? Is everything okay?"

She softly states, "Yeah. I'm fine." *But the timbre of her voice and words don't match up.*

"Abby—Hey, what's wrong?"

She stares at me with a gut-wrenching sadness that pierces me to the core. She doesn't speak. I feel tension in the room. She seems scared. It's as though she has something to tell me, but is hesitant to say it.

In a soft, calm tone, I say, "Abby. What's wrong, babe? Did something happen?"

Her reply comes in the form of a clipped whisper, "He got me."

What fills the room but remains unspoken is Abby's shame and defeat. It's standing in the room alongside us. I feel it.

Still calm, I reply, "What do you mean he got you?"

Abby extends both arms outward in the form of a cross, like she's trying to show me something.

I see bruises on both of her arms, near her elbows. The types of bruises that a person would likely have from being held down. *Oh hell no.*

"They beat you up?"

"No."

"So, what are the bruises from then?"

There is no verbal reply. Only sullen confirmation in the form of Abby's eyes diverting downward. One lone tear rolls down her left cheek before tracing its way down her chin and onto her neck. I attempt to tamp down my anger.

I watch as Abby unties her robe and opens it up to expose her nightgown, which she pulls down below her breasts. This moment is a confirmation of evil acts. There are five dark purple marks across the front of Abby's breasts.

"Are those bruises?"

"No."

"They're hickeys?"

"Yes."

"So, what the fuck happened?"

"He raped me."

"Him and Laura?"

"No, just him."

"Where was Laura?"

"Asleep."

I'm not sure what to believe at this point. Adrenaline courses through me. My vision blurs. I'm still trying to hold it together, because I know what Abby just admitted to me was major for her. That said, it's taking every ounce of my willpower to remain even half-way calm.

"I'm fed up with this shit, babe. We are gonna end this now," I say, while grabbing my phone out of my pocket.

"What are you doing?"

"I'm gonna call the cops."

"No. no. no."

"When did this happen? Last night?"

"No, over the weekend."

"We're gonna end it now. This is bullshit, Abby. It's not right."

"Well, what about the kids?"

"Let's just go. Let's get out of here."

"No. We can't. He's been passing by the house during the day. Checking up on me."

"I don't fucking care."

"No, Rudy—you don't know him. He's dangerous."

"Well, he doesn't know ME. He's a piece of shit." *Preying on her. Taking advantage of her because she is scared shitless. If he was gonna do something, he would have already done it.*

"Abby, there's no way a job would just let him leave to come drive by here all the time. He's just telling you that to scare you and make you think he's watching you. There's no way he's doing that."

My comment is met with silence.

"Abby, we've got to do something now." As those words fly from my mouth, I see that Abby is shutting down. She looks annoyed with me. My beautiful girlfriend sits before me on the bed, beaten, battered, and scared. *What do I have to do or say to get her out of here?*

I know this moment is not the one where I will convince her to leave. That said, I need her to realize how serious of a situation this is. I can't keep dealing with this—with knowing he is hurting her and not doing anything about it.

"Okay. I can see that you don't feel like you're ready to leave yet. If you change your mind—I'm here, okay? Anytime. All you have to do is say the word, babe, and I'll get you and the kids out. Period. There's nothing that Laura and Chevo can do about it."

"I know. I love you, babe. I do want to leave here. I really do. There's just a lot of stuff we have to figure out first."

I drop a gentle kiss on her right temple. "Babe, I've got to head to work now. It's time for me to go. But you check in with me later. I want to know that you're safe."

"Okay. I will. I love you."

"I love you, too, babe. So much. If anything happens, you call me. You've got your phone—you call me."

I walk my rage down the driveway and shove it into the driver's seat of my Mustang. I shift the car into drive and speed away from Abby's house with my anger consuming me at the edges as it smolders its way deeper inside.

All of this is pointless. I have accomplished *nothing* by waiting. I can't stand knowing that the woman I love got raped. Even *I* don't leave hickeys on her boobs. And here is Chevo—her adoptive dad—claiming her.

Me and my rage fly down the road toward work. I pull into a parking spot outside the building, where I remain in the driver's seat with the radio blaring for a few more minutes because I need to calm the hell down. I have no idea how that's even possible. Nothing about me is going to be calm right now, but there's no way I can walk into work this amped up.

My mom always used to say, "Mijo, you walk your anger." I'm most definitely walking it today. I'm not an angry person by nature, but this is just too much. I feel the street side of me returning. The side of me that used to get knocked down in a circle of gang members five times and would get up six.

How am I just supposed to stand by and allow this to happen to the woman I love? Why can't I convince her to get the hell out of there? What's it gonna take? Does she need to almost die before she'll leave? Does something need to happen to one of the kids before she'll get out? Really, what's it going to take?

I could call the cops, but I know that it would be her word against his. No doubt Laura and Chevo are smooth talkers—more like liars—to get away with all the messed-up shit that they do. I also don't want to do anything that would piss Abby off by going to the cops behind her back or we won't end up together. I really do want us to be together. I want her to be free of them.

I walk my barely quelled rage into work. We load postage machines and run envelopes through the slot at record speed. My body feels like it's buzzing with energy. The activity of feeding envelopes through the machine feels slightly therapeutic. The rage-induced adrenaline is making me a highly productive employee in the mail room.

Rock music blares through my earbuds. Envelopes fly into bins. The buzz of aimless energy remains. Alone with my own thoughts. Alone with my anger. Alone with my mind spinning in a thousand revolving patterns, all of which inevitably return to one central point: I need to get Abby the hell out of there. And soon. I don't have much patience left for this. I will *not* allow the woman I love to be raped by a psychopath. It can't happen again. And I need to make sure that it won't.

I just need to figure out how to convince Abby to leave.

ABIGAIL

A Saturday in June

One Week Later

I walk through each day in the week after the group rape by my
parents like the hollowed-out shell of a person. My life is not
my own. My body is not my own. All I do is exist within the walls
of this house, care for *my* stolen children, and answer to the beck and
call of two demented people. I just couldn't bring myself to tell Rudy
the full truth. Owning up to being raped by Chevo was bad enough.
Rudy would have flipped out if he knew my mom was also involved.

I don't have to wait long before it becomes clear when the next
attack on me will be, when I hear my mom call out, "I'm gonna go
lay down. I just took a Benadryl. My allergies are killing me today.
I'm not feeling well. Abby—come and rub my back."

In a normal household, her words would simply put others
on notice that she isn't feeling well and wants a massage from her
daughter as a favor to help her relax.

In this house, what it means is that I am probably going to get raped
tonight—by my dad. As soon as he thinks my mom is in a medicine
induced slumber, he will pounce. And I will attempt to defend.

Defeated, I get up from the couch and walk into my mom's
bedroom. My mom is lying on her stomach on the bed, naked and
ready for a rub down. My dad is lying beside her guzzling long

gulps of beer from a bottle. He's been drinking all day today, so he's undoubtedly drunk right now. As I enter the bedroom, he looks at me with a sadistic sneer on his face—one that leaves no doubt as to what it is he has in his sights. He takes another long pull from his beer and glances back at the TV.

I walk over to the bed, pick the bottle of lotion up off the nightstand and squirt a few pumps of lotion into my right hand. I rub my hands together to spread it into an even layer, then I begin rubbing my mom's back. The physical act of doing this is bad enough. I'm tired of doing it for them. I'm sick of them expecting me to. She moans as I gently rub my fingers across the middle of her back in a circular kneading motion.

Tonight, it's not so much the massaging that's killing me, it is the thought perched in my mind about what happens next. *She took a Benadryl. It's going to knock her out. I am going to be alone in the house— with him. He is going to try to attack me. For sure, he will. And I may not be able to stop it. I have to try to stop it though. I have to fight.*

The really messed up part is knowing that if my mom knew about my dad's sexually abusive plotting, it would upset her not because my dad wants to force himself inside of me, but because she would be jealous of him having sex with me alone, without her. How messed up is that? *How in the hell did I end up here? How are they this messed up in the head? How is this my life?* After about an hour of massaging my mom's back, neck, arms, and legs, she is almost asleep. She is relaxed and I am on edge. My attacker lurks in this house like a predator ready to pounce on its prey. Only in this house, it's a father getting ready to pounce on his adult daughter—me.

Not even an hour later, that's precisely what happens.

I am in my bedroom, alone, lying on my bed in my usual sleeping attire consisting of shorts, a sports bra, and a tee shirt. I prefer to wear shorts that have a drawstring to bed because they are harder to pull down and present more of a challenge for my attacker. I know he's going to be here soon. I'm surprised he's waited this long. I pull my blanket around me and clutch it tightly. I stare at the doorway. There is a beam of light spilling through the crack in the doorway.

I think I heard something. What was that? Maybe it was nothing. But maybe, it was him.

A moment later, he is standing in the doorway wearing nothing but a pair of boxers. I feel so vulnerable. There is no way for me to protect myself. But I'm still going to try. I have to.

He walks up beside my bed and lays down beside me. I attempt to push him, but he wraps his hands tightly around my wrists like a vise grip. This is what he always does to gain control over me. He then grabs at the top of my shorts and tugs them down. I am now pinned beneath his weight. His beer breath covers me first, followed by his body. "No."

"No?" he sneers.

"No. Stop. Don't. Please stop."

It isn't just me that I'm fighting for in this moment. It is my loyalty. It is me fighting against the betrayal of Rudy. But I can't stop it. He's too strong.

He says nothing and pounds into my flesh as he digs his fingers deeper into my wrists. His breath smells pungent. I am wiggling. It does not matter. He does not stop pounding into me. He never stops.

He is pummeling into me over and over again. I try to wrestle myself free of him, but I know that it's no use. I can't. The more I struggle to break free, the harder he rapes me as a form of punishment.

He is pounding into me. Over and over again. He is raping me. Tears stream down both sides of my cheeks. Unable to handle being consumed by him, I do what I always do. I pretend that I'm not here, in this room, with my abuser. I deny his physical presence and I deny my own.

I am at the beach. It's a sunny day. It's so beautiful out. Seagulls swoop down to pick up scraps of chips left by people on the sand. Kids are building a sandcastle and the waves keep washing over it, eroding it. Rudy is here. He is with me. It is Rudy that I'm with right now. It is Rudy. I love Rudy.

It has to be over soon. He has to be almost done. *Please just let him be done.*

With another few pumps into me, my dad releases himself into me before his shoulders drop down onto me and he shudders with a slight groan. He then pulls his boxers back up and walks out of my bedroom without glancing back. His departure marks his victory—and my defeat. This feels worse than any other time, like it is the ultimate betrayal of Rudy. This time was different for me in that way. It's not like this hasn't happened to me a thousand times, but this time was the worst. It shattered pieces of my soul that I may never be able to piece back together.

Unmoving from my spot on the bed, I roll onto my side. I tuck the blanket around me tightly, and I sob. For hours, I weep, held only by the darkness—the blackness that fills my room, as well as the darkness that sits heavy on my heart.

The next morning, sunlight pours through the window, filling my bedroom with warm light. I feel nothing but darkness, emptiness, and a longing for death because it would end my suffering. But I can only lie in bed and chase away dark thoughts for so long because I am a mom. I have three kids to care for. They depend on me. They are all that matters, aside from Rudy, whom I have unwillingly betrayed.

I hate my dad. I loathe his existence. I hate every single thing about him. As for my mom, I hate her, too. I hate her for allowing this to happen to me my entire life. I hate her for choosing not to believe me when this first started. I hate her for becoming a predator right along with him.

I finally manage to pull myself out of the warmth of my covers to head to the kitchen. Pulling out a skillet, I begin dicing potatoes to fry them. I crack eggs into a plastic bowl and whisk them to make scrambled eggs to fill breakfast tacos for the kids. *My kids. The only reason I am still alive.* Since it is summer, the children sleep in a little longer than they do on school days. My clueless mom and my rapist father eat a quick breakfast then head out of the house to work. My mom must be feeling good enough to work today or at least good enough to realize that she needs to work, so she can help pay the bills. I assemble breakfast tacos onto plates and set them on the table in front of my kids.

My phone starts blowing up with missed calls and missed texts. I do not care. I watch my children as they eat and ignore the pinging. Each missed incoming text and call is from my dad. Fury emanates from each text.

"You bitch."

"You fucking ho."

"You better answer your fucking phone, Abby. I'm not fucking around."

I fucking hate him. I'm done. I'm not doing this anymore.

Ping. Ping. Ping. Each text or voicemail is more of the same. He is literally calling every few minutes to the point it's unusual if my phone isn't pinging.

"If you don't answer your phone, you're going to get it tonight."

"I'm worried. Where are you?"

"You're nothing but a stupid bitch."

"You fucking whore! Answer your damn phone."

"You are good for nothing. You stupid ho. You better pick up this phone right now or you're gonna get it."

"Don't make me drive back home to show you who is in charge, you stupid bitch."

I ignore all of them.

Ping. Ping. Ping. One text or voicemail after the next.

I honestly don't care anymore. I can't go on like this. I'm not going to answer.

When I finally push the stroller through the entryway of the house, I call Rudy from the secret phone that he bought for me.

"Hi babe."

"Hey, Abby. How are you today?"

"I'm okay." *That's somewhat of a lie, but I'm not sure what else to say.*

Ping. Ping. Ping.
Ping. Ping. Ping.

"Abby—what is that?"

"What? That sound?"

"Yeah, the beeping. Is that your other phone?"

"Yes—it is."

"Who is it? It's him, isn't it?"

"Yep, it is him."

Ping. Ping. Ping. Ping. Ping. I didn't think it was possible, but he's now sending the texts even more rapid fire. *Ping. Ping. Ping. Ping.*

"Oh my God, Abby. What the hell is going on? "WHY is he blowing up your phone?"

"I need you to come get me."

"Babe—you know I'm already at work. I can't come right now. Why didn't you say something earlier, before I got here, if you wanted to leave? You know I'd come get you."

"I wasn't ready then. I'm ready now. I want to leave."

"I'll have my mom come get you and the kids. Give me a few minutes."

"Okay. Thank you. I love you."

"I love you, too, babe. She'll be pulling up to your house soon, okay? Be on the lookout for her."

Ping. Ping. Ping.

"Okay. I will be. I love you. Bye."

"Bye, Abby."

ABIGAIL

The Escape

*H*itting the button on my lime green phone to end the call, I immediately head down the hall to my bedroom to grab a small duffel bag and some trash bags. I grab three outfits to pack for myself, then I head to the kids' rooms to pull items from their closets to pack three outfits for each of them. I also grab a toy for each of them. "Kids, we are gonna go on a vacation! We're gonna have a slumber party with my friend and her son."

"We are? Oh, okay! That sounds fun, Abby!" is the response of my eldest daughter.

"My friend will be here to pick us up soon, kids. We're gonna leave as soon as she pulls up."

I tuck my lime green phone into the front pocket of my jeans. I toss the other one onto my bed because I won't be needing it anymore. I don't want them to be able to reach me or to use it to try to track me down. Standing beside the doorway in my bedroom, I keep glancing out the window hoping that Rudy's mom will pull up any minute. *Please let her get here soon. Please let her get here soon. Please just let us get out of here without any problems. Please just let us get out here.*

Rudy doesn't know what we are dealing with when it comes to my dad. I do. He is an evil, cruel, violent person. He will try to track us down. He could try to hurt us. He may even kill us. Rudy is oblivious to all of this, but I am not. My rapist father poses a threat that is formidable and real.

Finally, I see Rudy's mom pull up out front of our house in her small, white, four-door Ford Focus. She immediately gets out of her car, slams the door behind her, and runs up the driveway and across the yard to the bedroom doorway where I am standing, "Let's go, Mija. Are you ready? Let's go! Let's go!"

"I don't know if I have everything."

"It's fine. We will get you whatever you need. It's going to be fine. We have to go. We have to go right now. Let's go."

"Okay. Help me get the kids to the car."

Rudy's mom—with an air of much-needed authority and confidence—leads us down the driveway to her parked car with me and my kids in tow behind her. I look around to see if my dad is driving by or in the area watching us. I don't think he is. We pile the kids into the back seat of her car, secure their seatbelts across them, then I strap my son—a toddler—into his car seat. *No one is here to see us or stop us. Thank God.* With each mile of distance Rudy's mom places between us and my former house, I feel a surge of strong emotion. I feel nervous to be leaving, but for the first time, I also feel free. I am finally gone from the parents who rape me, betray me, and treat me like I am nothing.

Rudy's mom pulls up outside her white ranch style house and leads us up to it, holding the door open to allow us to step inside. Her daughter—Rudy's younger sister—is here. I know that she is aware of my situation, so I feel safe to be around her. The living room has white walls. There is a long black couch, black end tables, and a small black TV stand holding a fairly large television. A small computer desk is off to the side with lots of video games on top of it. There are beautiful, framed pictures of various saints embellishing the walls throughout her home and lots of candles—the tall cylinder kind that are encased in glass; the ones that Mexican Catholic people light when they pray to the saints and the Father. It looks like the typical Hispanic home. It has a lived in, cozy feel to it.

Rudy's mom shuts the door behind us, turns the deadbolt to lock it, and walks us further into the entry way to lead us toward the living room. Pointing us in the direction of the black couch, she says, "Y'all make yourselves at home. Keep the door locked. Don't answer the door for nobody. I don't care *who it is*. Don't go outside *for anything*. Y'all need to stay inside—where you'll be safe."

"Okay. We will. Thank you so much for coming to get us."

"It was no trouble at all. I'm just glad y'all finally got out of there. I've got to head back to work now. Make sure you stay away from the doors and windows, Abby."

"I will. Thanks again. I hope you have a good day at work."

Sitting on the couch with my beautiful children on each side of me, I catch a look of uncertainty on my eldest daughter's face. She isn't sure what's going on, that much is clear. At nine, she is old enough to piece together the bits of our conversations, the words of concern and my underlying fear to understand that something has happened.

Looking me in the eyes, she says, "What's going on, Abby? I'm scared." Turning toward her with that same air of calm authority that Rudy's mom exuded earlier, I tuck a loose strand of hair behind her ear. "It's okay. We're just on vacation, kids. Just like I said back at the house. We're just going to stay here tonight, at my friend's house, for the slumber party."

My youngest daughter, who is six and my little boy, age three, are easily convinced. My eldest seems slightly unsure as to whether she believes me, but she seems to buy the cover story enough, at least for now. The kids all start to talk and play in the living room. Cartoons are playing on the TV, which helps to distract them. Over the next several hours, my two youngest kids seem to intermittently take turns telling me, "I have to go potty!" So, I lead them to the bathroom in this house where they, like me, probably feel like they don't belong. It feels awkward every time we go to use the bathroom, like we are invading their private space because we must walk through one of their bedrooms to get to the bathrooms.

I feel safe around Rudy's sister, but I felt more protected when Rudy's mom was here. She's a take-charge, no-nonsense type of lady.

A strong Hispanic woman. She knows how to step in and get things done. Even in the short time I've known her, she feels like someone I can count on. I've never really had anybody like that in my life—someone who cared about me or wanted to do something nice for me—aside from Rudy. I guess maybe that's where he gets it from. I can't really count anything nice that my parents did for me because there was always some dark, ugly act waiting around the corner.

Their two-bedroom house is small, but clean, and it is well-kept. I have no idea how we're all supposed to stay here because there is so little space for us. Much like the kids, I occasionally glance over at Rudy's sister to ask, "Is it okay if I grab a drink?", "Is it okay if I go to the restroom?"

Chucking slightly, Rudy's sister quips, "Abby, it's okay—you don't have to ask me every time you want a drink or need to use the bathroom. You can just go. You live here now."

"Oh, okay. Thanks." *I wonder if she thinks I'm weird for asking. It just didn't feel right not to.* I feel out of place, especially without Rudy here.

While I am really grateful that Rudy's mom came to get us and that she is allowing us to stay here, I can't help but feel like *I* don't belong here—like *we* don't belong here. Like we are going be a huge burden on Rudy's mom because I don't have any way to support us or provide anything for us. I have no money at all for food, drinks, rent, or anything else. It's not because she has said anything to make me feel that way, it's just that the reality of me being unable to provide for us is a fact.

We are a burden, at least for now. I can provide nothing for us. One prominent thought clouds over my anxiety-filled thoughts. *I'm gonna owe these people—big time.* I don't even know where we are going to sleep tonight. There really is nowhere for us to sleep. There are only two bedrooms—their bedrooms—and one couch. When Rudy gets home from work tonight, hopefully, he'll help me figure things out.

I feel lost. I have no home. No car. No job. No money. No means of getting anything. I have nothing.

Still, today . . . I do have my freedom. Our freedom.

And this new, tangible freedom gives me the ability to make my own choices and to live my own life the way I want to live it. I'll just have to figure the big stuff out in time.

I sure hope Rudy doesn't change his mind about all of this when he gets home and sees all of us here, overcrowding their house. He already has two girls to take care of. How is he going to be able to take care of three more kids, plus me?

RUDY

Hell Yeah

I’ve never been more excited to leave a shift at work than I am tonight. I can’t believe Abby finally did it—she left! It makes me happy that she finally had the courage to leave there, but I’m sure she’s freaking out. I need to hurry up and get home, so I can reassure her that everything is going to be okay.

With a huge smile on my face, I impatiently sit through red lights, swear at yellow lights, and fly through green lights, until I finally make it home. Walking through the front door of our house, I make a beeline straight to Abby, who is sitting on the couch. She immediately stands up to greet me. I wrap my arms around her and pull her in to hold her close to me. We both cling to one another for a moment. I place a soft kiss on her left temple, followed by a gentle kiss on her lips. I’ve never felt happier to have Abby in my arms and to know that she is here, with us—that she is now safe.

“Hey, how are you, Abby?

“I’m good. Did you have a good day at work?”

“Yeah, I did. I couldn’t wait to get home to see you though.”

“Where are we going to sleep tonight?”

“With me—in my room.”

“Oh, okay. I’m glad we get to be together now.”

“I know. I am, too. I love having you here, living with me.”

I can sense how glad Abby is to see me when I get home from work each night. I know that my presence brings her comfort. It brings me comfort knowing that she can no longer be abused or hurt by them, that she is finally free. Even if Abby doesn't want to be in a relationship with me, I want her to be free to live her life on her own terms, to be happy. But it would kill me if she didn't want us to be together. I'm so in love with her that the thought of not being with her guts me. Either way, she deserves to have a good life, to make her own choices and live her life freely, whether that is with or without me. But I do hope that it's with me.

When the house is quiet at night, my thoughts often drift to the financial side of our current predicament. I am now going to have to take care of all of us: me, her, my two girls, and her three kids. Truth be told, I want to, but I know that it's not going to be easy. When Abby moved in with us, she brought with her just three trash bags full of clothes, mostly for her three kids. She left Laura and Chevo's with almost nothing for herself beyond the clothes on her back. It is on me to ensure that Abby and the kids have what they need to get by. The kids are going to be going to school here now. They're gonna need some new clothes, all of their school supplies, and new backpacks. It's a lot.

Lying beside Abby, I tell her, "This isn't going to be easy, you know. I don't even make 50 grand a year, Abby, but I know how to manage money right. I'm not a doctor or a surgeon or something. It's gonna be hard, but we can do it. We need to stick to the basics—just what we need. But I'll take care of us—all of us."

"I know it won't be easy. I know I can't really help out with that, since I don't have a job. We can do whatever we need to do to make it work. I love you and I want us to be together—for us all to be a family."

"I want that, too, babe."

"I love you."

"I love you, too, Abby."

In reality, this means that if we have to go to the store to buy soap, detergent, and some personal care items we need, we have to be really tight with money until my next bi-monthly paycheck. The financial struggles are going to be real, but I am so happy to have a good woman in my life, who is a good mom, that the financial piece feels secondary and seems tolerable. My girls now have another positive role model and more kids to play with. Abby and I can give *all* our kids the happy family life that we never had. And that thought right there makes the struggle part 100% worth it, necessary, even.

I am also excited to finally have a son! I get to be a true father to Abby's kids now. All they have ever known as a father was Chevo, and that guy's a piece of shit. I'm thrilled to take them in as my own. I work with some guys who know about me and Abby's situation and they've made comments like, "Man, I would just hit it and leave her," or, "Dude, you're just gonna take on three more kids like that? That's crazy." But what they don't understand is that I love Abby and we are going to be together. We are building a real family.

What we have between us is deep and real. I love her kids. They are not a burden. As a matter of fact, these kids are gonna help me to stay on my feet as a man. So, if we gotta eat ramen noodles, hot dogs, rice and beans, and sandwiches until we make it to payday, so be it. It's not like the kids care. They actually like the stuff. As for Abby and I, we can get by okay. We are gonna take care of our family. We will stretch things thin when we need to, so we can make this work.

One thing that does get a little odd is us all still living in my mom's house with my mom, my sister, and her son. My mom is cool and doesn't have an issue with it, but Abby and I would obviously like to live on our own at some point. My mom and my sister spend most of their time in their bedrooms on one side of the house, and Abby, the kids and I spend our time on the other side, in the living room and dining room that we've converted into makeshift bedrooms. With this many kids, you do what you gotta do to make the space work.

Abby doesn't seem to feel sure of where she fits in here, but she does seem pretty happy overall. I know that she'll be happier once we get our own place, but it is clear that she is grateful to my mom for all that she has done for her, and everything that she continues to do for all of us.

Ever since Abby got out, I've noticed that certain things seem to trigger her. She lives in a constant state of fear that Chevo and Laura will find her and hurt her and the kids. Even when Abby thinks that she's doing a good job of hiding that fear, I still see it. I know that it runs deep for her. At this point, it's almost instinct.

She stares at the doorway when a room is dark as though she is waiting for someone to appear. Anytime we are out driving, her eyes scan every passing car to make sure it isn't them. I see the flickers of panic and relief. She constantly glances in the rear-view mirrors of my car to watch the vehicles behind us. I miss none of these things. Her eyes scanning. Her face dropping. Her walking around on eggshells. Her worry and fear live in the house alongside us and have become palpable to me. I've also noticed that Abby can be really hard on herself if she makes a simple and honest mistake, or when she feels like she isn't doing enough around the house. I can tell that Chevo and Laura really did a mental job on her to make her this way. It's almost like she's been programmed by the abuse.

One morning, Abby's youngest son came into our room and softly bumped into the side of the bed and Abby immediately flew up out of the bed and up onto her feet, wide-eyed, fueled on terror and adrenaline. The simple bump of her little boy into the mattress immediately transported her mind back to that dark place and terrible time when she was raped. It's not easy to spot all of the fallout from a situation like hers, but day-by-day, I notice the little signs of self-doubt, lack of confidence, trying to always please people, and constantly asking permission to do any little thing.

It's as though she is now physically wired differently due to their brainwashing, manipulation, physical harm, stalking, and the way that they constantly made her believe that she was nothing. There are also times when she picks a fight or tries to push me to see if she can get me to abandon her. I never will. I know a lot of the things she now deals with are probably due to the mental and emotional duress Chevo and Laura caused.

I'm just happy that she got out. We can work together to get through all of the bits and pieces of pain that she has to unpack. I'll do everything in my power to not only protect her, but to help her move forward in life, learn to make her own decisions, find a way to one day heal, and to one day see herself as the incredibly beautiful, strong, fierce, kind, compassionate, and capable woman that she *is*.

ABIGAIL

Freedom

*L*ying in Rudy's bed, in Rudy's bedroom, with Rudy's body cuddling mine, I feel at peace. For one of the first times in my life, I feel genuinely happy, because I know that I am here, lying next to him, by my own choice. If it wasn't for Rudy, I'd still be in that house, being abused by them, being raped by him—by them. I shake the thought out of my mind and focus on the warmth that surrounds me. The protection that Rudy's presence next to me provides. I guess he really did mean it, after all, that he would get me and the kids out of there. I just don't want to be a burden. I know that it is a lot for his mom to take in one more adult and three small kids.

Rudy runs his fingers up and down my side in a comforting gesture. Not long after that, his breathing begins to slow, his fingers go still, and I know that he has fallen asleep. I'm sure he had a long, tiresome day at work.

I am wide awake lying in the darkness alone with my own thoughts. *Oh my God—what if they come after us? Will they be able to find us? Will they try to hurt us? They'll for sure try to make me come back. I took the kids—my kids. But there's no way they are going to stand for that. We could all end up in trouble.* My thoughts then flick to the positive side. *Relax. Everything is going to be okay. They're not going to find you. If they do come or do call, we won't answer the door. We'll call the cops. We won't answer. It's gonna be fine.*

The next day, we all pile into Rudy's car and head to Walmart to pick up some toiletries, snacks, and drinks for the kids. As we are making our way down a grocery aisle pushing a cart with the kids behind us, my younger daughter asks, "Abby, can we go look at the toys? Pleeeeease, can we?"

Rudy responds, "Sure. Y'all can go look. Just stay in the toy aisle and don't go anywhere else though, okay?"

"Okay!" they all exclaim.

I quickly jump in, "No. You can't go anywhere alone, kids. You have to stay here, by us. We are all going to shop together."

Seriously, what was Rudy thinking? Has he lost his mind to think that it's okay for the kids to just wander around the store alone when my mom and dad are looking for us?

"Aw. But Abby, Rudy said we can. Why can't we just go look at the toys? We just want to see what they have."

"Because I said so, that's why. And y'all need to listen to me. You need to stay with us. We will all go look at the toy aisle together in a little bit, okay? You have to be patient. You have to stay with us. Rudy didn't realize that I don't want y'all wandering off by yourselves. You're too young."

"Oooookay," the kids reply in defeat.

I don't even care if they're mad at me. I can't let them out of my sight. Ever. This is how it is going to be now. I have to watch over them, look out for them, and keep an eye out for my mom and dad. It's my job to keep us all safe.

"Now, let's hurry up and get this shopping done, so y'all can go look at some toys. Hold hands and stay right by us. I want you in my sight at all times."

Annoyed by my toy-aisle-adventure-thwarting outburst, we hold hands and walk down the chip aisle behind Rudy, who is pushing the cart. He probably thinks that I'm crazy and overprotective. I really don't care. He is so good to me and the kids, not only to help us to escape that house, but to be here now, buying us groceries and basic items that we need to live. He is the best man I have ever met. I am lucky that he is mine.

I fear that I can't really make it on my own, even with Rudy's help. It's hard to start over with nothing. But I know that we will be far better off with this fresh start, even if we only have the clothes on our backs, the last meal we ate in our bellies, and each other. To do my part, I can cook everybody's meals and wash all the dirty dishes. I can clean the kitchen and sweep and mop the floors. I will wash everyone's laundry. I can even change the oil in their cars or repair anything that breaks around the house. My dad taught me how to do all sorts of handyman jobs because he wanted me to be independent. I can fix a leaking toilet, hang a towel bar, paint walls, or lay tile. I can even babysit for Rudy's sister, if she'll let me. I need them to know that I don't want to be a freeloader. I want to help them out as much as they are helping me out. I am more than happy to do all the same chores at their house that I used to do at my parents' house. I'm so glad that I won't be abused anymore. I will happily do anything they need me to.

I want for Rudy, my kids, and his two girls to all be a real family now. I hope we can get our own place one day and that I can finally have the type of life that I always wanted. If Rudy gets tired of dealing with this situation, I don't know what I'll do. I am so in love with him. He is my savior. He is my best friend. He is my lover. He is my everything. Without him, I never would have found the courage to make it out. Without him, I never would have been able to get my kids out of there. The reality that my daughter is now the same age as I was when my dad first started molesting me is horrifying. No way was I going to allow what my dad has done to me to happen to my kids—any of them. No freaking way. I'd probably have ended up in prison for murdering my dad.

It is because of Rudy that we all have our shot at a new life, a different and better life, where we can grow together as a couple and raise our beautiful family.

I am finally free.

I am in love.

I am happy.

ABIGAIL

AGE 25
Mid-June of 2014

The Note

*M*y phone rings. I see that it's my brother, so I answer it, "Hey."

"Hi Abby. I just wanted to let you know that Dad left. He's gone."

"What do you mean he left? Where did he go?"

"I don't know where he went, but he left me a 'goodbye' note."

"What? He left?"

"Yeah, Abby— he's gone."

"Well, where did he go?"

"I don't know where they went. Dad already had his clothes packed in the car, and I just helped him load some other stuff into it earlier."

"Where is Mom? Is she with him?

"She went with him. I know Mom misses the kids, Abby."

"You have no idea where they went?"

"No, I don't know. They didn't say."

"Well, what did the note they left say?"

"Just goodbye and, hopefully, soon we'll be together again."

"And you have no idea where they went?"

"Nope."

In much the same way as they had so many times throughout my childhood with each CPS report that resulted in a house visit for an inquiry into my abuse—they did what they always do—they fled.

ABIGAIL

AGE 25
Early July of 2014

The Message

I log onto Facebook to see if I have missed anything recently and see that I have one unread message. It is from Laura.

"Oh my God. Rudy, look—Laura messaged me."

"What? Laura? She messaged you? What the hell did she say?"

"She said she's really sorry about everything, asked how are we are doing, and asked if she can see the kids. She said Chevo is gone and it's just her. She just wants to meet up to see the kids."

"See the kids? Are you fucking kidding me? Who in the hell does she think she is to see anybody after what she did?"

"I know. But the kids do miss her. They still ask about them all the time. She's their grandma, Rudy. They grew up around her their whole lives."

"I know, but that wasn't any type of a life. Fuck no. Why would you want her to see them? She's a lowlife, babe. She's no good. She's an abuser. A predator."

"I know you don't understand this, Rudy, but I feel like I should let the kids see her one last time."

"Are you serious?"

"Yeah. I'm serious. As long as my dad isn't gonna be there, I'm okay with it."

"Why? Why would you want to do that?"

"I'm not afraid of her anymore, Rudy. I'm trying to be a bigger person about it for the kids. But I'd want you to go with me, if I do go."

"Of course, I'd go with you. No way would I let you go meet her alone."

"Okay. Well, what should I tell her then?"

"You don't want to hear what I think you outta tell her. Tell her you'll meet her at the park—the one by Mission Church. You definitely need to meet her in a public place, where there are people around, with me there."

"Okay. I'll tell her we can meet up at the park."

"You can go and see what she has to say, but it's not gonna be pretty. I'll be there with you and the kids in case anything crazy pops off."

RUDY

The Next Day

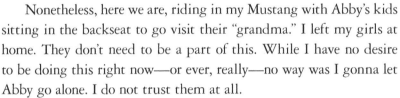

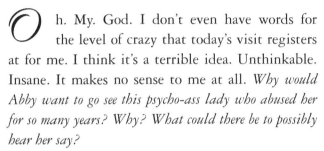

*O*h. My. God. I don't even have words for the level of crazy that today's visit registers at for me. I think it's a terrible idea. Unthinkable. Insane. It makes no sense to me at all. *Why would Abby want to go see this psycho-ass lady who abused her for so many years? Why? What could there be to possibly hear her say?*

Nonetheless, here we are, riding in my Mustang with Abby's kids sitting in the backseat to go visit their "grandma." I left my girls at home. They don't need to be a part of this. While I have no desire to be doing this right now—or ever, really—no way was I gonna let Abby go alone. I do not trust them at all.

Glancing over at Abby, I do my best to gear her up for the visit. "Remember, babe, you don't let your guard down. You stand up to her. You have the ball in your court now. You're the one in charge."

"I know," she replies softly.

I pull into the parking lot and drive the perimeter, looking for any suspicious looking cars, and especially, trying to spot their old beater, a gray Honda Accord. I don't see it, or anything else that seems out of sorts. I drive three more loops around the park, before pulling into an open parking spot. Abby and I get out of the car. Turning to the kids before shutting the driver's door, I say, "Y'all just stay in the car until we tell you to get out." Abby walks around for a bit, waiting to see if Laura shows up. I stay close to the car to keep an eye on the kids. I don't trust Laura or Chevo. If they come here today thinking they're gonna take these kids, they've got another thing coming.

It's then that we notice Laura sitting in a nearby pavilion filled with empty benches. Abby starts to walk over toward her. I walk back over to the car. "Okay, y'all can get out now. Laura is here." We all then make our way over to Abby and Laura. Laura and Abby hug one another, then Laura hugs each of the kids in turn, saying, "It's so good to see you. I miss you. I love you." Nausea washes over me as disgust thrums in my veins. Interestingly, the kids don't seem excited to see her. While they don't resist hugging her, their faces are flat and free of any readable expression. Hmmm. I find that interesting. Abby sits across from Laura at a picnic table, the kids sit a few tables behind them, and I closely stand guard, saying nothing. I hear Laura say, "I can't believe you left." I'm not sure if I feel more anger or disgust. It's a pretty even mix of both.

Abby replies, "I'm not coming back. All that is over. I'm NOT coming back."

Proud as hell, I keep listening, as Laura starts to spew her next wave of bullshit.

"Abby, I'm so sorry. Please forgive me. It was Chevo's fault that all of this happened."

Unbelievable. This lady is so full of shit. She's delusional. Proudly, I watch my beautiful girlfriend—who looks all dolled up today—standing tall and remaining firm in her position. I stand watch to make sure nothing crazy is gonna go down—that this isn't some type of set-up. If either one of them think they're gonna steal these kids today, they got another thing coming. Still no cars pulling in. No other people approaching. I hear Abby respond to Laura's bullshit.

"I'm done with it all. Even though I'm not gonna call and report anything, I never want to see you again—either one of you."

"I'm so sorry, Abby—for all of it. Y'all can come and live in the house. I'll move out into the chapel. You, Rudy, and the kids—all of you can live there and have your own house—a real home of your own."

"No. I'm done. I'm not coming back."

"We can continue [Miracle Girl's] work."

"No way."

"Come on, Abby. I'll help you fix up the house, to make it real nice for you guys—you and the kids."

Oh. My. God. This lady is fucking delusional. I feel like I'm listening to the devil trying to barter to steal a person's soul. Man, I should have taken both of 'em out when I had the chance to in that chapel that day. I should have beat both their asses. I really should have. It's hard as hell to stand here silently and not cuss this psycho ass lady out, but I'm gonna let Abby stand her own ground. It's important for her to be the one to do it.

"I left and I'm never coming back. I'm with Rudy now—me and the kids. That's it. We're done."

"I understand. Let me know if you change your mind about the house. Let's trade numbers, so we can stay in touch."

Laura leans in closer to Abby and recites her phone number. Shocked, I then see Abby do the same. *Why in the hell is she giving this psycho her damn number? Oh my God.* Utterly baffled, I manage to stifle my anger at the insanity of it all. *I'm just here for Abby. I can't flip out because of Abby.*

One week later, in the evening, Abby's cell phone rings and she picks it up. "Hello?" On the line she is greeted by only silence, followed by some quiet breathing. Someone sitting on the line. Listening. Waiting. "Hello. Is anybody there?" The moment I see Abby's face twist in confusion and the tone of her voice raise an octave, immediately, I know—it's them. It has to be. It is not a coincidence. We just met with Laura and now we're getting calls from a lurking breather at nighttime a week later. "Hello?" Abby ends the call. She turns to me and says, "I didn't want to bother you with this until I knew for sure, but this happened before. This is the second time I've gotten a call like this tonight. The first time I wasn't sure. It could have just been somebody playing a prank or something, so I didn't bother mentioning it to you. I didn't really think anything about it at the time. But now, I think it's Chevo."

"A random call with breathing happened before?"

"Yeah, earlier tonight, when you were still at work."

"What popped up on the Caller ID?"

"Unknown number," Abby replies.

"You know that was them, right? You gave them your number, and now, here we are."

"I know. You're probably right, but maybe not."

"Trust me, babe. It was them. We never should've met up with her."

Abby's lime green cell phone lights up with another call. She picks it up. "Hello?" "Hello?" This time, she hangs up.

"Abby, you know it's them. It has to be."

A minute later, her phone lights up with another call. Abby picks it up, "Hello?" She falls silent but leaves the line open so we can listen to the quiet breather. We stay on the line for about three minutes before hanging up, just to see if he would say anything.

Her phone rings again. Abby answers it, "Hello?"

I reach my arm out to indicate that I want to grab the phone from her. Lifting it to my ear, I answer with, "HELLO?" It is met with breathing. It's Chevo. I know it is.

"Look, *motherfucker*, I *know it's you*. I will find you and I *will kill you*. You better hope the cops find you first, *you sick piece of shit*. I said we were gonna leave you alone, but I'm gonna do everything in my fucking power to catch you and arrest you. You and your ugly ass bitch of a wife."

All I hear in response is quiet breathing, so I continue, "I'm coming for you Chevo. You fucked up. I'll see you in hell." I hit the button to end the call. A look of shock and pride flickers across Abby's face.

There were no more calls after that.

To The One:

Who, one day, will fall,
Only to RISE.
To crawl across the ashes,
Knees bleeding, soul bruised.
Over heartache,
Cloaked in silence,
Past the pain
With lightning in her soul,
Grit in her bones,
A storm in her veins,
A glint in her eye.
The mercenary of fate.
The carrier of hope.

Here
To
Burn
The
Whole
Thing
Down.
To step forward.
Rebuilder of her destiny.
The architect of her fate.

—JAMIE COLLINS
(For Abigail)

ABIGAIL

AGE 25
July 21, 2014

"*M*y name is Abigail Castillo."

Those are the first words I say after swinging open the door and walking into the brown brick building of the San Antonio Police Department.

The police officer led me away from the glass encased front desk at the entryway and the sterile waiting area filled with a throng of uncomfortable black plastic chairs, back to a rather non-descript office to hear what I came here to report. Sitting across the table from him, I take a deep breath, hoping to steady my nerves, and continue, "I've been abused—badly abused—for the past 16 years . . . my entire life. It all started when I was a child. I was beaten, stalked, and sexually abused. I was held prisoner for more than a decade. My abuser raped me almost every single day of my life—and it wasn't just him. I finally got away. I'm here to report the abuse—everything that happened to me—to make a police report . . ."

There are defining moments in one's life that serve as a poignant, unforgettable marker of the person you used to be, punctuated by the one you have become. That person, blurred at the edges, with her boundaries now clearly defined, stands in the room an entirely different woman than the one she otherwise might have been. One who feels weaker in some regards, but stronger in others. A survivor of evil acts. A teller of brutal truths. An echo in the darkness not to be forgotten. One forged by another's sins and standing strong to hold the space of survival. That's who I am today: a survivor. And this was the moment where I would stand up, step forward, and take my power back.

It was daunting to say it all aloud, but necessary.

**All typographical and grammatical errors are contained in the original report. Some names intentionally withheld. **

NARRATIVE LEGEND
    DET = MARTINEZ, SVU, 2594
    SUP = B. BRADLEY, SPA, 3338
    SP1 = CASTILLO, EUSEBIO
    V1 = CASTILLO, ABIGAIL O.
    J1 = [name of child one]
    J2 = [name of child two]
    J3 = [name of child three]
    O1 = CASTILLO, LAURA

NARRATIVE INFORMATION
I WAS DISPATCHED TO THE POLICE SUBSTATION TO TAKE THIS
REPORT. UPON MY ARRIVAL, I CONTACT V1 [Abigail]. V1, A
25-YEAR-OLD FEMALE, STATED THAT SHE WANTED TO REPORT
THAT HER ADOPTED FATHER SP1 [Eusebio Castillo, Jr.] HAS
BEEN SEXUALLY ASSAULTING HER SINCE SHE WAS NINE OR TEN
YEARS OLD. V1 STATED THAT WHEN SHE WAS NINE YEARS OLD,
SHE WAS PLACED WITH SP1 AND O1 [Laura Castillo], HER
UNCLE AND AUNT, BY CHILD PROTECTIVE SERVICES. V1 STATED
THAT SP1 WOULD WAIT UNTIL NIGHTTIME, AND WOULD TOUCH
V1 WITH HIS HANDS ON HER LEGS AND VAGINA, AND WOULD
PENETRATE HER VAGINA WITH HIS FINGERS. V1 STATED AT NINE
YEARS OLD, SHE TOLD O1 [Laura], SP1'S WIFE, BUT O1 WOULD
CALL V1 A LIAR. V1 STATED THAT THE FIRST SEXUAL ASSAULT
OCCURRED WHILE THEY LIVED IN HAWAII. V1 STATED THE
FAMILY THEN MOVED SEVERAL TIMES TO HOUSTON TX, LAREDO
TX, MISSION TX, THEN FINALLY TO SAN ANTONIO TX. V1 STATED
THE SEXUAL ASSUALTS CONTINUED THROUGHOUT THE YEARS, AND
WOULD INCLUDE SEXUAL INTERCOURSE. V1 STATED THAT POLICE
REPORTS WERE MADE IN HOUSTON TX, LAREDO TX AND MISSION
TX, BY OTHER FAMILY MEMBERS THAT WERE SUSPICIOUS, BUT

V1 WOULD DENY IT TO THE INVESTIGATORS OUT OF FEAR. V1 STATED THAT SP1 IS THE BIOLOGICAL FATHER TO HER THREE CHILDREN . . . AND FEARED THEY WOULD BE TAKEN AWAY IF THE TRUTH CAME OUT. V1 STATED THAT SHE CAME FORWARD TO POLICE NOW, TO STOP SP1 FROM DOING THIS TO OTHER GIRLS. V1 IS ALSO FEARFUL THAT SP1 WOULD EVENTUALLY HURT HER CHILDREN. V1 STATED THAT SP1 HAS BEEN TRYING TO LOCATE V1 AND V1'S CHILDREN, SINCE V1 HAS RECENTLY MOVED OUT OF SP1'S RESIDENCE. DET AND SUP WERE BOTH NOTIFIED ABOUT THE DETAILS OF THIS CASE. I GAVE V1 A CASE NUMBER, AND ADVISED V1 OF THE FOLLOW UP PROCEDURE. V1 RECEIVED INFORMATION ON COUNSELING, PROTECTIVE ORDER AND CRIMES VICTIMS ACT SERVICES. ADVISED V1 TO CALL POLICE IF ANY DISTURBANCES OCCUR WITH SP1.

The detective told me that the focus of the criminal charges would need to be linked to my three pregnancies, since that abuse was provable through DNA evidence. For that reason, age 15 became our anchor, since that is when the pregnancy-inducing-threesomes began.

It feels weird to see the sanitized sexual words typed in black keystrokes across several pieces of paper depicting the despicable acts that had, for so long, defined me. The moments of my life that, for so long, he—my depraved uncle and adoptive dad—had owned me. As the swirled brushstrokes of ink bled onto the paper, I felt liberated. It was time for both of my adoptive parents to pay the criminal penalty for what they had done to me and all that they had taken from me.

It was time for them to pay in years of their lives trapped behind black iron bars for what I had paid through physical abuse, emotional neglect, and the soul-destroying theft of my flesh for 16 years. It was time for them to answer for the type of people they had chosen to become. Sadistic people. Evil people. People who robbed me of my self-worth and stole every social milestone, every "first" experience that I should have had if I'd been lucky enough to have led a normal life. Instead, they forced me to live as their personal handmaiden and household servant in every way within the twisted confines of their depraved world. Their home became my prison. It seems fair that prison should now become their home.

When the officer was done interviewing me about the abuse, he walked me out to the lobby where Rudy sat waiting for me. Without Rudy, I don't think I would have had the strength to do any of this—to leave that house, to report my abusers, to pick up the splintered pieces of my life and move forward. But with Rudy by my side—my fierce protector, constant companion, tireless supporter, and unwavering ally—I could do these things, and I did.

I didn't have to name myself publicly. It was a choice, both then and now. As a survivor of sexual assault, the authorities would happily have agreed to shroud my identity comfortably within the black-ink keystrokes of anonymity to keep my name out of the public record.

But in the sweltering Texas heat of that day in July, eight years ago, I was prepared to own my identity.

It was finally time to own the shame-filled-ugliness that had consumed my life. It was something I wanted—and needed—to do after enduring 16 years of hell at the hands of two demented people masquerading as normal that I somehow managed to survive. Some in positions of power would call it one of the worst cases of child abuse they had ever heard. I would call it my life story.

For me, the interview at the police station and signing of my statement were the defining moments when, for the first time, I truly realized that I was the one who had done nothing wrong in this situation. I wasn't going to be arrested. I hadn't committed a crime. They had. The DNA test would seal my rapist adoptive father's fate, not mine. I was simply an innocent child, now a resilient woman sitting in a plastic chair, signing her way from pen to power to reclaim the situation. Prison is exactly where they deserve to be. And I am the only one who can put them there.

**All typographical and grammatical errors are contained in the
original affidavit. Some names intentionally withheld. **

STATE OF BEXAR   Case Number: 14148771
COUNTY OF BEXAR   Date and Time: July 21, 2014 10:38 AM
                               Taken by: DET. D. Cartwright 2438

Page 1 of 4

BEFORE ME, the undersigned authority in and for the
State and County aforesaid, on this day personally appeared
Castillo, Abigail who being by me duly sworn upon oath,
deposes and says:

My name is Abigail Castillo and my date of birth is
09/04/1988. I live at 307 E. White Ave and my phone number is
210-###-####. I came down to SAPD headquarters to give my
statement about what has been happening to me since I was
about 9 years old. My adoptive father, who is also my uncle,
Eusebio Castillo, has been sexually assaulting me. He is the
biological father of my children.

I was placed in Eusebio care by Child Protective Services
when I was 9 years old. We lived in Honolulu Hawaii on
Scofield Barracks, the military base where Eusebio was
stationed. He is married to Laura Castillo. My sister [first
name intentionally omitted] Castillo and my brother [first
name intentionally omitted] Castillo were also adopted and
lived with us. We moved to Laredo, Houston, and Mission TX
over the years. We settled in San Antonio about 5 years ago.

The first time I remember being assaulted was when I was
about 9 years old. We lived in Hawaii. Eusebio would sit me
on his lap. He started to rub my feet and worked his way
up to my vagina. He rubbed my vagina and put his fingers
inside my vagina, over my underwear. This happened when he
and I were the only ones home. I don't recall the number of
times he did this. I do recall after one of the times he did

this, I told Laura what Eusebio had done to me. She told me I was lying so I never told her again.

As we moved to Texas, Eusebio would do the same things to me. He would penetrate my vagina with his fingers. This happened when we were alone. He would also grab on my breasts with his hands. He would tell me not to say anything to anyone about what he was doing or I would get in trouble.

When I was 15 years old, Eusebio started to place his penis inside my vagina. I don't recall the first time it happened but I know I was 15. I am not sure of the exact location, but I believe we were in Laredo, TX. We lived in a house then. I do not recall if he used a condom or not, but I think he did. This would happen about once a month. No one was home when this happened. It would happen in his room or my room on the beds.

Sworn and subscribed before me, Det. Dennis Cartwright, a Peace Officer in the State of Texas, and pursuant to No. 602.002, Texas Government Code on this 21st day of July A.D., 2014.

STATE OF BEXAR   Case Number: 14148771
COUNTY OF BEXAR   Date and Time: July 21, 2014 10:38 AM
                        Taken by: DET. D. Cartwright 2438

Page 2 of 4

BEFORE ME, the undersigned authority in and for the State and County aforesaid, on this day personally appeared Castillo, Abigail who being by me duly sworn upon oath, deposes and says:

I know one time when we lived in Laredo, TX my sister called Child Protective Services to report Eusebio for what he was doing to me. I was 17 years old. CPS came out to talk to me but I denied anything was happening. By this time Eusebio was telling me I would go to jail for what was going on. I was scared so I did not tell the truth. Shortly after CPS left I found out I was pregnant. The father of the baby is Eusebio.

I was not sexually active with anyone else. He was happy about the baby but he said it was my fault I was pregnant. We moved to the valley before I had the baby and the assaults occurred there as well. I had two children while living in the valley. Both are Eusebio's. [First name intentionally omitted], Castillo, 11-16-05 and [first name intentionally omitted] Castillo, 7-11-08 were born in Mission TX.

During one of the assaults, I looked up and I saw Laura peeking in the door. I know she saw what Eusebio was doing to me. After he was done, I started to cry and Laura came up to me and told me she "would deal with it". She never did because he kept doing this to me.

One time while in Mission TX when Eusebio penetrated my anus one time with his penis. I was able to push him off when he did this. This is also when he started to perform oral sex on me. He would force me to perform oral sex on him as well.

After about 5 years we moved to San Antonio, TX. The sexual assaults continued to occur here also. The sexual assaults would occur more often here in San Antonio. I ended up having another baby here. [First name intentionally omitted] Castillo, 4-12-11. Eusebio is the father also.

There were times when we first moved here to San Antonio where Laura and Eusebio were having sex and Laura would call me into the room. Laura would tell me to get undressed and get in the bed. I didn't want to but I was scared so I did. Eusebio would then penetrate my vagina and Laura would "play" with herself. Eusebio would then start to have sex with Laura. He was going back and forth. Eusebio would force me to suck on Laura's breasts and vagina. Laura would then suck on my breasts and vagina.

Sworn and subscribed before me, Det. Dennis Cartwright, a Peace Officer in the State of Texas, and pursuant to No. 602.002, Texas Government Code on this 21st day of July A.D., 2014.

STATE OF BEXAR   Case Number: 14148771
COUNTY OF BEXAR   Date and Time: July 21, 2014 10:38 AM
                        Taken by: DET. D. Cartwright 2438

Page 3 of 4

BEFORE ME, the undersigned authority in and for the State and County aforesaid, on this day personally appeared Castillo, Abigail who being by me duly sworn upon oath, deposes and says: happened about every other day for about 2 months. The last time this happened was about 2 months ago.

I was pregnant about 4 months ago and Laura gave me some unknown pills. I took them and I had a miscarriage about a week later. I am not sure if the pills had anything to do with it.

During this entire time he would tell me I would go to jail if I told anyone. Eusebio became more violent and threatening as time went on. He would threaten to kill our kids if I told anyone. There were also times he could pour gasoline around the house and threatened to set it on fire. A few times he poured gas on himself and said he would kill himself if I told. Eusebio hung himself one time, but Laura was able to cut him down. The police were never called about this.

I am finally coming forward to report this because I know what he did to me is wrong. I am scared for my life and my children's life. I currently live with [Rudy Alvarado]. I left Eusebio about 1 month ago. I have not seen him since then. Eusebio has not assaulted me for about 7 months now.

When I was living with Eusebio and Laura my kids called Laura mom and they called me Abby. Eusebio and Laura both wanted the kids to do that so there would not be any suspicion about what was really going on with us. Since I moved out the kids now know that I am their mom. Before this happened, they didn't know.

I have not been threatened in any way or promised anything in return for giving this statement. I have given this statement freely and voluntarily. I have told the truth. Everything in this statement is what I told Det. Wilson and it is true and correct. I understand that lying is a prosecutable criminal violation of Texas Law. This is the end of my statement.

Sworn and subscribed before me, Det. Dennis Cartwright, a Peace Officer in the State of Texas, and pursuant to No. 602.002, Texas Government Code on this 21st day of July A.D., 2014.

STATE OF BEXAR   Case Number: 14148771
COUNTY OF BEXAR   Date and Time: July 21, 2014 10:38 AM
                        Taken by: DET. D. Cartwright 2438

Page 4 of 4

BEFORE ME, the undersigned authority in and for the State and County aforesaid, on this day personally appeared Castillo, Abigail who being by me duly sworn upon oath, deposes and says:

Signature *Abigail Castillo*

SUPPLEMENTARY REPORT

**All typographical and grammatical errors are contained in the original report. Some names intentionally withheld. **

ASSIGNMENT NO: 14148771

OFFENSE NO: 110041

DATE REPORTED: 07/26/14

SYNOPSIS: The Complainant went to the police station to report she has been sexually assaulted by the Defendant 1 since she was 9 or 10 years old. C is now 25 years old. C stated the assaults happened in Hawaii, Laredo Tx, Houston Tx, and Mission Tx. C said she told Defendant 2 but she was accused of being a liar.

DOCUMENTATION OF INVESTIGATION

07/30/2014—I called O1 [Abby's older sister] and recorded our conversation on an audio CD. Below is an overview of that interview. [See audio CD for complete details.]

- Defendant 1 is her biological mom's half-brother. He adopted them while in Hawaii. While their C [Abigail] came crying to her saying Defendant 1 got on top of her and put his penis inside her and white stuff got on her stomach. They told Defendant 2 who called C a liar. She went to school C stayed home and when she came home Defendant 2 told her C admitted to lying.

- In Houston she woke up one morning and saw a large black vibrator. C was crying and told her Defendant 1 put the black vibrator inside her. She confronted him and he made her get out of his room. She told Defendant 2 who dismissed her.

- Someone called CPS because they went to the school. She told them C was being sexually assaulted but C denied the allegations to CPS. This happened on a few occasions.

- She left the home in 2005. She says in 2007 Laredo PD subpoenaed Defendant 1 & 2 and C. C did not outcry to them either.

08/18/2014—I ran both Defendants via CLEAR [a database]. [See CD reports] I talked to a Linda [last name intentionally omitted] at [number intentionally omitted]. She is the owner of the home the Defendants lived in here. She said they had moved out and she does not know where they went to. She also said they formerly worked for her but no longer do. She said all their belongings were gone. I received the copies of the 3 previous sexual assault allegations. No new information the Defendants were found on CLEAR.

08/27/2014—I still could not find any current address for the Defendants. I put a BOLO [Be On The Lookout] in Visinet Mobile alerting officers to contact me if the Defendants were found. If found I would attempt to obtain a buccal [DNA swab] warrant from Defendant 1. The BOLO was entered for two weeks.

09/15/2014—I run the Defendants via CLEAR and again no new current address information was available.

CONCLUSION:

During the investigation of this case I received and reviewed the reports. I interviewed and received a statement from the Complainant and first outcry. The Complainant related the elements of Sexual Assault and states she is eager to cooperate in the prosecution of this case. Both Defendants cannot be located. A BOLO was placed in the Visinet Mobile for Defendant 1. Due to the lack of outcry when the assaults were committed and the Defendants unable to be located, the case will be closed PFI [Pre-File Investigation] at this time.

ABIGAIL

On The Run

I wish this was the part of my story where I could tell you that Laura and Chevo were arrested for what they did to me, but that isn't what happens next. Chevo fled, once again, revealing his true form: a coward on the run.

I learned from an uncle that Laura ran off to reunite with the coward. Nobody knew for certain where they fled to, except for maybe my brother. However, if he does know, he refuses to tell me. It seems like he wants to protect them. Does he know what they've done? I know Rudy told him about it, but it still seems like he doesn't want to believe it. He's tried to get me to tell him *exactly* what Chevo did to me, but I just don't see the point. He knows enough. There was abuse. There were rapes. There are my three beautiful kids born of it.

I guess he is probably worried about what may happen to them, but I'm certainly not. They deserve whatever they get. They need to pay for the terrible things they have done.

Although I felt both nervous and brave walking into the police station to finally report my abuse, it was empowering. Unfortunately, it just doesn't seem as though anything is going to happen to them. They always seem to find a way to get away with the heinous things they do. They spin stories, create lies, sell people a completely alternate version of reality.

They are cowards.

They lie. They run. They hide.

It is, after all, what they do best.

ABIGAIL

AGE 25
Early August of 2014

Telling the Kids

I am sitting at the table eating cereal with my kids this morning, when my son—the youngest—asks, "Abby, when are we going home? I miss Mom and Dad." My heart drops like one of those rides at a carnival that jolts your entire body. I cringe at his words, not only because it is a loaded question, but because the words that he uttered to me are no longer our reality, not really. I deflect by saying, "I don't know. We'll probably see them sometime soon . . ." before diverting their attention to something interesting on the cereal box. It is in that moment that I decide it is time to tell my kids— ages nine, six, and three—the truth that I am their mother. I went to the police several weeks ago. We are safe. It is time.

While I'm not sure how they are going to receive this news, it is a reality that we can no longer continue to dance around. We are out now and away from my mom and dad. We are safe here with Rudy and his mom. I am happy here and we aren't going back, so it is time that they know the truth. I'll tell them as soon as Rudy gets home from work tonight.

About five minutes before Rudy typically arrives home, I start to watch for him from the window. When I see his Mustang pull up, I step outside on the front porch to greet him, "Hi babe. How was your day?" Looking slightly confused, Rudy wraps his arms around me, pulls me in to a hug, plants a soft kiss on the top of my head, and replies, "It was good. What are you doing out here? Did something happen?" His tone holds an edge of worry that I feel compelled to override.

"No, nothing happened. Everything is fine, babe. I just decided that it's finally time that I tell the kids the truth about me being their mom."

"Really? Okay, are you sure?"

"Yeah. I'm sure."

"Okay. And you want to do it tonight, or when?"

"Yes. I want to do it right now."

"Okay. I'll follow your lead, babe. I'll be right there beside you."

I make my way back into the house with Rudy trailing behind me. Pulling open the front door, I say, "Hey kids, I need to talk to you and tell y'all something. Gather around, here in the living room. Everybody, come sit down, over here, by me." My two youngest—my son and daughter—take a seat beside me. My eldest sits next to her little sister. Rudy is standing in the living room near us but is giving me space to sit with them and tell them. "So, I need to tell y'all something and it's something really important. It's something that you need to know. It's something that we've been keeping from y'all, but you need to know the truth. And the truth is—that I am y'all's mommy." I pause to assess their reaction. My little boy says, "What? You're really OUR MOM?"

Keeping my voice calm, I continue, "Yes. I am all of your mommy. And that means that makes Laura and Chevo really y'all's grandparents." I volley the words into the air, then sit silently, awaiting their reaction. It comes quickly, in the form of a short silence as they glance around the room at each other, taking in the weight of my words. My eldest chimes in, "So, you are *really* our mom? And you have been this entire time, but we just didn't know about it?"

"Yes. That's right. That is the truth. Remember when my belly was all big? That's when I was pregnant with your little sister. I am y'all's mom. I always have been—you just didn't know about it. I gave birth to each of you at the hospital. You are really *my kids*. I'm not really your sister, like you always thought I was. I'm your mommy."

A flicker of recognition crosses my daughter's face. "Oh, yeah. I do remember when you had a big, round belly. So, you're our mom then. Okay," my eldest daughter replies, her brows furrowed with a twinge of confusion before reality and acceptance fully sink in. Her expression softens, "Yeah. So, you're our mom then."

Upon hearing my eldest daughter's confirmation of this fact, the two youngest seem to take the news in stride right along with her, as though it's no big deal at all. But it is a big deal! They finally know the truth, after all these years! Here I was, braced for major fallout and they took it like a report about the day's weather. I continue, "So, like I said, I am y'all's mommy. And I'm with Rudy now. And I'm really happy with Rudy and y'all seem to like it here. So, we are gonna all stay here, and live with Rudy and his mom, until we can afford to move out and get a place of our own." My little boy excitedly asks, "Our own place? Can we get a big house?"

"Maybe. I don't know yet, but we'll see. The important thing is that we are all going to be together, as a family. I know y'all probably miss your grandma and grandpa because it's been a while since you've seen them. Maybe we can see them sometime soon, okay? But I'm not sure yet. That's something that we will have to figure out."

Sensing that my kids are unfazed by this news and getting more fidgety by the second, I tell them, "So, that's it. That's all that I wanted y'all to know. That I'm your mom. And that everything is gonna be okay. We're all gonna be okay here, together. And we're gonna be happy. Once summer is over, we'll get y'all enrolled in school here. We'll get y'all some school supplies. Everything is going to be good for us here." Losing interest, my son scuttles off of the couch in search of a toy to play with, accompanied by my younger daughter, who is also done with this discussion. Rudy and I exchange a quick glance of relief at how well the kids took the news.

We then resume normal family life for the evening, eating dinner together and watching TV with the kids buzzing through the living room, loud and playful. As Rudy and I sit together on the couch, I feel both relieved and grateful. I am relieved that the delivery of this news was so well-received by my kids. And I am grateful to be here, with Rudy and our children, where we are safe, cared for, and happy.

I never knew whether this day would come—the day when they would finally know the truth. I guess we'll just have to wait and see whether they keep calling me "Abby" like they always have, or whether they start calling me that sacred title that has always been biologically mine by right, but never uttered aloud, "Mom."

It only took a day or two for my little boy to start calling me Mom. At first, he would break into a huge smile any time he said it, like he found it amusing. I would smile right back at him because it made me happy to be acknowledged in that way.

My daughters eventually began calling me "Mom," too, but it was harder for them to break themselves of the habit of referring to me as "Abby" because they had called me that for so many years. It was a title that I had been robbed of for far too long. One of the most beautiful words that I have ever heard spoken to me. And now that they know the truth—that I am their Mom—I am going to do everything in my power to ensure that I am a good one.

ABIGAIL

AGE 34

Present Day

This brings us to all the things that I, as a grown woman, never realized. While I certainly knew CPS made occasional appearances at our home and in our lives in nearly every city where we dwelled in Texas, I had no idea the level of documentation that CPS possessed in its file. I also did not realize the damning picture that all those CPS reports painted when viewed collectively. It as the story of a little girl moved from one city to the next, often in the middle of the night, so that her parents could flee investigations and potential charges. I learned to live within layers of heavy truths tucked within a smattering of lies that I had to tell for the sake of self-preservation. My entire childhood was built upon a foundation of lies carefully crafted by my abusive parents to cover up their horrific wrongdoings.

All of the things they claimed that *I was*.

All of the things they claimed that *they weren't*.

The words sit heavy upon the pages to help piece together some of the jagged, ugly parts that comprise my life story. I must now accept these things—all of them, even the ones I did not recall about my former life with Real Mom—they are all unfortunate pieces of my reality.

As for my failure to "outcry" to CPS, I knew that I had to return home to my abusers that night. That, coupled with the persistent brainwashing they started at the age of nine, rendered me too petrified to admit to the abuse. I suspect that such brainwashing is fairly common among abused children. But, even with CPS finding "moderate reason to believe" that I was being sexually abused, the system created to protect children failed me. CPS never managed to put the pieces of the abuse puzzle together. All my parents had to do was run. And it apparently wasn't difficult to outrun CPS. Report after report, city after city, within the state of Texas.

INVESTIGATION REPORT

[Pertinent portions included below]

**All typographical and grammatical errors are contained in the original report. Some names intentionally withheld. **

Case Name: Laura Castillo
Case #:   25014731
Intake Legend:
SXAB = sexual abuse
MO = mother
FA = father

Intake Narrative

Intake Received: 4/21/2003
Reporter Name: [reporter]
Stage ID: 28672678
Rel/int: Anonymous
Stage Type: SXAB1
Person ID: 31907571

Person Notes: A neighbor. The child told this person about the SXAB [sexual abuse] nine months ago. The caller went to MO [mother]. MO contact off contact between the caller and the child. Caller said she made report to a teacher with the last name of Fox last year at Stuchberry Elem.

———

Household consists of MO [mother], FA [father], 16 yr old [sister's name omitted], 15 year old [stepbrother's name omitted], 14 yr old Abigail, and 13 yr old [brother's name omitted]. The 16 yr old, 14 yr old, and 13 yr old are adopted. The children were FA's sister's children.

Nine months ago, the 14 yr old reported that FA was sexually abusing her. The 14 yr old reported that FA was having sexual intercourse with her. The 15 yr old [stepbrother] was in the hospital with cancer a year ago. MO would stay at the hospital with the 15 yr old. FA would go to school and pick up the 14 yr old and take her home and have sex with her. FA would have the 14 yr old to shower and then take her back to school. MO was made aware of the SXAB nine months ago.

FA left the home for two days. MO states she has paperwork saying the 14 yr old was sexually abused previously. MO said the 14 yr old lived in a fantasy world. MO said she sought counseling for the children and they were put on medication. The 16 yr old said they were not on meds and MO did not take them to counseling.

The parents do not allow the children to have contact with anyone outside of the home. MO said she doesn't want the 14 yr old to make sexual abuse allegations against other people. The two oldest children are allowed to come outside about once a month. The children have to stay within the house with the blinds drawn when the parents are not home. The children are not allowed to have friends or receive telephone calls.

FA was kicked out to the Army about two years ago for having contact with a minor over the Internet. This happened while the family was in Hawaii. The minor's parents made a report to the police. FA was arrested. His computer was confiscated. The parents watch pornography on the Internet in front of the children. FA has child pornography on his home computer.

The 14 yr old got in trouble two or three months ago for kissing a boy. For a while FA would make the child walk out of the home with her head underneath his coat. They didn't want the child looking at boys. Last year FA would walk the

14 yr old into her classroom to make sure she didn't talk to anyone. The parents make the 14 yr old sleep on the floor in their bedroom. The parents lock the 14 yr old inside of the bathroom when they have sex. Six months ago, the 14 yr old wrote a note stating she wanted to commit suicide. The 14 yr old is told she is stupid and ugly.

The children report that they are beaten. The kids are slapped to face, choked, and clawed to the neck. The 14 yr old had claw marks on her neck six months ago. It is unknown if marks or bruises have been left on the other children. MO and FA smoked marijuana with the 15 yr old when he was undergoing cancer treatment to help his cancer.

The parents allegedly lied to adopt the children. The parents had the 15 yr old to say the parents use time out as discipline.

Janet Clayton, PSIS IV

CONCLUSIONS:

P1/sxab [sexual abuse] and PHAB [physical abuse]. FA having sexual intercourse with 14 yr old female. AP also has pornography and child pornography on the Internet. AP has been arrested previously for contact over the Internet with a minor. Children allege they were beaten.

LOCATING INFORMATION: Directions. When the family is home. Where the victim can be seen.

Abigail and [brother's name omitted] attend school at Thompson Intermediate. [Sister's name omitted] and [brother's name omitted] attend school at Dobie High School. The schools are in Pasadena ISD.

IMPACT History for All Principals

Castillo, Abigail Olga

Case:	25014731
Stage:	16462798
Intake Date:	5/28/1996
Allegation:	Neglectful Supv. [CPS]
Role:	Victim
Disp:	Ruled Out
Sev:	
Allegation:	Sexual Abuse
Role:	Victim
Disp:	Ruled Out
Sev:	

Castillo, Abigail Olga

Case:	25014731
Stage:	24209226
Intake Date:	3/23/1998
Allegation:	Physical Abuse
Role:	Victim
Disp:	Reason to Believe
Sev:	Moderate
Allegation:	Physical Neglect
Role:	Victim
Disp:	Reason to Believe
Sev:	Moderate
Allegation:	Sexual Abuse
Role:	Victim
Disp:	Reason to Believe
Sev:	Moderate
Risk Finding:	Risk Indicated
Removal[s):	

Castillo, Abigail Olga

Case:	25014731
Stage:	24336123
Intake Date:	5/14/1998
Allegation:	Neglectful Supv. [CPS]
Role:	Victim
Disp:	Reason to Believe
Sev:	Serious
Allegation:	Physical Abuse
Role:	Victim
Disp:	Reason to Believe
Sev.	Moderate
Allegation:	Physical Neglect
Role:	Victim
Disp:	Reason to Believe
Sev.	Moderate
Allegation:	Sexual Abuse
Role:	Victim
Disp:	Ruled Out
Sev.	
Risk Finding:	Risk Indicated
Removal[s]:	

Castillo, Abigail Olga

Case:	25014731
Stage:	29333423
Intake Date:	12/9/2003
Allegation:	Physical Abuse
Role:	Victim
Disp:	Family Moved
Sev:	

Risk Assessment

Rationale for Risk Finding:

Area of Concern:	Child Vulnerability
Scale of Concern:	Somewhat
Concerns:	Not addressed.
Area of Concern:	Caregiver Capability
Scale of Concern:	None
Concerns:	Not addressed.
Area of Concern:	Quality of Care
Scale of Concern:	None
Concerns:	Not addressed.
Area of Concern:	Maltreatment Pattern
Scale of Concern:	Very Little
Concerns:	Not addressed.
Area of Concern:	Home Environment
Scale of Concern:	Somewhat
Concerns:	Not addressed.
Area of Concern:	Social Environment
Scale of Concern:	Very Little
Concerns:	Not addressed.
Area of Concern:	Response to Intervention
Scale of Concern:	None
Concerns:	Not addressed.

Investigation Contacts

Date of Contact:	4/22/2003
Date Entered:	4/22/2003
Case Name:	Laura Castillo
Case #:	24828539
Case Worker:	Andrea Chapman
Date Completed:	5/19/03

Structured Narrative

Interview and Examination of Children:

4/22/03 FTF Abigail Castillo/OV

I spoke to Abigail at her school, Thompson Intermediate.
Abigail is 14y/o in the 7th grade. Abigail enjoys doing art
and crafts. The people that live in the home with Abigail
are [names of siblings omitted]. Eusebio and Laura adopted
Abigail, [brother's name omitted], [sister's name omitted]
in 1989. Their biological mom is [mom's name omitted].
Eusebio is the biological uncle of the kids. The children
were adopted because their biological mother had a drug
addiction. [Name omitted] is their biological child. Abigail
says that her two brothers sleep in the same room, she sleeps
with her sister, and mom and dad sleep together.

Abigail demonstrated that she knows the difference
between a truth and a lie by giving and example. Abigail
described the parts of her body that no one should touch as
her top and bottom; pointing to breasts and vagina. Abigail
says that no one has touched her on her top and bottom,
and no one has asked her to touch them on their private
parts. No one has put their mouth of her private parts and
no one has asked her to put her mouth on their private.
Abigail says that if someone did touch her, she would tell
her mom or the principal. Abigail doesn't know anyone who's
been touched.

Since Abigail made no disclosure, I questioned her as
to why someone would think that Eusebio was touching her.
Abigail said that she told Kylie [last name omitted], her
best friend, and her best friend told her mom. Abigail said
that Eusebio was abusing her because she was mad at him.
After it she said it, her parents talked to her about whether
it actually happened, Abigail said no. Abigail said that she

was grounded for a long time. She was in serious trouble. Abigail says that her dad stopped talking to her for a week.

When Abigail gets into trouble she gets grounded or gets a whipping with a belt on her butt. She says that Eusebio drinks beer and smokes cigarettes.

4/22/03 FTF [Brother's first name omitted] Castillo/SB

I spoke to [brother's name omitted] at his school, Thompson Intermediate. When he gets into trouble, he gets grounded to his room for a while, or he gets a whipping on his behind with a belt. [Brother's name omitted] says that Eusebio drinks beer and smokes cigarettes. [Brother's name omitted] says that he sleeps in the room with [stepbrother's name omitted], two sisters sleep in the same room, and his mom and dad sleep together. [Brother's name omitted] appeared to be very shy when asked about his private parts. He called his private parts, front and back. No one has touched him on his private parts and no one has asked him to touch them on their private parts. No one has put their mouth on his private parts and no one has asked him to put his mouth on their private parts. [Brother's name omitted] says that if someone did touch him, he would tell them not to do that and he would tell his mom and dad. [Brother's name omitted] says that he doesn't know anyone who's been touched before.

4/22/03 FTF [Stepbrother's name omitted]/SB

I spoke to [stepbrother's name omitted] at his school, Dobie High School. [He] is 15 y/o in the 9th grade. He was born on October 8, 1987. When he gets into trouble, he gets punished; sometimes a whipping with a belt on his butt. [He] says that Eusebio drinks beer and smokes cigarettes. The cops have never come to their house. [He] says that he likes about his home is that they watch movies and his dad is fun to hang out with. He says that his mom is always there to talk to if he needs help. When asked about private parts, [he] pointed to his penis and his butt. No one has touched him on his private parts that he didn't want to and no one has asked him to put his mouth on them. [He] says that he would tell his mom and dad if someone were touching him. He doesn't know anyone who's been touched. [He] says that he always says no to drugs.

4/22/03 FTF [Sister's name omitted]/SB

I spoke to [name omitted] at her school, Dobie High School. [Name omitted] is in the 10th grade. When she gets into trouble, she gets grounded and the younger ones get smacked on their butt with a belt. She says that her dad smokes and he drinks on Holidays. When asked about her private parts, [sister] named her breasts and vagina. No one has touched her on her private parts that she didn't want to, and no one has asked her to touch them on their private parts. [Name omitted] denies any type of abuse. She said that Abigail was sexually abused when she was younger. [Name omitted] doesn't know of Abigail being abused lately. She says she don't think so; she hopes not. [Name omitted] says that her mom and dad get along good with each other and with all of the kids. She says that if someone was touching her or her sister, she would tell an adult.

4/22/02 FTF/Laura Castillo/MO

I spoke with Laura Castillo at her home. She denied a criminal history and a history of abuse. Laura denied a CPS history. She did talk about a CPS incident that happened in Hawaii. She also mentioned that she and her husband adopted [sister's name omitted], Abigail, and [brother's name omitted].

After I discussed the current allegations with Laura Castillo, she seemed to know immediately how the report was generated. She explained that her neighbor's daughter and daughter got into it because a black guy raped the neighbor's daughter. Neighbors don't like black people and Laura's son dates a black girl. Laura says that [sister's name omitted] was going to fight, but she kept her inside. Laura says that her children come first. Laura says that this is the exact reason why she keeps the children inside. They don't go out by themselves. The neighborhood is filled with crime and people wanting to start problems. Laura says that recently, two days ago, she was called to the school because Abigail was caught making out with a little boy. Laura says that it wasn't a peck on the lips, they were French kissing passionately. Laura says that she is concerned about Abigail, because she doesn't want her to become a teenage mom like she was. Laura also said that before she and her husband adopted the kids; it was thought that Abigail had been touched by one of her biological mom's guys. Laura says that after they adopted Abigail, the put her into counseling on their own; she went a long time. Abigail just got tired of it.

Laura says that when the kids get into trouble, they go to timeout or get privileges taken or by not being able to go outside. She says that they don't go outside without her or her husband period. The environment is not good. People are robbed and getting into fights; they don't feel safe. They've been living in the apartment complex since October of 2001. Laura expressed grave concern for moving; buying or renting a house. She doesn't think that they would have so many problems if they were out of an apartment complex.

In July of 2001, she found out that her biological son, [name omitted], had cancer. He's been in remission since July 2002. She says that they have a good family and they all love each other. She says that her husband would not do anything like that to Abigail. She said that another problem that they are having is trying to adapt as a family. Everybody seems to be fine except Abigail. Abigail is known to steal and lie, and she's always been caught making out with little boys. Laura expressed a concern for counseling referrals that might be able to help them adjust as a family.

4/29/03 FTF Eusebio Castillo Jr./AP

I spoke with Eusebio at the CAC. Mr. Castillo denied a criminal history. He denied a history of abuse or neglect. He also denied a history of drug or alcohol abuse.

Mr. Castillo said that the person who reported it, had it all wrong. The incident didn't actually happen 9 months ago. Someone was always in the home. Abby initially said that Mr. Castillo had touched her back in 2001. Mr. Castillo said that Abby had gotten mad because they wouldn't allow her to have a boyfriend. Abby told their neighbors that same story. The neighbors confronted them, and they took measures to control the issue. Mr. Castillo says that he would never do anything to hurt his children.

Mr. Castillo says that they have a lot of problems in that apartment complex. He says that they moved from one apartment to the next and because of what people saw them moving, people started saying that they were rich.

Mr. Castillo says that he has never been arrested, but when he was in the army there was a big investigation. He was close with a soldier and the soldier came to their home and looked at pictures on the Internet and was also messing with an under-aged child. Mr. Castillo says that because he was involved, due to the soldier being at his house a lot, Mr. Castillo requested to be dismissed from the army.

Mr. Castillo says that Abby used to get into trouble at school and he made her walk next to him. So Abby was embarrassed, she would cover her face. He admitted to walking her to her classroom, but it was because he wanted her to be embarrassed and wouldn't get into trouble. Mr. Castillo says that he tries to get involved in her education. He's always told his kids that he wanted them to be better than him. He buys educational materials and books, even material for the computer.

Mr. Castillo says that they don't beat their kids. They removed privileges; trying to motivate them. He says that he did spank Abby twice on her butt with a belt.

4/22/03 STA Gerri Feld/Staff with supervisor
Worker explained that there was no disclosure made. Abigail admitted to saying that her dad touched her because she was mad. Gerri said to talk to the rest of the children.

4/29/03 LTF Donna Hare/COC
Donna has known Abigail and [brother's name omitted] for 3 years combined. At no time has she ever see any marks or bruises on them. Their behaviors in class are excellent. She finds these children well-behaved and have exemplarily behavior records. Their parents have been involved with their academic work and have been a major part of helping with the children's education.

4/29/03 STA Gerri Feld/Staff with supervisor
It was explained that Mr. Castillo denied all allegations and had a reasonable explanation for the allegations made. Gerri said to give them counseling referrals.

8. Observations of Home Environment [if home visit was made]:
Describe the home environment and identify conditions that involve risk to children.

The Castillo's were living in a three-bedroom apartment. There were two small dogs on the inside of the home. The home appeared to be very small and crowded for a family of 6. The home had an odor that could've been from inside pets and mild uncleanliness. The apartment environment was over all OK. The outside environment was concerning. There was numerous people hanging outside the apartment. Basketball goals and activities for children were broken and lacking. The apartment grounds were filthy with paper and residue.

———

Home Environment: Somewhat Parents are having problems with Abigail trying to keep her away from boys. She's been caught several times at school kissing passionately. Parents are also having trouble with the neighbors starting trouble. Neighborhood isn't suitable for children. Home was unsanitary, but there were two dogs and a lot of stuff. Crowded.

Laura and Eusebio both seem to love their kids very much. They spoke openly about family issues and expressed concern for referrals. The kids were open to talk and had great things to say about their parents.

CASE CONCLUSION
There was no disclosure of abuse. Abigail admitted that she made a false allegation because she was mad. Disposition: R/O; No Significant Factors

———

The case will be closed, but the family has received referrals for counseling concerns.

ABIGAIL

AGE 26

The Ring

I am so happy living with Rudy and our kids—his two and my three. It is the life that I always imagined for myself. A big, fun, loud, crazy, busy, loving family with kids running all around. Now, I finally have it.

The moment I met Rudy, it was love at first sight—at least for me. I loved his style, his confidence, his kindness, his strength, his compassion, and the unjudging, unconditional way that he has always loved me. I love this guy. I want to marry him!

Rudy's mom isn't working today, so I wait until I think she's up and I go to her bedroom to talk to her.

"Good morning. I wanted to ask you a question."

"Okay, Mija. Ask me anything."

"Well, I'm kind of scared and nervous, but I wanted to see if you could help me on getting a ring for Rudy because I want to marry him."

"What?!" she exclaims. She seems shocked, but happy.

"I really love him. I think he's the one for me. The kids are all good together, so I think we'll be good together."

Her face lit up with excitement, she replies, "Of course!"

She and I end up heading to a local jewelry store. I pick out a plain silver band for Rudy. It's simple, but it's perfect. It's exactly what I had in mind. Then we head back home, where I begin to plan how I'm going to pull this off when Rudy gets home from work later tonight.

I am going to make enchiladas with rice and beans for dinner. I start to lay out some of the ingredients I will need. I am watching the clock constantly. I feel slightly anxious, but more than anything, I am excited for this—for the start of our future.

About five minutes before Rudy usually gets home, I manage to herd all the kids into Rudy's mom's bedroom. I want everyone to be a part of this special moment between us. The plan is for me to stay in here with the kids and for his mom to go out to approach Rudy when he gets here to lure him into the bedroom. "He's here, Mija!" She heads to the living room. I hear the door open and shut.

Rudy's mom then says, "Rudy, I need to talk to you" in a serious tone.

"Uh, you need to talk to me? What about? What's going on?"

"Come with me. I need to talk with you in my room."

"Uh, okay."

I hear them approaching. The kids are all eagerly clamoring, waiting for them both to walk into the room. They do.

Rudy's mom walks in with a big smile, followed by her son, who wears a serious expression. He has no idea what is going on. Rudy glances around, sees that we are all in the room, looks directly at me and says, "Uh, what's going on?"

I tell him, "I just wanted to ask you a question."

"Uh, okay." From the look on his face, I can tell he is clueless.

I slide my hand into my back pocket to grab the ring and I go down onto one knee. "You are the love of my life. I'm very happy to be with you. Rudy, will you marry me?"

"Yes, of course! But I'm the one who's supposed to be asking you."

"But I wanted to ask you!"

I slide the ring onto Rudy's finger. He pulls me up from my downed knee, kisses me on the lips with a gentle peck, and pulls me in for a tight hug. In this moment, I feel the happiest that I have ever felt. I feel loved. I feel safe. And I feel like I am home.

As we take a step back after embracing, the kids run up to us, the little kids are jumping up and down cheering and everybody hugs one another. Rudy's mom has a big smile on her face, adoration in her eyes, and seems genuinely happy for us. Rudy's eldest daughter and my eldest daughter actually seem to truly understand what is going on, the younger ones don't really get it, but are happy to be jumping around, hugging us, and celebrating this moment with us.

I feel like I am floating on a cloud. I am finally blessed with the big family that I always wanted. I am going to have a loving, caring, supportive, hardworking husband who will be a great father to all of our kids. This moment is a lifelong dream.

I will be a wife.

I will have a husband.

We will have a big, beautiful, happy, blended family.

Me and Rudy, together.

My soulmate. My lover. My friend. My future.

ABIGAIL

AGE 26
Late 2014

Phantoms and Babies

udy and I want to have a baby together. We aren't necessarily trying to have a baby, but we aren't doing much to prevent it either. We are in love and excited to add to our blended family.

Today, I realized that my period is almost two weeks late. Rudy doesn't know that yet. Plus, I've noticed that my breasts feel tender and I have had some nausea in the mornings. Rudy is still asleep beside me, so I quietly untangle my body from the comfort of the cool sheets and thin blanket and slide out of bed. Quietly creeping into the bathroom, I pull open the cupboard door to grab the small rectangular box of a pregnancy test inconspicuously sitting in there waiting for me. Like so many times in the past, I pee on the stick, only this time, alone and at my own direction. Only this time, I am filled with the hope that it will be positive. I hope that there is a baby growing inside of me. There is nothing ugly or evil intertwined with this moment. It is only mine.

Time never runs more slowly than when a woman pees over a pregnancy test stick. Each minute that ticks by seems to take forever. But after only a few minutes, up pops the second line. I am pregnant! Rudy and I are going to have a baby!

Far less quietly, I amble back to the bed where my handsome fiancé is still asleep. I sit down beside him on the bed and his eyes pop open. He glances up at me. I eagerly greet him with a "Good morning, babe. It's time to get up!"

"Good morning. It's time to get up? I'm still sleepy, babe."

"It's time to wake up! I need to tell you something."

"To tell me something? What do you mean? To tell me what?"

All at once, the words rush out on a wisp of exhilaration, "I'm pregnant!"

"No way."

"Yeah. I'm pregnant!"

Rudy sits up in bed and pulls me into a strong embrace with his arms wrapped around me. He plants a soft kiss on the side of my head.

"Really?"

"Yes, babe. Really. We are going to have a baby!"

"Oh wow. I mean, it's not like I didn't think this would happen, but it's such big news. Another baby. Together. That's great, babe. Seriously. I'm really happy."

"I am, too. I am so excited to have a baby with you."

While we are already a family, this feels different, like we will truly be a blended family in the best ways possible.

During our next trip to buy groceries, soap, and detergent, I eagerly explore one of the baby aisles of the store. I have never felt so excited to embrace everything about motherhood, the entire experience, to truly enjoy every moment of it. This time, I don't have to pretend that I am in love. I do not need to create a fake boyfriend in my mind to help get me through it. I don't have to bend to the whims and wishes of two twisted people who fully intend to steal the child growing within my womb. This time, I am in love. This time, I am engaged to the man I love. This time, I will be a mom to this baby from the moment that it draws its first beautiful breath on this earth. Mine.

Admiring an endcap of stuffed animals, I pick up a small blue teddy bear that has rubber teething feet for a baby. With a big smile on my face, I set the blue teddy bear into the cart for my baby. I have never felt more calm, happy, and at peace. I am in charge of my own life now. I will decide how this baby will live in this world. I will be the one not only taking care of him or her, but fully owning motherhood. The Mother's Day gifts made at preschool will finally go to me. There will be no one to step in and domineer my decisions, my actions, and the way I choose to raise this baby—*my* baby—our baby.

I am nearing the end of the first trimester in my pregnancy. Rudy has been amazingly supportive and beside me every step of the way. If I don't feel well or am struggling on a particular day, he steps in to help cook, clean, and tend to the kids. He is a partner in the truest sense of the word. I've never had anyone genuinely care about how I feel before. In the past, my feelings or level of exhaustion never mattered. It feels different living in a home where I am treated with respect, like I matter. Where I have the freedom to make mistakes and own them. I am hard on myself in that way.

Anytime I feel like I mess something up, I still hear the faint echoes of Laura chiding me or Chevo scolding me in my head. "You're so stupid. You're so dumb. You aren't good for nothin'. You are never gonna amount to anything." It can be hard to be in a new home and free of the people who tormented me to still sometimes find that their voices have the power to permeate the space around me.

The other day, Rudy said, "Babe, it's like you're always on edge, like you're walking on eggshells, waiting for something bad to happen. You don't have to be that way anymore. Things are different for you now. You don't have to be afraid. You don't have to worry anymore."

But the fear and anxiety live inside of me, just as much as the blood, bones, and cells that comprise my body. I constantly battle with the feeling that I am not good enough. I worry that I will do something wrong and it will upset Rudy, his mom, or his sister. None of them have ever done anything to make me feel this way, but the deep roots of trauma continue to twist and bind me.

Today, Rudy and I are headed to our first appointment with an OB-GYN. The kids are in school, so it is just the two of us. I am floating on happiness as we make the short drive to his office. Glancing at him, I see the strong, handsome, caring man that is my fiancé. He is my biggest supporter and has always been right alongside me for whatever craziness that has stood in our way. I don't know many men who could deal with the things that Rudy has had to deal with in order to end up with me.

Walking into the doctor's office, I check in with the receptionist and we both take a seat in the adjoining waiting room. It is a typical OB-GYN's office with green chairs and pale pink walls covered with candid shots of smiling babies, end tables covered with a slew of parenting magazines, and ladies in varying degrees of pregnancy all around us. I am nervous to finally see a doctor, but I am excited to finally hear our baby's heartbeat. Since this is my fourth (technically, my fifth pregnancy, if you count the one where Laura had me take some random pills that terminated it), I know exactly what to expect. Only this time, everything feels so much lighter and happier.

"Abigail Castillo—" the medical assistant calls out, as she props the door open with her hip to hold it open for us. I follow along behind her down an interior hallway of the office with Rudy trailing behind me. I glance back at him and am met with a grin. She has me step on a scale. She measures my height. She measures my belly. Then she ushers us into a nearby examination room.

I hop up onto the side of the flat, slightly tilted examination bench and Rudy takes a seat in a green chair on the other side of the tiny room. Following two brief knocks on the door, the doctor walks in. He greets us—a rail thin, elderly doctor with glasses—introduces himself, and dives right into the typical pregnancy banter in the form of a question-and-answer session. "How long ago was your last period?" "You had a positive test?" "How are you feeling?" "Have you had any morning sickness?" "Are you having any problems that you've noticed?"

"Okay, now let's have you lie down, and we'll listen to your baby's heartbeat." He lifts my shirt up to expose my bare belly and places the wand of the device on my flesh. This part is always exciting—to hear the baby's heartbeat for the first time and to realize that a tiny human being is actually growing inside my body. The doctor moves the wand to another spot on my belly. Rudy and I look at one another as we patiently await to hear the swoosh, swoosh that we have both heard before with our other babies. Part of me feels weirded out about having a male doctor, but with Rudy beside me, I feel safe. I know the doctor is just here to do his job and to help me.

The doctor moves the wand to another spot on my stomach. And then another one. There is no *swoosh, swoosh*. The room is silent. *Maybe he's just in the wrong spot. He will find it in the next spot.* A heavy silence settles in all around us. He moves the wand over another inch. *Where is the heartbeat? Why can't he find it?* Rudy is looking over at me with a flicker of solemn concern upon his face, yet stoic, with his brows furrowed, but otherwise a look of gentleness across his features. I can tell that he is trying to look like nothing is wrong right now, but he is unable to fully mask his worry. *Where is the heartbeat?*

The doctor looks over at Rudy, then at me, "I'm so sorry to have to tell you this, but it appears that there is no baby—there is no heartbeat. It looks like you had what we refer to as a 'phantom pregnancy.' Sometimes, the body can mimic a pregnancy when a person really wants to be pregnant, when the body isn't actually pregnant, to the point that a person will have many symptoms of pregnancy. Unfortunately, there is no baby. I'm so sorry . . ."

I hear the rumble of voices—the doctor's and Rudy's. I cannot make out the garbled words. *No baby. Not pregnant.*

"It's important for you to understand that your body truly believes that it is pregnant right now. It has even grown a placenta to hold the baby. If we don't intervene, your body could carry this phantom pregnancy to term. Let's give you both a bit of time to process all of this—to deal with this news—and then you may end up needing to go to the hospital for a procedure to remove the placenta. Let's see how things go and give you some time."

More garbled words. *No baby. Give us time.* Hollow. That is the best word to describe how I feel right now. And like a total failure. Like I can't do anything right.

I cry the entire way home, sobbing with my head in my hands and my body curled up into the seat. Rudy holds my hand, runs his thumb tenderly across my hand, and attempts to say kind words to me to comfort me—the right words—but there are no "right" words, and there can be no comfort. My body is literally ready for a baby, but there is no baby. There is only pain. Only loss.

Maybe I'm not good enough to have a baby with him. Maybe God is punishing me for my past—for all the things that have happened to me in my life. Maybe I don't deserve another baby.

Two weeks later, my water broke on its own, so Rudy drove me to the hospital. The doctor had to ensure that my body expelled the entire placenta that my body had formed to protect and nourish my precious, non-existent, phantom baby. I was crushed by this entire experience. I felt so angry, frustrated, and sad, like it was my fault somehow. Lying in that hospital bed overnight, I felt so alone, even with Rudy right beside me.

Nobody else around me seemed to understand that, for me, there was an actual loss of a baby—in my heart and in my mind, not just a betrayal by my own body. To Rudy, there was never a baby—not really. To me, there was one, and I was looking so forward to everything that would come along with it.

In the months that followed, Rudy and his mom were a resilient, unshakeable force of support tethering me to the here-and-now on a daily basis. Without them, I would not have made it through this difficult time. While I still felt as though my body had betrayed me, I tried to cling to the fact that I needed to be grateful for the amazing family and home life that I now have.

I am not without. I am with everything. All of it. I have so much.
If God ever wants us to have another baby together, then it will
happen. But I worry that something like this could happen again if
we try for another baby, and that fear, once again, rules my thoughts.
This time, it is a different type of fear. It is the fear of loss.

ABIGAIL

AGE 26
March 7, 2015

The Wedding

*T*oday is the day that I will marry my best friend. As I pull on the beautiful, fitted white bridal gown made of an intricate white lace, my stomach flutters with excitement as I glance into the mirror to give myself a final once-over. Then we climb into the car and drive to the church. I guess you could call us non-traditional because Rudy and I saw one another at home while we were getting ready. Our wedding is a small affair and the church was already decorated, so we didn't have to pick anything out.

My four-year-old son—Baby Three—who looks adorable sporting a black tuxedo, walks me down the aisle. I am nervous, but in a good way. I see Rudy standing at the altar, waiting for me, looking remarkably handsome in a black suit. The sight of him takes my breath away. I feel so happy and so lucky to be here. With each step we take toward the altar, I fight back tears. Standing beside Rudy at the front of the church are two tall columns decorated with beautiful yellow and white flowers. There is a small table topped with a unity candle and more yellow and white flowers to the left of us. It is simply decorated, but beautiful. While I normally don't like being the center of attention, today feels different. Today, I happily bask in the glow of this moment.

As Rudy and I recite our vows to one another, what I feel is unconditional love coupled with pure happiness. The type of love that I had never known to exist prior to meeting this amazing man who now stands before me, handsome as ever, with my hand tucked in his hand, and my heart also tucked inside of his. Forever. Unconditionally, from this moment on. I always imagined myself here. Not just the ceremony part of things, but right in the thick of it—the love story. The good times, the spats, the annoying habits, the children, the loud house, the memories—I love all of it. It took so many years for me to make it to this moment. To my soulmate. To a family. To a real life. To live out *my* life.

Once the ceremony is finished, we make our way to a nearby room filled with our family and closest friends. Much like my eighth-grade dance and senior prom, I find myself taking in the energy of room and smiling, talking, and laughing. Only this time I know the magic will not end. When the lights go down and fade into blackness, the happiness will remain. This is my life now. I am in charge of my future.

Sitting in the room filled with round and rectangular tables each bearing a candle and flowers, we dine on forkfuls of meatloaf, brisket, mashed potatoes, and corn. It's a simple meal, but it is delicious.

While we didn't pick out the decorations or do much to plan our wedding, the cake is one item that I put a lot of thought into. When it is time to cut our cake, Rudy and I walk to a table holding a beautiful two-tiered wedding cake covered in thick white fondant piped in frosting made to look like a fancy ribbon and topped with a cluster of chocolate-dipped strawberries, two of which are decorated to resemble the attire of a bride and groom. Tucked inside the layers of luscious vanilla cake hides a strawberry jam filling.

Rudy and I cut the take together and take turns feeding each other a piece of it in a respectful manner without smearing each other's faces. Considering the amount of time that I invested into perfecting my makeup today, I am grateful for the lack of fondant and cake crumbs on my face. You know what they say: "Happy wife, happy life!" Rudy made a good choice going the mannerly route.

After hanging out with our guests for a while, we drive to a historic setting nearby, the Mission San Jose Church, to take wedding photos of the two of us and us with our children alongside the remarkable architecture. Once the last of the pictures are taken, we hop into the car and head home to spend the rest of what will be a relaxed evening with our kids. I guess you could say our honeymoon was filled with normal family life and a few romantically stolen moments.

This was a beautiful day. A happy day. And one of the most important days in my life. It is the day that, at long last, I finally feel complete—and loved, like I have a true family, and I am home.

ABIGAIL

AGE 27
March 20, 2016

Hello, Baby

O n March 20, 2016, I give birth to my first child with Rudy—my fourth baby, his third. This day is calm, peaceful, beautiful, and filled with so much positivity and love. This day is everything that a birth experience for any woman should be.

I look down at our handsome baby boy, cradled in a white hospital blanket—the new owner of the pale blue plush teddy bear with rubberized feet that I once bought while filled only with hope. I now hold the baby that I prayed to God to give to me—and to Rudy.

I feel like God has given me a second chance, like maybe my "phantom pregnancy" just wasn't the right time for me and Rudy to have a baby, and now is the right time. When Rudy and I visited my doctor throughout this pregnancy, I made him check for the heartbeat three times during each appointment, just to make sure the baby was still there, as I eagerly listened to the tiny *swoosh, swoosh* that filled a no-longer-silent room.

Interestingly, although this is now my fourth baby, I feel like a first-time mom, like I have no idea what I am doing. With my other babies, Laura was always lording over me, watching my every move, dictating my every action, and with this baby, I am the one in charge. Me and Rudy. It is an awesome responsibility, but a lofty one that comes with a slight twinge of paranoia. *Am I doing this right? Did I put this diaper on tight enough?* I suspect this is how I would have felt with my first baby if I had her under normal circumstances. While I love each of my beautiful babies equally, the way they came into the world was undeniably different.

Rudy and his mom are a daily presence in my life to perpetually remind me that I am loved, I am worthy, I am capable, and most importantly—I am enough.

What I now know is this: evil can only consume you if you allow it to change who you are. Evil touching you does not become you. It does not tarnish you. It does not diminish the essence of who you are as a person. When that evil takes a step away, and it is scrubbed off of skin, and it is shed from your soul, what is left behind is still YOU. The "you" that existed before the evil. The "you" that survived in spite of the evil. The "you" that surmounted the face of evil and still stands.

Evil is a tyrant that rules by fear. It buries seeds of doubt. It grows roots that ensnare you at the core, wraps around your soul, and stretches its reach outward to alter a person's existence. But much like weeds, evil can be cut out, the same way that it is removed from a bed of shrubs and flowers. Pruned. Pulled away and stripped of its existence. And that flower? It never had anything wrong with it at all. It was breathed into existence by God himself, fully intended to bloom. People aren't much different. Once you cut the evil out of your life, that beauty that was always held at the core—begins to bloom.

Each of us is a tiny piece of God's work that helps to create the full masterpiece.

With free will, we make our own choices. We choose the type of people we will be, and who we will become. We each walk our own path.

Even when some of us have been planted to stand involuntarily in the darkest of days whether suffocating in the midst of weeds, hell, or evil—we still can triumphantly bloom.

Every. Single. Day.

By choice.

ABIGAIL

2016

Finding Them

$\mathcal{A}$fter more than two years of calling the detective in an effort to check the status of my case—and the status of the arrest of Chevo and Laura—Rudy and I feel frustrated and defeated. The first detective assigned to my case is never in when I call. Sometimes, he's out of the office working on other cases, other times, he's out of the office on vacation. Then when he's in, he's generally not available to talk. It feels like no one is taking this seriously, which amplifies my shame for even bringing it up.

To make emotions more complicated, while scrolling across recent posts on Facebook today, I come across a GoFundMe campaign for my mom. It is dated September 27, 2016, and was created by Chevo to collect donations for Laura's medical bills. The update reads:

> *Laura A Castillo a 45 year old female fighting Lupus. Laura was diagnosed in December 2011. Since then she has undergone various surgeries. She is currently having to undergo two additional surgeries, one in particular which will allow her to finally have an MRI that she so desperately needs to treat her Lupus. Lupus is also affecting her jaw bone and causing her to have severe TMJ and problems with her right ear for which she will need to undergo another surgery. Laura currently has no medical insurance. Even through the pain Laura still continues to go to work, have her weekly prayer meetings and*

visit with the elderly in her community. She has always given to so many people. That is to include the 13 Bravo field artillery soldiers and their families which she holds so dearly to her heart. Now its time that we help her out. Laura is a strong woman and will not go down without a fight. We ask that you please help with a donation. Laura is a very humble person and doesn't like to ask for help, those of you who have been touched by Laura know just how kind and loving she is, and how she is always willing to help anyone in need. There is no cure for Lupus, so this is a battle Laura will be fighting for a long time. WE pray for a CURE!

The post is end-capped with the following:

One of the oddest things is trying to explain how a Lupie can go from their 'good' day to just needing to be in bed because you just can't really function. This is a cruel reality for most Lupies.

A wave of nausea hits me full force, as I continue to scroll down to see an image of a large magenta butterfly accompanied by the words "LUPUS WARRIOR" hanging above it. Next is a picture of Laura lying in a hospital gown wearing a fancy, blue, Mardi Gras-style eye mask bearing large sparkly stones around the eye slits and donning tall white bunny ears—apparently from using one of those creative app filters—along with words, "I Fight Like a Girl—Lupus Warrior," and, "I'm in the fight of my LIFE and I'm going to WIN!".

It appears that they have raised $250 of their $3,000 goal. While I do believe Laura has Lupus, their ploy for other people's money just makes me sick.

Unbelievable. The gall of them to post this online. And for them to say all those nice things about her as though she is a good person. As the past keeper of her secrets, I know her true form. The part that really gets me is the part with the words, ". . . those of you who have been touched by Laura." Did they really say that and not notice how weird that reads based on the things that she has done? It is yet another ploy for money at the expense of others to further themselves. It looks like their own greed won out over their desire to remain undetected. That part may actually be a blessing because it led me to this post. It led me to them.

My initial bout of nausea is replaced with a ping of excitement. Maybe this information will help the police find them! Maybe this will be the thing that finally gets them caught.

I immediately pick up my cell phone and dial the number for the detective at the San Antonio Police Department to share what I found with him and learn that a new detective is assigned to my case. He seems eager to hear the news and says that he is going to look into it. Maybe he will actually do something and maybe they will finally be arrested.

SUMMARY OF DOCUMENTATION AND INVESTIGATION

On Saturday, December 10, 2016. I was assigned to investigate further into the case by my supervisor after the Victim had contacted me, while I was answering phone calls for the day, with information about her case. The Victim told me that she had gotten married since the report and her new last name was Alvarado. The Victim told me she saw a GoFundMe ad posted on the internet with Defendant 2, Laura Castillo, listed as the subject for requesting funds for her medical diagnosis. The Victim said the ad shows that Defendant 1, Eusebio Castillo, created the ad on September 27, 2016 and his location where he posted the ad was listed as San Juan, TX. The Victim directed me to the web page and I confirmed that the ad was in fact posted. I printed the web page containing the ad for documentation. I pulled the case file from the file room and checked the details of the case, see Det. D. Cartwright #2438's documentation included in the case file for further details . . .

On Wednesday, December 14, 2016, I called the San Juan Police Department and left a voicemail for one of the detectives to call me in regards to this case for assistance.

On Thursday, December 22, 2016, I was able to speak with Corporal M. Martinez of the San Juan Police Department over the phone and he advised me that he would be able to assist me in trying to contact Eusebio and obtain a DNA sample after I sent them the search warrant. I obtained a search warrant for a DNA sample of Eusebio and emailed a copy of the warrant to Corporal Martinez . . .

On Wednesday, December 28, 2016, when I returned to my office from my days off I received an email from Corporal Martinez saying they were able to obtain the DNA sample from Eusebio. After checking with my supervisor, I requested Corporal Martinez to mail the sample to our property room so we could send it off to the crime lab for testing . . .

In Review —
I was assigned to investigate further into this case by my supervisor after receiving information from the Victim of a possible location where Defendant 1, Eusebio, could be found. I looked into the case file for information about the case. My review of the information: the Victim had been sexually assaulted by Eusebio, her biological uncle and foster parent at the time, since she was nine years old and had given birth to three children that she states were from the result of the sexual assaults; the Victim had gotten pregnant with her first child when she was 16 years of age and states Eusebio is the father; the Victim stated that they had moved to San Antonio about five years before she filed the police report and previously had lived in multiple areas within Texas; Eusebio had made threats to the Victim of killing her children if she told anyone about what happened to her and also overtly made threats by pouring gasoline around their house and even on himself, saying he would burn the house and himself if she told anyone; the Victim indicated that Laura, Eusebio's wife, partook in some of the sexual assaults after they moved into San Antonio; DNA samples were collected from the Victim and her children. Eusebio and

Laura were unable to be located at that time and the case was closed PF1.

I checked the information given by the Victim and researched around it to determine that San Juan, TX was a good area to check for Eusebio to collect a sample of his DNA. I contact the San Juan Police Department and became in contact with Corporal Martinez who assisted in getting a sample of Eusebio's DNA after a Search Warrant was obtained. The DNA sample was mailed to the San Antonio Police Department's Property Room and then submitted to the Bexar County Crime Lab for testing/comparison with the DNA samples from the Victim and her children. The results came back to conclude that Eusebio is the most likely match [99.9% per the DNA testing] to being the father of the children involved. I then obtained two arrest warrants for Eusebio's arrest [Sexual Assault and Prohibited Sexual Conduct/Incest] and notified the San Juan Police Department of the active warrants. I was notified by the San Juan Police Department that Eusebio was arrested for the warrants. I reached out to the authorities in Hawaii, Houston, Laredo, and Mission to advise them of the case and provided them with the proper information.

Upon reviewing all statements, reports and related information, I find the information to be credible and consistent with Texas Penal Code Violations 22.011 Sexual Assault. This case is being sent to the district attorney's office for prosecution.

Case No. 16-03108
SAN JUAN POLICE DEPARTMENT
Incident # 16-03108
Martinez, M

On December 22, 2016, Corporal Michael Martinez checked his voicemails from the December 21, 2016 just after starting his shift. Cpl. Martinez had left the early on the 21st of December and is why he had not check his voice mails sooner. Cpl. Martinez received a voice message from a Detective Miles McPeak of the San Antonio Police Department. Detective McPeak requested assistance from the San Juan Police Department in obtain DNA samples from a suspect that was currently living in the city of San Juan, Texas.

At around 8:25 a.m., Cpl. Martinez returned Det. McPeak's phone call but there was no answer. Cpl. Martinez left Det. McPeak voice message informing him, he would assist him and provided his email so that Det. McPeak could forward any information regarding his case. At around 9:50 a.m., Cpl. Martinez received an email from Det. McPeak informing Cpl. Martinez that he was going to get a search warrant for buccal membrane [DNA swab]. Det. McPeak later provided the subject's information being Eusebio Castillo Jr. [D.O.B. 03-06-1970 TxDL 09198133] with an address of 700 Hwy. 83 Apt. D. The email explained that Mr. Castillo is a suspect in an Aggravated Sexual Assault from 2014.

After viewing the address provided by Det. McPeak, Cpl. Martinez noticed that address was incorrect due to his knowledge of his jurisdiction. Cpl. Martinez then conducted a search on Mr. Castillo through LexisNexis. Cpl. Martinez found that Mr. Castillo had a current address at 400 N. Iowa

Rd. Apt 7 San Juan Tx. Later that morning, Cpl. Martinez receive the search warrant from Det. McPeak. Cpl. Martinez decided to wait on serving the warrant until December 27, 2016 due to the Christmas Holiday and now knowing how the mail system would be operating during the holiday in order to mail Det. McPeak the DNA samples.

On December 27, 2016 at around 11:00 a.m., Cpl. Martinez along with Investigator C. Kazan proceeded to 400 N. Iowa Rd Apt 7 in attempt to served the search warrant. Upon arriving at the location Cpl. Martinez attempted to make contact at apartment 7. There was no answer. Cpl. Martinez observed a door hanger from a furniture rental store with Mr. Castillo's name on it, which indicated no contact was made with Mr. Castillo and requested a return call. Cpl. Martinez then saw a gray Mazada license plates [TxPl BWK9086]. Inquiry returned showed that Mr. Castillo was the registered owner. Cpl. Martinez then suspected that Mr. Castillo was not answering the door intentionally. Cpl. Martinez then made contact with a neighbor and asked if she knew Mr. Castillo. The neighbor then said she did and that Mr. Castillo was the maintenance man for the apartment complex.

Cpl. Martinez then proceeded to the apartments' main office and made contact with the reception. Cpl. Martinez asked for Mr. Castillo. Mr. Castillo was called into the office. Mr. Castillo arrived and Cpl. Martinez made contact with Mr. Castillo outside the office. Cpl. Martinez informed Mr. Castillo of the search warrant issued for his DNA out the Bexar County in reference to a sexual assault report made against him. Mr. Castillo informed Cpl. Martinez that he was unaware of such a report and did not know of any sexual assault. Cpl. Martinez observed Mr. Castillo became distress[ed] and was breathing heavily. Cpl. Martinez then escorted Mr. Castillo back to towards his apartment where his unmarked police unit was parked. Mr. Castillo was provided with a copy of the search warrant. Cpl. Martinez then used two cotton swabs to obtain buccal membrane from Mr. Castillo's inner right and left cheeks. Each swab was secured in an evidence box. Cpl. Martinez later submitted swabs into the evidence room. Cpl. Martinez also sent an email to Det. McPeak informing the search warrant had been served and asked him where he wanted the evidence to be sent.

On 12-28-2016, Cpl. Martinez received an email from Det. McPeak. The email stated that the evidence was to be mailed to the San Antonio Police Department Property Room at 555 Academic Ct., San Antonio, Tx 78204 in reference to case SAPD14148771. Cpl. Martinez then informed Evidence Technician S. Benitez that he need the evidence pertaining to this case be mailed to aforementioned address. The same afternoon Cpl. Martinez was informed by Officer J. Galindo that he responded to the 400 N. Iowa Rd in reference to an information report. Officer Galindo added that an employee for the apartments had found a noose in one of the vacant apartments that Mr. Castillo had been working on. Officer Galindo also informed Cpl. Martinez that surveillance video in the area captured Mr. Castillo walking away from the apartment during the night hours. Officer Galindo then added that Mr. Castillo had been transported to the hospital earlier in the morning for unknown medical reasons. No other information was provided. Officer Galindo generated an incident report #16-18276.

SUMMARY OF DOCMENTATION
AND INVESTIGATION

CONTINUED

On Friday, January 6, 2017, I received information from my supervisor that the samples were delivered to the property room. I then submitted DNA samples collected from Eusebio, the Victim, and her three children to the Bexar County Crime Lab for comparison . . .

On Thursday, February 2, 2017, I received the results from the crime lab indicating that Eusebio is the father of the Victim's children . . .

On Saturday, February 4, 2017, I walked two arrest warrants on Eusebio for sexual assault and prohibited sexual conduct and notified the San Juan Police Department of the active warrant . . .

On Wednesday, February 15, 2017, I returned from special assignment [2/5-2/14] and received a voicemail from an Officer R. Gonzalez of the San Juan P.D. saying he arrested Eusebio on the warrants from his residence.

• • •

Laura Castillo was arrested on June 1, 2017, nearly three years after I walked into the police station.

Lawyers often say, "Lady Justice can be found hiding in the courthouse." In my case, I think Lady Justice got lost somewhere along the way. But when it comes to justice, late is certainly better than never, and the time has finally arrived for justice to be served to Laura and Chevo. They must pay for all the horrific things they did to me.

NO. 2017CR5376A

THE STATE OF TEXAS	§	IN THE DISTRICT COURT
V.	§	187TH JUDICIAL DISTRICT
EUSEBIO CASTILLO JR	§	BEXAR COUNTY, TEXAS

STATE'S NOTICE OF INTENT TO INTRODUCE EVIDENCE OF EXTRANEOUS OFFENSES PURSUANT TO TEX. R. CRIM. EVID. 404(b), AND TEX. CODE CRIM. PROC. ART. 12.42, 38.37 AND 37.07, 12.42.

TO THE HONORABLE JUDGE OF SAID COURT:

NOW COMES NICHOLAS LAHOOD, Criminal District Attorney of Bexar County, Texas by and through the undersigned Assistant Criminal District Attorney, and files this Notice of Intent to Introduce Evidence of Extraneous Offenses. The purpose of this notice is to give the Court and defense counsel notice of extraneous offenses for the purposes of punishment and to give notice for enhancement purposes pursuant to Texas Penal Code Sec. 12.42. In support thereof the State would show the Court the following:

I.

The State hereby gives notice to the Court and to counsel for the defense, ANTHONY B. CANTRELL, that the State intend to offer evidence of other crimes, wrongs and acts in the case-in-chief at the Guilt/Innocence phase in the above numbered cause. This

Notice is given pursuant to Rule 404(b), Texas Rules of Criminal Evidence and Art. 37.07(g) and 38.37, TEX. C.C.P., as amended effective Sept. 1, 1995.

II.

The State also gives notice to the Court and to counsel for the defense that the State intends to offer evidence of other crimes, wrongs, and acts in the case-in-chief at the punishment phase in the above numbered case. This evidence is to be tendered pursuant to Article 37.07.

III.

The State specifically gives notice that upon a finding of guilt, at the punishment phase of the trial the State seeks to enhance the Defendant's punishment pursuant to Texas Penal Code Sec. 12.42.

IV.

Such other crimes, wrong or acts that the State intends to introduce in its case in chief in the guilt phase and/or punishment phase are:

- On or about June 12, 2000, in Honolulu County, Hawaii, the defendant committed the offense of wrongful possession and distribution of child pornography.

- On or about August 2, 2001, in Honolulu County, Hawaii, the defendant was discharged under honorable conditions from active duty of the United States Army due to misconduct.

- On or about 2003, the defendant in concert with Laura Castillo scammed the Make a Wish Foundation by holding his step son, [name intentionally omitted], out as terminally ill in order to receive a free trip to Disney World.

- On or about August 2010 through on or about June 2014, the defendant in concert with Laura Castillo fraudulently held our [first name intentionally omitted] Castillo as a "miracle child," capable of curing or helping those afflicted with cancer. As part of this fraudulent activity, the defendant and Laura Castillo would solicit donations.

- On or about June 2014, the defendant in concert with Laura Castillo scammed Linda Whitener out of her property by holding out the property as his own and selling appliances and various items to a third party without her consent.

V.

To the extent any additional wrongs or acts of Defendant not set out above or contained within the State's file become known, additional written notice will be given.

WHEREFORE, PREMISES CONSIDERED, the State of Texas requests that the Court allow in the State's case-in-chief and at the punishment phase all evidence of other crimes, wrongs, or acts as outlined in this motion.

Respectfully submitted,

_____

Brittany Byrd
Assistant Criminal District Attorney
Bexar County, Texas
Cadena-Reeves Justice Center
300 Dolorosa
San Antonio, Texas 78205-3030
Phone No. ***
State Bar No. 24094574

The Deal

October 13, 2018

Laura Castillo entered into a plea bargain with the State of Texas on Counts VI, VII, and VIII—three first degree felonies for Aggravated Sexual Assault in the first degree.

DEFENDANT'S WAIVERS AND AFFIDAVIT OF ADMONITIONS

TO THE HONORABLE JUDGE OF SAID COURT:

I, LAURA A. CASTILLO, the Defendant in this cause, having this day appeared in open court with my counsel and having been duly sworn, represent to this Court that I have received a copy of the indictment or information in this cause, that I fully understand its contents; that I know that I am charged with the felony offense of AGG SEXUAL ASSAULT and that I waive formal arraignment and the reading of the charging instrument.

• • •

I, the Defendant, hereby enter into a plea of ~~GUILTY/~~NOLO CONTENDERE to this charge.

1. I have had my Constitutional and legal rights explained to me by my attorney, and have decided to waive my Constitutional right of trial by jury and enter the plea before the judge. I hereby request the consent and approval of the State's Attorney and of the Court to my waiver of trial by jury. I further represent to the Court as follows:

2. I am mentally competent now and was legally sane at the time that this offense was committed.

3. I have not been threatened, coerced or placed in fear by any person to induce me to enter my plea.

4. If I have a plea bargain agreement with the prosecutor, its terms are fully set forth in the attached document. I have received no promise from the prosecutor, my attorney or the Court which are not set forth in that document, and I realize that no one else would be empowered to make me any promises.

5. ~~If I am pleading GUILTY, it is because I am guilty, and for no other reason.~~ If my plea is one of NOLO CONTENDENDERE, it is because I have considered all aspects of my legal situation and discussed them with my attorney and have determined that the entry of such plea is in my own best interest.

6. If applicable, my attorney has explained to me the requirements and consequences of Chapter 62 of the Texas Code of Criminal Procedure Sex Offender Registration Program.

7. I understand the Courts admonishments as contained in this waiver.

8. I am satisfied with the advice and representation of my attorney in this case.

9. I have been explained my immigration consequences by my attorney.

I certify that: __X__ I am a United States citizen.
_____ I am NOT a United States citizen.

• • •

The Defendant and his counsel further agree with the State's Attorney that the Defendant is the person named in the indictment Count VI, VII, and VIII of this indictment, that all of the acts alleged therein occurred in Bexar County, Texas, and that the allegations are ~~true and correct~~ not contested.

I further judicial swear and affirm that I committed the above offense with Eusebio Castillo in that I aided, assisted, encouraged, solicited, encouraged, directed, or attempted to aid Eusebio Castillo in the commission of the offense.

No. 2017CR5376B

I, LAURA A. CASTILLO, do not contest that I intentionally and knowingly, in Bexar County, Texas,

Count VI
Paragraph A

on or about the 12th Day of August, 2010, LAURA CASTILLO, hereinafter referred to as defendant, did intentionally and knowingly act in concert with EUSEBIO CASTILLO by causing the MOUTH of Abigail Castillo to CONTACT the SEXUAL ORGAN of THE DEFENDANT, and during the course of the same criminal episode, EUSEBIO CASTILLO did intentionally and knowingly cause the SEXUAL ORGAN of Abigail Castillo to CONTACT the SEXUAL ORGAN of EUSEBIO CASTILLO, said act having been committed without the consent of the complainant, in that THE DEFENDANT COMPELLED THE COMPLAINANT TO SUBMIT AND PARTICIPATE BY THE USE OF PHYSICAL FORCE AND VIOLENCE.

Paragraph B

on or about the 12th Day of August, 2010, LAURA CASTILLO, hereinafter referred to as defendant, did intentionally and knowingly act in concert with EUSEBIO CASTILLO by causing the

MOUTH of Abigail Castillo to CONTACT the SEXUAL ORGAN of THE DEFENDANT, and during the course of the same criminal episode, EUSEBIO CASTILLO did intentionally and knowingly cause the SEXUAL ORGAN or Abigail Castillo to CONTACT the SEXUAL ORGAN of EUSEBIO CASTILLO, said act having been committed without the consent of the complainant, in that THE DEFENDANT COMPELLED THE COMPLAINANT TO SUBMUT AND PARTICIPATE BY THREATENING TO USE FORCE AND VIOLENCE AGAINST THE COMPLAINANT, AND THE COMPLAINANT BELIEVED THAT THE DEFENDANT HAD THE PRESENT ABILITY TO EXECUTE THE THREAT;

Count VII
Paragraph A

on or about the 12th Day of September, 2010, LAURA CASTILLO, hereinafter referred to as defendant, did intentionally and knowingly act in concert with EUSEBIO CASTILLO by causing the SEXUAL ORGAN of Abigail Castillo to CONTACT the MOUTH of THE DEFENDANT, and during the course of the same criminal episode, EUSEBIO CASTILLO did intentionally and knowingly cause the SEXUAL ORGAN of Abigail Castillo to CONTACT the SEXUAL ORGAN of EUSEBIO CASTILLO, said act having been committed without the consent of the complainant, in that THE DEFENDANT COMPELLED THE COMPLAINANT TO SUBMIT AND PARTICIPATE BY THE USE OF PHYSICAL FORCE AND VIOLENCE;

Paragraph B

on or about the 12th Day of September, 2010, LAURA CASTILLO, hereinafter referred to as defendant, did intentionally and knowingly act in concert with EUSEBIO CASTILLO by causing the SEXUAL ORGAN of Abigail Castillo to CONTACT the MOUTH of THE DEFENDANT, and during the course of the same criminal episode, EUSBIO CASTILLO did intentionally and knowingly cause the SEXUAL ORGAN of Abigail Castillo to CONTACT the SEXUAL ORGAN of EUSEBIO CASTILLO, said act having been committed without the consent of the complainant, in that THE DEFENDANT COMPELLED THE COMPLAINANT TO SUBMIT AND PARTICIPATE BY THREATENING TO USE FORCE AND VIOLENCE AGAINST THE COMPLAINANT, AND THE COMPLAINANT BELIEVED THAT THE DEFENDANT HAD THE PRESENT ABILITY TO EXECUTE THE THREAT;

Count VIII
Paragraph A

on or about the 12th Day of October, 2010, LAURA CASTILLO, hereinafter referred to as defendant, did intentionally and knowingly act in concert with EUSEBIO CASTILLO by causing the MOUTH of Abigail Castillo to CONTACT the SEXUAL ORGAN of the DEFENDANT, and during the course of the same criminal episode, EUSEBIO CASTILLO did intentionally and knowingly cause the SEXUAL ORGAN of Abigail Castillo to CONTACT the SEXUAL ORGAN or EUSEBIO CASTILLO, said act having been committed without the consent of the complainant, in that THE DEFENDANT COMPELLED THE COMPLAINANT TO SUBMIT AND PARTICIPATE BY THE USE OF PHYSICAL FORCE AND VIOLENCE.

Paragraph B

on or about the 12th Day of October, 2010, LAURA CASTILLO, hereinafter referred to as Defendant, did intentionally and knowingly act in concert with EUSEBIO CASTILLO by causing the MOUTH of Abigail Castillo to CONTACT the SEXUAL ORGAN of THE DEFENDANT, and during the course of the same criminal episode, EUSEBIO CASTILLO did intentionally and knowingly cause the SEXUAL ORGAN of Abigail Castillo to CONTACT the SEXUAL ORGAN of EUSEBIO CASTILLO, said act having been committed without the consent of complainant, in that THE DEFENDANT COMPELLED THE COMPLAINANT TO SUBMIT AND PARTICIPATE BY THREATENING TO USE FORCE AND VIOLENCE AGAINST THE COMPLAINANT, AND THE COMPLAINANT BELIEVED THAT THE DEFENDANT HAD THE PRESENT ABILITY TO EXECUTE THE THREAT...

A nolo contendere plea (also known as an "Alford Plea") is a plea by which a defendant in a criminal prosecution accepts conviction as though a guilty plea has been entered against him or her but does not admit guilt. In other words, Laura was willing to accept the punishment for the crimes she committed but wasn't willing to admit guilt for those crimes. One advantage of this type of plea is that it cannot be used against the defendant in another cause of action. Under this "deal" for the three counts admitted, Laura knew that she would be sentenced to a term between five years and 99 years or life, plus pay a possible fine of up to $10,000. Under the agreement, she also waived her right to appeal.

Laura was ultimately sentenced to 33 years in prison for the three counts of Aggravated Sexual Assault in the first degree—each a felony charge—with credit for the 415 days she had already served behind bars from the date of her arrest.

Court costs of $584.00 were assessed.

Laura would be required to register as a Sex Offender.

A no contact order was also entered to prohibit Laura from any contact with Abigail Alvarado and her three children due to the affirmative finding of family violence.

SENTENCING HEARING—IN ITS ENTIRETY

The State of Texas v. Eusebio Castillo
Trial Court Cause No. 2017-CR-5376-A
October 23, 2018

**All typographical and grammatical errors are contained in the original transcript. Some names intentionally withheld. **

On the 23rd day of October 2018, the following proceedings came on to be held in the above-titled and numbered cause before the Honorable JOEY CONTRERAS, Judge Presiding, held in San Antonio, Bexar County, Texas.

Representing the State: Mr. Steven Spier & Mrs. Brittany Byrd
Representing Eusebio Castillo: Mr. Tony Cantrell

THE COURT:	The State versus Eusebio Castillo, Junior.
	All right. Mr. Cantrell is here with us. Everybody is here.
	Mr. Castillo, on October 1st, 2018 you entered a plea to the indictment, or most if not all of the counts. The record reflects which ones you did in this case, and I put it off—I put off sentencing in order to have a PSI [Pre-Sentencing Investigation] generated. One has been generated and has been given to both sides.
	Both sides, I presume, have had time to read and review it?
MR. SPEIR:	Yes, Your Honor.
MR. CANTRELL:	That's correct, Your Honor.

THE COURT: All right, then. Let's proceed with the
                 sentencing. Who wants to lead off?

MR. CANTRELL: Your Honor, we'd ask that you consider a 35
                 year sentence in this case. It's appropriate
                 for the offense that was committed that
                 my client has taken full responsibility
                 for. It's also appropriate because of his—
                 because of my client's condition.

                 Just to remind the Court, he has renal cell
                 carcinoma [cancer of the kidneys]. His five
                 year survival rate is forty percent. So, most
                 likely he won't be alive in five years.

                 He's truly remorseful for his actions. And
                 he can't really give a good explanation as
                 to why he did his actions.

THE COURT: Maybe alcohol involved.

MR. CANTRELL: Most definitely.

THE COURT: I got that from the PSI.

MR. CANTRELL: Most definitely alcohol involved. But even
                 then there is no good explanation.

THE COURT: No.

MR. CANTRELL: So we'd ask the Court to just consider that.
                 It's within the area which the state was
                 asking. We think it's appropriate.

MR. SPEIR: Your Honor, the state has two witnesses.

THE COURT: You want to put some testimony on? Okay. Go
                 ahead and call your first witness.

MR. SPEIR: State would call Linda W. [last name
                    intentionally withheld and denoted as "W"].
                    Come on up here, Mrs. W, around here.

                    Step up, Ma'am, and raise your right hand.

THE COURT: Have a seat, Ma'am. They are going to ask
                    you some questions.

DIRECT EXAMINATION

BY MR. SPEIR:

Q.   Mrs. W, I want to make sure I told the court reporter
      correctly. Your name is spelled how?

A.   [witness spells last name]

Q.   Okay, and Mrs. W, you live in San Antonio?

A.   I do.

Q.   Are you related to a Laura Castillo?

A.   Yes, I am.

Q.   Explain to us how you are related to her.

A.   Distantly. Her Dad was my first cousin.

Q.   And do you know who Eusebio Castillo [is]?

A.   Yes, I do.

Q.   And who is he in relationship to Laura?

A.   Her husband.

Q.   Okay. Now I want to draw your attention back, it's been
      several years ago, say, back around 2000 and—well, let
      me just ask you. When did you and Laura, I guess, bump
      into each other in San Antonio, approximately? What
      year?

A. I would have to say probably five or six years ago.

Q. Okay. So in 2012, 2013, thereabouts?

A. Uh-huh.

Q. Where did you bump into Laura?

A. We were at a family funeral.

Q. And at that time did you learn about Laura and her husband Eusebio's need for new living conditions?

A. Not immediately.

Q. Okay.

A. At that time she just explained to me that she was working and that she had a very special daughter that she thought I needed to come visit.

Q. And that special daughter, did that turn out to be [name of Abby's eldest daughter, intentionally withheld and denoted below as "Abby's Eldest Daughter"] Castillo?

A. Yes.

Q. This special daughter, what type of setting did you go visit that special daughter in?

A. The very first time I visited their home they were having a rosary outside and there was chairs situated in the back yard. It was kind of drizzly morning— evening, I'm sorry. And people just kept arriving. I didn't know who they were.

Q. Was this a make-shift religious service?

A. Yes. Yes.

Q. How many people were there?

A. I would say somewhere between twenty and thirty.

Q. And was Abby's Eldest Daughter being held out to be something?

A. Yes.

Q. What was she being held out to be?

A. That she had special healing powers. That she could lay hands, as the story goes. That she was able to cure people.

Q. Okay. Cure people of what?

A. Mostly of cancer.

Q. Now at this service, was Eusebio collecting any money?

A. At the end of the service they passed a basket.

Q. Okay. And were people putting money in this basket?

A. Yes.

Q. Did you ever go back to any other of these services?

A. Yes.

Q. How many?

A. Well we actually had one at my office. And then we had several at my parents' home, which is where they ended up living.

Q. Okay. Your parents' home where they ultimately ended up living. How did they come to live there?

A. Laura told me that they had to move from the rent house because the—they were going to sell it. Immediately. So they moved back into Eusebio's grandmother's house, temporarily, but there was so many of them and they didn't get along with the grandmother and so they needed a place to stay. As it happened my stepmom had recently passed away. And so my father's house became my property.

And at that time I talked it over with my husband and I said would you care if I let them stay at grandpa's house. And he said no, of course not. You know.

Q.   Did you charge them any rent?

A.   No. They didn't pay rent. All they had to do was pay utilities.

Q.   Did these religious services, did they continue at that house?

A.   Yes, they did.

Q.   How often would they take place?

A.   I would say at least once or twice a weekend.

Q.   And the ones that you attended, was the collection plate passed around every time?

A.   Yes.

Q.   And was money placed in that collection plate?

A.   Yes.

Q.   Now, ultimately, when these—when—what came to light about what Eusebio and Laura were doing to Abby, in this case, came to light, did Eusebio and Laura leave your house?

A.   Yes.

Q.   And when—and actually—I neglected to even talk about this. Did you also provide Eusebio and Laura a job?

A.   Yes, I did.

Q.   What did you have them do for your company?

A.   We own a commercial flooring covering installation company. Eusebio worked in the warehouse. And Laura worked in the office doing payroll and insurance and things like that. She had done that before, is what she told me.

Q. Now, the interior of the house that you were allowing them to stay in, was that their furniture or yours?

A. No, that was—stayed with the property, would have been my Dad's and stepmom's.

Q. Now when Laura and Eusebio left the location, did you ultimately go back to the house?

A. We were called on the phone by the police department that there was a woman there claiming that Laura had sold her all of the furniture and fixtures in that house and she was there to pick it up but she couldn't find a key so she called the police because she had given Laura cash.

And we were on our way back from Dallas so we actually got them to wait 'til the next morning. My brother and my son and my nephew went that same day when the police were there. And after we talked to them against and told them we were in Waco, that we couldn't possibly get there in time, they agreed to have the woman come back the next morning to get the furniture.

Q. What did you observe inside the house?

A. It was pretty much trashed. They had sold the refrigerator, or the freezer, excuse me, a big stand—upright refrigerator—freezer. And they had taken all that food that was in there and threw it in the sinks. They had put some in ice chests but the ice had already melted so everything was a mess.

Q. What was the state of the furniture?

A. It was gone. The police had actually let the woman come back in and pick up everything that Laura sold her, which was everything in the house.

Q. Did you give anybody permission to sell that furniture?

A. No.

MR. SPEIR: Thank you, Ma'am. I'll pass.

MR. CANTRELL: I don't have any questions.

THE COURT: Thank you.

MR. SPEIR: State would call Abby—Alvarado is her last name.

THE COURT: All right.

ABIGAIL

The Courtroom

A lady walks into the small room where they have me waiting near the courtroom until it is my turn to testify. She pulls the door open, "Okay. It's time."

Today, I will see him—the monster behind the mask—for the first time since my escape. I am terrified. My stomach is clenched, my heart is pounding fast and hard in my chest, my legs feel wobbly with each step I take, anxiety floods my body, and I feel like I want to throw up. When I went to the police, I knew that this was going to be a part of it: turning that asshole in—turning *them* in. I always knew this day would come, and that when it did, I would be forced to see him.

Is he going to look at me? Will he stare me down? Will he stand up while I'm speaking and call me a liar? Will he glare at me in the form of a silent threat? I know that he is in prison, but he still poses a threat. He knows people—in prison and out of prison—bad people who would probably be happy to earn some extra money by taking me, my kids, or all of us out. Rudy always says, "He's behind bars now, babe. He can't hurt you now." But Rudy doesn't understand the things that Chevo is capable of. He still doesn't realize how evil he truly is. I do.

I shakily make my way behind the lady toward the courtroom. We are almost there. When we walk in, everyone stares at me. Fear fills my veins the closer we get. He is here. Waiting. A bunch of people are. I hate being in front of people. I don't like being the center of attention. The idea of speaking in front of a bunch of people, like this, makes me want to turn around and run as fast as I can out of this courthouse. But I am here to tell the truth today.

We walk into the courtroom. The lady gestures with her hand to indicate to me that I should approach an empty seat not too far from the judge. I raise my right hand as I am told to do. I place my other hand on the Holy Bible, and I agree to tell the truth.

That is exactly what I am going to do here today. I can't believe I have to talk about all of these sexual things in front of a crowded room full of people. These things are not only difficult to talk about, and to confess, but to actually own. In spite of all that, I am going to share the secrets that I have been hiding since I was a little girl.

I do not look directly at Chevo, who is seated at a table with his lawyer catty-corner from where I am seated. From his blurry silhouette in my peripheral vision, I can see that he looks old. His hair is gray now. He is rail thin. But I do not chance a direct glance his way. I try to blot him out of my mind. Being in the same room with him is terrifying. The fear floating inside my body holds the space that he still seems to invade—even from across a crowded room, without even touching me. That is the power he still wields over me. Fear. But afraid or not, I am here today to take back that power. To strip it away from him, the same way he stripped all the pieces of me away over the years.

The District Attorney, a Hispanic man clothed in a dark suit, walks up closer to where I am seated. I am just going to focus on what I am saying—on his questions—and on my answers. Just questions and answers. That's all it is.

Just me and him.

And Rudy. And Chevo.

This room full of people I don't know.

The judge.

A lady typing everything we say.

And the truth.

DIRECT EXAMINATION

**All typographical and grammatical errors are contained in the original transcript. Some names intentionally withheld. **

BY MR. SPEIR:

Q. And for the record, you are Abigail Alvarado, correct?

A. Yes.

Q. And you're the victim in this case?

A. Yes.

Q. Now when were you—what age were you when you were first adopted by Laura and Eusebio Castillo?

A. Around eight or nine years old.

Q. And where did you go, which state did you go to when you were adopted?

A. Hawaii. Honolulu.

Q. Now approximately how long had you been in Hawaii until Eusebio started abusing you?

A. About a month after we got there.

Q. Okay. So only about a month into it?

A. Yes.

Q. Now you stayed in Hawaii for a couple of years, correct?

A. Yes.

Q. Was there ever a time in which the abuse ceased during that time between Eusebio and yourself?

A. [No response]

Q. I guess understanding it didn't happen every day, correct?

A.   No.

Q.   But was there ever a time where he just stopped touching you at all?

A.   No.

Q.   No? Okay.

Now after Hawaii where did you move?

A.   To Houston.

Q.   Okay. And eventually when you moved to Houston initially Eusebio didn't come 'til a little bit later, correct?

A.   Right.

Q.   Now when Eusebio arrived did the abuse continue?

A.   Yes.

Q.   Did the level of abuse ramp up?

A.   Yes.

Q.   From not just touching to other things?

A.   Yes.

Q.   Now eventually did Laura, Eusebio's wife also start to join in on the abuse?

A.   Yes.

Q.   Now after—while you were in Houston you actually made an outcry about this abuse, correct?

A.   Correct.

Q.   At that time did anything happen? Did it stop?

A.   No.

Q.   Did you end up ultimately moving to another city?

A.   Yes.

Q.   Where did you move?

A. We moved to Laredo, Texas.

Q. To Laredo? And during that time in Laredo did the abuse continue?

A. Yes, it did.

Q. From both Eusebio and Laura?

A. Yes.

Q. And at the tail end of the time that you were in Laredo, did Laura and Eusebio use you as a surrogate to have children?

A. Yes.

Q. Did you become pregnant?

A. It was later on in the valley. Mission.

Q. Okay. In Mission?

A. Yes.

Q. You were under seventeen at the time?

A. Yes.

Q. When you became pregnant?

A. Yes.

Q. Did you ultimately give birth?

A. Yes, I did.

Q. What was the name of the child?

A. [first name intentionally withheld] Castillo

Q. Was [she] held out as the child of Laura and Eusebio?

A. Yes.

Q. And what did they hold you out to be in reference to [her]?

A. Her sister.

Q. Was after that, also still in the valley in the Mission area, did Eusebio impregnate you a second time?

A. Yes.

Q. Did you end up ultimately having that child?

A. Yes, I did.

Q. What's the name of that child?

A. [first name intentionally withheld] Castillo.

Q. Did Laura and Eusebio hold that child out to be their own?

A. Yes.

Q. Did they hold you out to be that child's sister?

A. Yes.

Q. Now later at a third time did Laura and Eusebio—or I guess Eusebio impregnate you?

A. Yes.

Q. Was that in Mission?

A. No. This was here in San Antonio.

Q. In San Antonio? What's the name of that child?

A. [first name intentionally withheld] Castillo.

Q. Did they hold [him] out to be their child?

A. Yes.

Q. Now were there ever times in which you tried to break away from the situation?

A. Yes.

Q. Were you always pulled back in?

A. Yes.

Q. Did Eusebio ever make threats to you about if you told anyone?

A. Yes, he did.

Q. What would he threaten you with?

A. He would threaten to beat me up, threaten to slice mine and the kids' throats.

  Burn the house down.

Q. Did he ever threaten to do harm to himself if you told anyone?

A. Yes.

Q. What would he do?

A. He poured gasoline on himself and he hung himself.

Q. But he ultimately was saved, did not die, obviously, correct?

A. Correct.

Q. But when you moved to San Antonio you still lived with Laura and Eusebio and the three children correct?

A. Correct.

Q. Was there a time that Laura and Eusebio held out your oldest child, [first name intentionally withheld], as some type of miracle child?

A. Yes.

Q. Explain to the Judge, what was this ploy?

A. That [first name intentionally withheld] was able to talk to the Virgin Mary and lay hands on anyone who had cancer or any illness and cure them from it.

Q. Did Laura and Eusebio receive money from these desperate people hoping for this?

A. Yes.

Q. Ultimately, did you even with this money have the church pay to fly you out to California?

A. Yes.

Q. Where did they take you?

A. We went to California and then on Thanksgiving day—we went to Disney World.

Q. Disneyland in Anaheim?

A. Disneyland.

Q. And was this done through the funds collected for these services?

A. Yes.

Q. How long did these services last? How long did Laura and Eusebio hold [eldest daughter] out to be this miracle child?

A. It was days.

Q. How many years?

A. Oh, since she was at least nine or ten 'til we got out.

Q. So we are talking about three or four years?

A. Right.

Q. How many services would they hold weekly? Or would it vary?

A. It would vary. Varied on—

Q. Would they always collect money at these services?

A. Yes, they did.

Q. Now ultimately the day that you were finally able to break away and get out of this situation, who did you notify to help you get out?

A. My husband, Rudy.

Q. Okay. And at the time you were not married to Rudy, correct?

A. Correct.

Q. And was Rudy able to come to your house and pick you up or was it someone else?

A. He was not able to. His mom was.

Q. And did his mom come and pick you up?

A. Yes, she did.

Q. And the three children?

A. Yes.

Q. Was that when you were finally able to get away from this?

A. Yes.

Q. So this abuse lasted from age nine to age 25?

A. Yes.

Q. Is it fair to say that you were sexually abused over a thousand times?

A. Yes.

Q. Now, how old are you now, Abby?

A. I'm 30.

Q. Are you still dealing with this?

A. Yes, I am.

Q. Now, your three children; [all first name intentionally withheld], they are with you, correct?

A. Yes.

Q. Are you seeking any counseling right now?

A. I've been trying to get some counseling.

Q.   And has your husband been trying to help you through this ordeal?

A.   Yes, he has.

MR. SPEIR: Your Honor, we'll pass.

THE COURT: Questions, Mr. Cantrell?

CROSS EXAMINATION

**All typographical and grammatical errors are contained in the original transcript. Some names intentionally withheld. **

BY MR. CANTRELL:

Q.   Just curiosity, and this is just for my own self. You said—was it the Catholic church that got involved somehow?

A.   It was—I believe it was the Catholic or—it was an archbishop got ahold of us.

Q.   And so did the church believe also that your daughter was special?

A.   Yes.

Q.   And could heal people?

A.   Yes.

Q.   Was that ever verified to be true?

A.   No.

Q.   I'm truly sorry for what happened to you. And finally you're able to get on with your life.

MR. CANTRELL: No other questions.

MR. SPEIR: Nothing further.

THE COURT: Thank you, Ma'am.

MR. SPEIR: And Judge, the state did file a motion to
              request for consecutive sentence last week.
              Count One and County Two of this indictment
              the victim was under seventeen years of age.
              Count One under Penal Code 22.021 and Count
              Two under Penal Code 22.011. Both of those
              the Court has the authority to stack the
              sentences. The other eight sentences are not
              stackable because she was over seventeen
              years of age.

              Judge, I have never encountered a situation
              where somebody has been sexually assaulted
              easily over a thousand times in her lifetime.
              The threats, the physical abuse that she
              endured, I've told her many times when I
              pre-trialed her before, she's one of the
              strongest people that I've ever come across
              to be able to survive this and to be able to
              come through with this.

              The level of perversion that she was
              subjected to by Eusebio and Laura, people
              who are supposed to be her adoptive parents,
              is unreal to me.

              And then, of course, as I wanted to present to
              you today, that that reach was even further.
              They took advantage of desperate people who
              were dying of cancer and took their money
              as opposed to these people going and seeking
              medical care. They did this for a period of
              years using this young child. [Abby's eldest
              daughter] was only nine when this began in
              this farce to defraud these folks.

Mr. Castillo—honestly, even the life sentence is—it will be something if I could, I'd ask for more. But by law I can't go any further.

What I would like the Court to do is sentence him to life on the five counts that are first degree, except I'd like the Court to stack him on the first two counts as you are allowed to do by law and give him 20 years on the other five counts that are second degrees.

This is the worse case of sexual abuse that I've ever seen in my life and I hope I never see one that's worse.

THE COURT: Mr. Castillo—

MR. CANTRELL: Just briefly, Your Honor, before you pronounce.

THE COURT: Oh, yes. Sorry. I'll let you respond.

MR. CANTRELL: I think on the stacking sentence the statute says I'm supposed to be given notice on that. And I have not been given notice of.

MR. SPEIR: We did file notice on—it was October 19th. It was done by efile.

THE COURT: So you would have gotten electronic notice.

MR. SPEIR: Yes, sir. It was not hand delivered. It was electronic notice.

MR. CANTRELL: Okay.

THE COURT: Anything else, Mr. Cantrell?

MR. CANTRELL: Only that, you know, I understand the
seriousness of this case. No doubt it's
horrific. It's hard to measure how horrific
more—one case can be more than another.
I've been a lawyer for 30 years. There's
countless cases that are just awful, and
this is one of those type cases.

And I understand why the state wants to
give him a life sentence and why they would
want to stack that. But other than publicity
and show, which I think should never be a
part of a sentence, it's not appropriate in
this case.

A life sentence is a life sentence. If you
gave a life sentence he's going to be in
prison for the rest of his life. You don't
need to stack it. If you give him 35 years,
which I think is more than sufficient, he's
going to do a life sentence.

So I just worry that the state, when they get
these types cases and they want to make—
whether it's publicity or otherwise, I think
it's wrong in the judicial system when you
hear people get 200 years in prison in
other states, it's just—you know, you can
only die once. Until somebody can be brought
back it's pointless to do these ridiculous
sentences that really have no merit in our
system of justice. The way I look at it.

But I respect the state's position very much.
It's a horrible case. But we'd ask the Court
to consider 35. If the Court needs to go
higher than that, 40 years is sufficient.

MR. SPEIR: Judge, how do you measure over a thousand
                sexual assaults? I think if anybody deserves
                life it's certainly somebody who committed
                crimes like that, especially on somebody so
                young.

THE COURT: Mr. Castillo, you took a little girl and
                you took her into your home with your
                wife. And you pretended to offer her a
                loving home. And you had her call you Dad,
                I'm sure, and your wife had her call her
                Mom. And then you began doing unspeakable
                damage and harm to that little girl. At the
                age of nine, an age I still consider just
                not very far removed from being a baby
                because they are so dependent on you for
                support and love and nurturing of their
                parents.

                Instead you began having sex with her at the
                age of nine. And you did it over, and over,
                and over, and over, and over. Day after day.
                Year after year. This was your blood niece.

                That woman somehow has to get—find the
                strength to heal and get past the fact
                that her first sexual experience came at
                the hands of the man who she considered her
                father. I don't know how she can heal from
                that. But what you did was unspeakable. And
                it's not forgivable. And it boggles my mind
                how anybody with any sense of decency could
                do that to their own baby.

                I don't just pronounce sentence. I speak for the
                community. And I pronounce the judgment of
                the community. And sometimes the judgment of

the community contains a powerful component of symbolism that represents outrage and a strong request for retribution for the sake of retribution.

You will die in prison. And then you will have your maker to deal with.

On Count One I assess a sentence of life imprisonment.

Once you have completed that sentence and served it all, you can begin serving Count Two. I assess a sentence of life in prison. Those sentences will be stacked.

Once you have completed those two sentences— well the next, the court—Six cannot be stacked, but I assess a sentence of life.

Count Seven, I sentence you to life in prison.

Count Eight, I sentence you to life in prison.

Count Three, I sentence you to 20 years in prison, the maximum I can give you.

Count Four, I sentence you to 20 years in prison, the maximum I can give you.

Count Five, I sentence you to 20 years in prison, the maximum I can give you.

Count Nine, I sentence you to 20 years in prison.

And Count Ten, I sentence you to 20 years in prison.

And if I could make you suffer in a way that approaches the way this beautiful young lady has, I would do it. But that's left to God. Anything else?

MR. SPEIR: Judge, we have impact.

THE COURT: We are in recess.

                  Do we have impact?

MS. BYRD: Victim impact, Judge.

THE COURT: Stand to the side.

ABIGAIL

AGE 30

Victim's Impact Statement

R ising from my seat on a wooden bench beside Rudy, I walk to the front of the courtroom to take my place beside the attorneys. "Stand right over here, Abby." Standing before the judge is an elderly, rail thin, whitish-gray-haired man with dry, slicked-back hair who looks about twenty years older than I know him to be. He looks pale and sickly. In his current form, one might be left with the mistaken impression that he couldn't hurt a soul. Fooling absolutely no one in this courtroom of his *true* form today, he is now known to be the evil, manipulative monster who destroyed my childhood. The deranged psychopath who rearranged the fractured pieces of me to the point that I felt worthless and unrecognizable. Before him today, the broken, rebuilt woman now stands. Nervously, but filled with immense pride, I begin to read my statement from the sheet of lined paper that I tore out of one of my children's notebooks. Clutching it in my hands, I take a deep breath. And I read.

"So, everyone here in the courtroom knows you as Eusebio Castillo, but I know you as Chevo, and here is what I have to say to you. You were supposed to be my guardian and my father. To raise me, to care for me, to love me, but yet you did the opposite. You took my childhood away from me. You tormented me and tortured me for more than a decade. You are a monster. You will not hurt me anymore, or my two beautiful, wonderful daughters and take anyone else's innocence away from them. Where you are going you will never get that chance. You got what you deserve, and it took so long for you to get caught, but I'm happy that it has finally come to an end. You thought you could beat me into submission, keep me for the rest of my life. Chevo, you put me down so much I believed I was not good for nothing.

Now, I'm a wonderful mother and wife. I have done things you said I could never do. The punishment you receive today is the punishment you deserve for being so evil. I have spoken my piece. One more thing though—I want to thank the people who worked so hard on helping me put you away."

Once I am finished, I walk out of the courtroom and into the women's restroom down the courthouse hallway to gather myself. The fear I felt facing Chevo was a powerful undercurrent, hitting my soul as hard as a tsunami, threatening to not only crush me, but to engulf me and to pull me down. I somehow managed not to bow to that fear. Moments later, that same fear is replaced by pride. Thoughts of how old and sickly he looked, interlaced with horrific memories of everything that he had done to me throughout the years flood my mind. He is just an old man who looks pathetic, sickly, and harmless now, but he is the predatory monster who made my life a living hell.

Standing within the private confines of the public courthouse restroom, I sob—a deep, soul-shifting, guttural, ugly cry. The kind where faint lines of snot drip down your face mixed with long lines of tears that run down your neck. I find myself crying for the little girl I used to be. I also cry for the woman that I am today. I cry for all of it for about a solid ten minutes straight. Then, glancing into the mirror, I take myself in. The skin beneath my eyes is slightly swollen and my face is flushed from crying. Holding a wad of toilet paper in my hand, I begin blotting it around my eyes to hide the evidence of my ugly cry.

I take a few deep breaths to steady myself. Abigail Alvarado. Mom to six beautiful children: four who are biologically mine, and two beautiful girls I inherited through love. Rudy's wife. Survivor. Then I stand up tall and walk myself out of that fancy bathroom into the hallway, where Rudy tucks me inside his outstretched arms, and we both cry. Together. For all of it.

ABIGAIL

AGE 30

Life After Justice

*F*or the next three days, I fight a variety of competing emotions. One moment, I feel shame for allowing the abuse to go on for so long and not getting out earlier. The next moment, I feel pride for finally standing up to Chevo and Laura. I try to be strong and hold it together when I am around Rudy and the kids. The shower is the one place where I allow myself to fall apart. Then, just as I did that day in the courthouse restroom, I blot beneath my eyes with a tissue, I take a few deep, steadying breaths and pull myself together to emerge a stronger person. A person who, somehow, managed to rearrange the shards of my broken past into a colorful mosaic pulled together from the broken, sharp edges of the pain that I managed to survive, even when I didn't think I would. A woman who continues to wade through and learn from the twisted feelings lodged deep within me for so long—feelings of sorrow, resentment, shame, hurt, betrayal, and utter worthlessness. I shove those broken, sharp edges into that invisible box in my mind. I acknowledge them, almost in the way one would pay respect to someone at a funeral, for closure. Then I shut the lid. This time . . . for good.

Rudy probably has no idea that it feels as though I am at war within my own flesh—within my heart and mind, although I suspect he might sense it, like he always does. He's perceptive in that way—he just knows things without being told them. Much the same way he knew there was more to me and my situation than any other person would have ever noticed or realized back at that broken down chapel where I stood with my "parents" and my "sisters" and my "brother."

Each night as I lay my head upon my pillow, I am so grateful that Rudy walked into my life. That I was able to escape my 16 years of hell. That I am now free to live as I choose. Free to raise my own children, speak my mind, indulge in things I enjoy, and start my new normal on a positive path filled with light, love, and laughter.

And free to live this life—*my life*—on my own terms.

THE APPEAL

Following the sentencing hearing, Eusebio "Chevo" Castillo, Jr., filed an appeal with the Court of Appeals of Texas.

On April 1, 2019, with his appeal still pending, after serving a little over two years in prison, Chevo died of renal cell carcinoma (kidney cancer) that had metastasized to his lungs.

The irony of him dying on April Fool's Day was not lost on me.

LAURA

Laura continues to serve out her 33-year prison sentence. I stood before her at her sentencing hearing to give my impact statement, just as I did at Chevo's. Here is what I said to her that day in the courtroom:

"Hello, my name is Abigail Alvarado, also known as Abigail Castillo. I'm here to speak my piece. All I want to say is, Laura, you were supposed to protect me and be my mother. But instead y'all abused me emotionally and physically. You allowed him to molest me as a child and rape me as he pleased. You disgusting person, you even joined him.

It took me 16 years to tell someone about what y'all did to me. That someone is now the love of my life, Rudy. I was scared to tell him 'cause I didn't think he would believe me. He did. And he promised to love my children like they were his own and to help me get out. To this day he has kept his word.

Laura, I just want to say, you and Eusebio would tell me I was not good for nothing. Also, you would tell me I was dumb, that I wouldn't be able to take care of my kids, I wouldn't be able to keep a job . . . LOOK AT ME NOW!

I have six children that I love very much. I have a good job and I'm about to pay off my truck and I did it all by myself. The judgment you will receive is the punishment you deserve for being the evil person that you are. You hid behind curtains, but you were finally caught."

The last time I saw or communicated with Laura was that visit that we had at the park, when I allowed her to see the kids—my kids—one last time a few weeks before I walked into the police station.

I have no positive feelings for Laura. I honestly don't even hate her, although a lot of people probably think that I should. What I feel for her is absolutely nothing.

As far as I am concerned, Laura is exactly where she needs and deserves to be, suffering behind bars for the crimes that she committed against me. I am grateful that she is now locked far away from the children and cannot possibly harm anyone else the way that she harmed and sexually abused me.

Laura,

There are no viable reasons, excuses, or credible words that will ever help you to evade all the disgusting things that YOU did to me.

But you hold no power over me today.

I am free of you.

ABIGAIL

AGE 34

Present Day

*T*oday, Rudy and I share a home with our six beautiful children: my three beautiful kids fathered by Chevo, the young son that Rudy and I had together in March of 2016, and my two beautiful stepdaughters, our eldest kids—Rudy's daughters from his prior relationship. Our kids span in age from Rudy's eldest daughter at age 18 to our youngest son together, who is five. I finally have that home and beautiful life that I always dreamed of and never thought that I would get to have.

As for my biological mom, we connected on Facebook in 2016. She was happy to see that I had gotten married and had kids of my own. Not long after reconnecting, we found ourselves on a call for several hours one day. I told her about everything that had happened to me at the hands of her half-brother and Laura—the abuse, the rapes, the kids—all of it. We both cried during the call for all that had happened. Upon learning the news of my abuse, my mom was furious and seemed ready to kill Chevo with her own hands. She told me she would "send people after him." I told her not to do anything and to let the police handle it. She said, "I trusted them. I thought you had a good life." Interestingly, she still seems to remember my childhood a bit differently than I do, but I guess that is probably true for each of us in any family dynamic. There is a collective smattering of memories and then our own individual pieces. The only person who can account for one's life, in totality, is the person who lived it.

In February of 2017, I learned the identity of my father, Ruben Lopez, from my biological mom. I was so excited to finally know his name and have the opportunity to meet him. My dad and I spent some special times together in the year and a half that I got to know and appreciate him as the wonderful man that he was, before he passed away in 2018.

I will carry a piece of my daddy in my heart always. He was an amazing man who was short in stature, but big in personality. He was handsome, full of life, always had a knack for making people laugh, and loved to dance. My only regret is not getting to know him sooner. I am proud to be his daughter.

A lot of people seem to wonder if I still have a relationship with my brother and sister. I do. What happened to me isn't their fault. In a way, we each lived our own separate lives inside of that house, in much the same way as we live our separate lives as adults with our own families, today.

My sister reported my abuse to a teacher once. Since I refused to make an "outcry" to the CPS worker who visited me, she said there really wasn't anything else that she could do to help, if I wasn't going to expose Chevo's abuse. My brother obviously now knows what happened to me and that there is DNA proof, but I think the weight of that reality is probably a difficult thing for him to fully reconcile, since he lived with us throughout so many years of my abuse.

Each of us is now left with our own unique paths, and our own unique stories, despite the fact that we all grew up under the same roof—or in our case, a whole lot of different roofs. Where we choose to go from here, as siblings, is up to us.

I have chosen to forgive both Chevo and Laura for what they have done to me. Not because they deserve it. It is quite the opposite, really. It's because they *don't* deserve it, but as a Catholic woman, it is anchored to my belief that I must forgive those who have trespassed against me to one day make it into heaven. So, I forget nothing. I remember every single scar. None of that is diminished. It does not ever go away. But I choose to move forward in positivity and happiness, to move past all that has transpired with an open heart and a forgiving mind. (And I'm pretty sure I won't be seeing them in heaven when I eventually get there.)

Since that time, I have learned that the triggers associated with trauma run hot, surge fast, and throw down roots to live within those of us who endure and survive it—whatever our "it" happens to be. The trauma becomes as much a part of us as blood and bone. The triggers take over us before we even know what happened. Emotional flashbacks are instigated by a familiar sight, sound, smell, or sensation that can prompt us to abruptly act, react, or freeze. It takes a lot of time and intentional thought to realize that the anxiety has nothing to do with the present moment. What I know now, as a survivor, is that I get to choose how I carry that trauma. I get to decide how much I learn from it, how hard I work to unpack it, and how I choose to sort it so that my load will be a little lighter and more comfortable moving forward.

Despite life's challenges, I graduated from the University of Cosmetology on September 17, 2020, with the biggest smile on my face—and Rudy by my side, as he always has been. Rudy left his job at the mail processing facility where he had worked for 20 years. He was ready for a change. He now works for a company doing power washing for commercial businesses and is quite successful at it. He is also studying to earn his GED. As for me, I now spend my days working at a center for autistic children of all ages in San Antonio—the most amazing kids who require a little extra time, love, and attention. I am so happy to be a positive influence in their daily interactions and lives. I love my job.

Rudy and I now live in a large older home in San Antonio with our six kids. I have definitely put my "handy woman" skills to work fixing it up. Our life is always busy, fun, loud, and full, but in the best way.

In the end, I am happy that I found the bravery and vulnerability to allow myself to emerge from the dark shadows to tell this story. I have always believed that everything happens for a reason. While I spent my entire life having *no idea* why God would allow me to be abused in such horrific ways for so many years, I am now able to see the good that can emerge from the horror.

I am alive. I made it.

I succeeded even though they told me that I never would. It is for that reason I am standing with my head held high sharing my deepest, darkest truths. It is with the hope that this story—*my story*—could potentially help others who are bound by their own endless shame, ugly truths, and pretty lies. We are not bound by these things. They do not define us.

The Woman I Am . . .

To the one who fell.
Who rises again.

To shed her shame.
Rearrange the splinters of misplaced blame.
Upended.
Reborn.

Beautifully torn.
To stand upon ashes.
The past's barren heap.
Fearless.
Shameless.
A caster of fate.

Leaving my former self.
Shedding her skin.

Untethered.
Anchored.
Behind she leaves it.
The heir to her own life.

Unbridled.
Unburdened.
Unbroken.
Reclaimed.

As the woman that I am.
Bearing no shackles of the woman that I used to be.
Emboldened. Fearless. Free.

That is who I am.

—JAMIE COLLINS
(For Abigail)

I AM ABIGAIL

AGE 34
January 21, 2023

I was the little girl named Abigail no-middle-name Rodriguez. I was also Abigail Olga Castillo.

Today, I am Abigail "Abby" Alvarado.

I am a woman.

I am a daughter.

I am a sister.

I am a friend.

I am a coworker.

I am a neighbor.

I am an aunt.

I am a wife.

I am a mother.

I am the little girl whom society failed to notice.

I am a victim of sex crimes who CPS failed to protect, over and over again.

I am the teenager who rebelled, and yelled, and struggled, and fought, and silently clawed her way across seventeen years of horror at the hands of the two discreetly evil people who promised to love me.

I am one who was robbed of nearly every normal "first" or major life choice a person has the privilege and personal agency to make.

I am also the woman who one day stepped through an open doorway to depart hell.

I am the one who chose to share the words of this story—*my* story.

I AM A SURVIVOR.

Now here to take back my power word by word, line by line, page by page.

I AM ABIGAIL ALVARADO.

Free.

Happy.

Loved.

Beautiful.

Worthy.

Proud.

No longer afraid.

Standing before the world.

Fearlessly.

As all that I have been,

And all that I AM,

UNBOUND.

Last day at the shelter, 1998

Abigail as a child

Abigail as a child

Abigail as a teenager

March 7, 2015

Abigail and her eldest son, 2015

Abigail and Rudy

Rudy, Abigail, and their five eldest kids, 2015

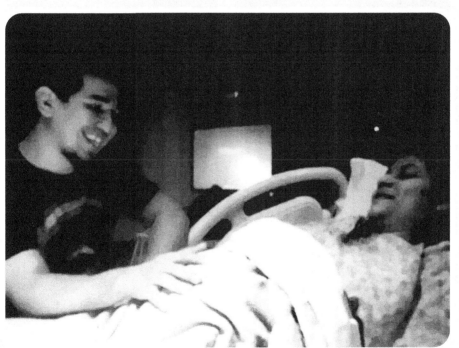

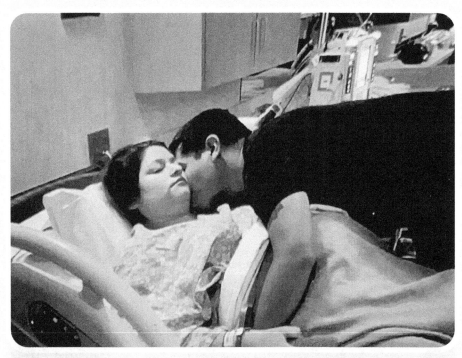

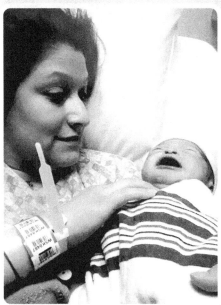

Abigail & her youngest son

Rudy & Abigail, two months after sentencing hearing, 2017

Rudy, Abigail, and their six kids, 2017

Abigail with the truck referenced in her
Victim Impact Statement, 2018

Abigail graduating from
cosmetology school, 2020

2018

2018

(Photo by Christi Anderson Photography)
Abigail & Rudy, 2023

The Survivor

(Photo by Christi Anderson Photography)
Abigail Alvarado, 2023

THE STATISTICS

- ► Every 68 seconds, an American is sexually assaulted.

- ► Every 9 minutes, that victim is a child.

- ► From 2009-2013, Child Protective Services Agencies substantiated, or found strong evidence to indicate that 63,000 children a year were victims of sexual abuse.

- ► On average, it takes a survivor of abuse seven attempts before he or she is able to permanently leave their abuser.

According to RAINN's website (rain.org)

DO YOU NEED HELP?

If you need help, please don't hesitate to reach out to a trusted family member, friend or one of the many organizations that can help you. Help is available. Don't be afraid to reach out. Everyone needs help sometimes. There are even ways to text for help if you aren't ready to talk about it yet.

It is worth it to get out of a bad situation. There *is* a way out. You will be happier.

NATIONAL RESOURCES

If you or someone you know is struggling with sexual violence, mental health and well-being, self-harm, or suicide, visit: wannatalkaboutit.com

» **National Suicide and Crisis Hotline:** 988

» **If you are contemplating harming yourself, text** 741741 at any time.

» **National Domestic Violence Hotline** (800) 799-SAFE (7233)

» **National Child Abuse Hotline** (800) 4-A-CHILD

» **Rape, Abuse, and Incest National Network** (800) 656-4673

To find mental health services and support in your area, contact:

» **National Mental Health Association Information Center,** nmha.org

WE NEED YOUR HELP!

If you enjoyed this book, it would mean *everything* to us if you:

- » Post an online review (where you bought the book, on Goodreads, etc.).
- » Share a picture of this book with a link to it on social media. Tag it #IAmAbigailBook
- » Call your local library or bookstore to ask if they have *I Am Abigail* available.
- » Tell someone about it!

We are so incredibly grateful to every single one of you who steps up to help us with promoting Abigail's story. Every book needs a "street team." Thank you to you for *anything* you do be a part of ours, to help us spread Abby's important story of healing and hope. You. Are. Amazing. We are forever grateful.

To inquire about speaking engagements or share feedback with us, email: contact@boldwhisperbooks.com

FOLLOW US!

Facebook: I AM ABIGAIL BOOK
Instagram: Abby—@abigails_dreamworks
                  Rudy—@renodelioncourt_cp
                  Jamie—@jamiecollinswrites

DO YOU HAVE AN IDEA FOR THE NEXT BOLD WHISPER BOOK?

» Would you like Jamie Collins to write *your* story?

» Bold Whisper Books is in search its next inspiring story!

» We are interested in sharing the raw, real stories of remarkable people who find a way to survive the unfathomable. We are open to all ideas.

Write a summary of 3,000 words or less.
Include your name, telephone number, and e-mail.
Put "Story idea" in the subject line.
Send it to: ideas@boldwhisperbooks.com

BOLD WHISPER BOOKS, LLC

BOLD WHISPER BOOKS

Where stories breathe on paper.™

VISIT JAMIE'S AUTHOR PAGE:

JAMIECOLLINSWRITES.COM

E-mail: jamie@boldwhisperbooks.com

ACKNOWLEDGMENTS

Abigail Alvarado

TO RUDY:

You are my hero. If it wasn't for you, I don't think I would be here. You mean the world to me. I'm so happy God put you in my life. We do have our ups and downs, but we always get through it. Our kids have a wonderful dad. Thank you for being by my side when I needed you the most. You helped me through a lot. I love you to the moon and back 100 times.

TO MY BEAUTIFUL CHILDREN:

You all mean the world to me. Thank you for choosing me to be y'all's mom. God knew that I would need y'all in my life. If it wasn't for y'all, I would not be here today. My babies—I try my best to give you everything you need and want. I do that because I didn't have a good life, so I want y'all to have the best life. I love y'all to the moon and back 100 times. I wake up every day for you. Y'all make me so happy.

TO ALL WHO HELPED TO CONVICT
LAURA AND CHEVO:

I would love to thank everyone who helped me to convict these ugly ass people: the Bexar County District Attorneys, the paralegals, and the hard-working court staff. A special thank you to Judge Jose "Joey" Contreras who did the sentencing. Thank you so much. I feel like they got what they deserved and I got my justice. I also want to thank the detectives at the San Antonio Police Department, as well as the San Juan Police Department for taking the time to go get the DNA test and arresting them.

TO MY WRITER, JAMIE:

Thank you so much for writing this beautiful book for me. You have helped me through a lot, too. I was never able to talk about what happened to me, but now I can. Talking to a female about this for two years helped me a lot. I'm so happy that we are going to get my story out there because I'll be able to help people out.

TO EVERYONE ELSE:

I just want to thank everyone else who has helped me through all of this. The ones that came with me to court. That meant a lot to me. I know it took time out of your own lives, but y'all came. You know who y'all are . . .

ACKNOWLEDGEMENTS
Jamie Collins

TO ABBY AND RUDY:

Thank you for trusting me to tell your remarkable story. It was fate. I believe your story was meant to be told, by me, in this way. It was one of my life's greatest honors to write this book. Not only are you "friends," you are now *family*. Good luck getting rid of me now. :) Family is for life.

Rudy—You are a man among men.

Abby—You are one of the most beautiful people with the purest soul. You deserve every good thing in this life. I look forward to seeing where this journey takes you.

TO GAVIN:

To my teenage son, Gavin, for so kindly "allowing" me to use "your" computer when mine crashed mid-way through this project. Good times. I didn't do anything to make it run slower. (Swear). I hope one day that you will find the thing that sets your soul on fire—and when you do, I hope that you chase that thing like it is *everything*. Because living out your dream? It will be—*everything*. I am living proof. I am so proud of the person you have become. I look forward to watching you walk your path in life. May the world be prepared to step aside for you—and all the greatness that you bring to it.

TO CHRISTOPHER:

To my husband of 15 years, I must admit that you took this book— my second one—a bit more in stride than my first. You are now a seasoned pro when it comes to being this author's husband. The ups. The downs. The tribulations. The expenses. Hearing me talk about the same thing over-and-over-and-over again. The journey. Thank you for living with a creative, crazy, busy author/wife/mother who somehow manages to keep our household running—a little less spotless at times, and a bit more chaotic. I salute you for all the "quickie" dinners, pizzas, and delivered meals you ate while I was obsessively working to write this story. Thank you for being my best friend and always supporting my side hustle. I truly am "living the dream." I appreciate you.

TO MY DAD:

You are the greatest man I've ever known. I am lucky to call you Dad. I am proud to be your daughter. Thank you for always telling me that I could be anything or do anything if I was willing to put in the work. You were right. (As a teenager I never would've thought I'd put that phrase in writing—but there you have it.) You were the first person who ever believed in me. You are my biggest cheerleader, but more like a badass Cobra pilot in a flight suit, sans pom-poms. Without *you*, I would not be *me*.

TO OUR CREATIVE TEAM:

To our dream team—the most amazing creative team on the planet: Autumn Jade Monroe (editing), Najdan Mancic (cover and interior design), Christi Anderson (cover photo), and Kris Gallagher (illustrations)—without you, this book would not be what it is today. And to the world's greatest publicist, Emi Battaglia—without you, not as many people would know about this book and read Abby's important story. Thank you to all of you, one thousand times, for *all* that you *are*, and all that *you* brought to this important project. We are forever grateful.

TO JEFF FERRIS:

I am forever grateful to you for introducing me to Abby and Rudy. I look forward to following your future writing endeavors and wish you every good thing in life.

TO OUR BETA READERS:

Thank you for being the first eyes to grace these pages. Your feedback was crucial. Your commentary was helpful. As always, you helped us to spot issues, fix plot lines, and make this story everything that we hoped it to be. A special shout-out to Sally Kane—you win our MVP award, hands down. Thank you for making us better, making me work harder, and for taking the time to read for us.

TO WOMEN WHO WRITE:

To every women writer who ever had to publish under a male pseudonym or write anonymously to conceal their powerful written words in conformity to societally accepted standards—until the 1840's when this became an "acceptable" profession for women—it is upon your shoulders that I, and every female author, now stand. We now claim what we will in our own names, loud and proud, word by word, page by page. May we do it boldly and unapologetically.

To every girl who dreams of one day becoming a writer—you *can*, and if you want to—*you will*. Let nothing stop you. The only permission you need is your own.

TO THOSE WHO WONDERED:

To those who ever wondered if I was going to be a "one hit wonder—" The answer to that question is now officially "no." :)

TO JESSI:

To my amazing cousin, Jessica Toronjo—without you believing in me and allowing me to write *your* story, *I Am Jessica*, NONE of this would exist. Your book. Abby's book. None of it. You will be one my closest connections until the end of time. I am forever grateful to you for trusting me to tell your story—our family's story. Love you forever.

TO THE DREAM CHASERS:

And lastly, to all the light bringers and dream chasers—to those who feel inspired to shake the world in some way. You can. And you should. Don't let anyone stop you.

Be authentic. Be inspired. Be fearless.

And don't ever let *anyone* tell you what you *can't* do.

Seize the damn thing.

Whether you are working to overcome past trauma or listening to the voice within telling you to pursue your life's dream—just like Abby, who stepped into hope when there was none—find a way to keep going! The world needs *you* in it. No matter what obstacles you encounter along the way, you *can* find a way to shine.

Be the light.

THE
~~END~~ *Beginning*

Made in United States
North Haven, CT
17 January 2024

47606450R00251